The Complete Guide to Garden Center Management

D1086874

The Complete Guide to Garden Center Management

John Stanley

 Ball Publishing
Batavia, Illinois, U.S.A.

Ball Publishing
P.O. Box 9
335 North River Street
Batavia, Illinois, 60140, U.S.A.
www.ballpublishing.com

Copyright © 2002 by John Stanley. All rights reserved.
Photographs, unless otherwise noted, copyright © 2001 by John Stanley.
All rights reserved. Used by permission. Photos 2-1, 4-1, 7-4, 7-5, 7-6,
7-7, 20-1 copyright © Ball Publishing. All rights reserved. Used by permission.
Cover photograph by Chris Beytes. Copyright © 2001 by Ball
Publishing. All rights reserved. Used by permission.
Chapter 9 is modified from *The Nursery and Garden Centre Marketing
Manual* by John Stanley (Plum Press, 2000).

Designed by Christine Victor, Batavia, Illinois.

No part of this book may be reproduced or transmitted in any form by
any means, electronic or mechanical, including photocopying, recording,
or any other storage and retrieval system, without permission in writing
from Ball Publishing.

Reference in this publication to a trademark, proprietary product, or
company name is intended for explicit description only and does not
imply approval or recommendation to the exclusion of others that may
be suitable.

Library of Congress Cataloging-in-Publication Data
Stanley, John.
  The complete guide to garden center management / John Stanley.
     p. cm.
  ISBN 1-883052-31-9 (alk. paper)
  1. Garden centers (Retail trade)—Management. I. Title.
SB454.6 .S72 2002
381.4159'068—dc21
                                        2001007898

Printed in Canada.
07 06 05 04 03   2 3 4 5 6 7

Contents

Acknowledgments

This book would not have been possible without the help and support of a number of people.

Anne Sugden is recognized as the top consultant in catering for garden centers, and her chapter on this growth sector in centers is appreciated. I have known Anne for a number of years, and her enthusiasm for introducing a "refreshment" concept into garden centers has inspired and helped many of my clients.

My wife, Linda, is the computer guru in our family, and she has written the chapter on marketing using this medium. This chapter was written between study for a M.Sc., and I am especially grateful for her input at such a pressured time.

Jenni Passmore, my assistant and typist, had to decipher my thoughts, many of which were brought together on overnight flights around the world and often needed to be rewritten in plain English. I am therefore especially grateful for her input.

Finally, Rick Blanchette, who edited this book, which was no mean feat when you consider that the author and editor were at the two furthest points away on the globe.

Thank you.

Introduction

Retailing is in constant change. The global events that took place when preparing this book during the fall of 2001 have highlighted how rapid and dramatic these changes can be.

In a world of uncertainty, retailers who provide products that enhance and secure the home are finding that consumers are looking to them more than ever. Horticultural retailers who are progressive, open-minded, and aware of their customers' needs can benefit from the changed economy.

The aim of this book is to stimulate ideas. Whether you are starting from scratch or have an established garden center, you need to look forward and obtain ideas from around the globe, which you can then adapt to your local scene.

I hope this book will help you with ideas on developing your garden center. Enjoy its contents and remember that the key is to find new ideas and then implement them in your business. All the great ideas in the world will not help you if you do not put them in action.

John Stanley
Perth, Western Australia
December 2001

Chapter 1

Retailing Horticultural Products in the Third Millennium

"The only constant in business is change." Never has this statement been so true as it is today. In today's retail world, everything is changing and changing at an ever-greater speed. Larry Downes and Chunka Mui in their book *Unleashing the Killer App* (1998) highlight the changes rather dramatically. According to the authors, the killer apps are the inventions that change our lives. The first such an invention was the wheel, and those who did not believe in the wheel were soon out of business. It took 5,000 years before the next killer app, which was the stirrup, and so the process went on until the present. The difference is that in this year alone there will be about twenty-five killer applications that will change the way we do business. Most of them won't affect your business this year and may take a number of years before you even become aware of them, but they will eventually catch up with you.

This means that you have to keep up with new technology if you plan to be in business for a number of years. The problem is keeping up. Researchers tell us it takes four years to keep up with one year's events. In other words, none of us is ever going to be completely up to date. So what's the answer?

First, you must work *on* your business, not *in* your business. Let me explain. To be successful, you need to be constantly reviewing what you are doing and what is happening in the market place. If you bury yourself in paperwork and day-to-day necessities, trends will pass you by and you will soon find yourself in a business with no customers. I work with a lot of businesses where it is part of their culture to ensure that the decision makers take at least a day out every three months and review where the business is now and where it should be going.

It used to be good business practice to have a five-year plan and to stick to it. That is not the way to do business today. Can any of us imagine what the gardening industry will look like in five years' time? We don't even know what technical, digital, and horticultural inventions are going to come along. Don't get me wrong—I'm not saying that you shouldn't plan. What I am saying is that if you are not flexible in your planning and keeping up to date, then you will not survive. I accept that the bank may want to see a five-year business plan, but not even the banks can forecast the killer applications that are going to come along in the next five years.

Be Focused

If you want a successful business in the next few years, there is one requirement: You must be focused. Focused on what? Focused on your customers and their needs. Gardening in the U.S. over the last few years has gone through some changes. According to Ian Baldwin at Nursery Business Consultants, the customer count is down by about 10%, while the average income for garden centers has increased. In other words, there are fewer customers, but those that come are spending more dollars.

Our industry is now firmly positioned in the leisure industry and has to compete with restaurants, vacations, and other leisure activities. We target the more affluent members of the population and they are being offered more ways to spend their leisure dollar and we therefore have to fight harder for a share of the leisure wallet. This means that your competition is not just the garden center down the road. It's also the travel agent, baseball team, and local restaurants.

To be successful today, you have to create an impression. Al Ries, the coauthor of the book *The 22 Immutable Laws of Marketing,* talks in that book at length about "focus." He believes that every single communication you get involved in must carry a consistent message about your company and its brand. Remember, you are competing with some large leisure companies who spend megadollars on getting their brand image across to their target market. This target may also be your target.

The Garden Advantage

We have an ace up our sleeve. Our market is looking for lifestyle statements. They used to use clothes or the interior of their homes as lifestyle statements, but now they are looking toward their outside room or garden to reflect those statements. They will achieve this in one of two ways: They will employ a landscaper to do it for them, or they will do it themselves. I have held the view for a long time that there should be closer links between the landscape company and the retailer, as they are aiming at the same customer base.

1-1. Lifestyle statements can sell the complete garden package. Create lifestyle gardens and change them with the seasons. They will sell the complete garden package and show customers how to incorporate plants with the rest of their décor.

Contemporary versus Traditional

Your view on the market place and where you fit into it can affect what you do and how successful you are. We can all sell the same things but position ourselves at different points along the same scale.

A traditional garden retailer would consider their role would be to offer the customer product, e.g., plants. They would therefore often concentrate on the product rather than the customer, and their only line of defense when times get difficult is to play the price game. This means that if they are an independent, they are often squeezed out of the market by mass merchandisers, as the consumer tends to judge the retailer solely on price.

The next level of retailing is where the retailer perceives their market as one where their role is to help the consumer improve their garden. This retailer has a different view to the previous retailer and, therefore, merchandises and sells in a slightly different way. Price is less of an issue in this retailer's mind.

Levels of Retailing

Contemporary Retailing	Lifestyle Retailer: Provides ideas based on the target market's lifestyle
	Enhancer Retailer: Provides matchmaking ideas
	Problem Solver Retailer: Provides solutions to customers' dilemmas
Traditional Retailing	Plant Retailer: Provides plants using displays organized on an A-to-Z system

The next level of retailing is where the retailer views their role as one of helping the customer to enhance their garden. This retailer will group plants differently and will provide the customer, both verbally and visually, with more ideas. Price is now a lot lower on the list of priorities in both the retailer's and the consumer's mind.

Finally at the opposite end to the market to our product-led retailer is the lifestyle-led retailer. This retailer groups plants in room settings based on their customer profile. The sales team is aware of garden fashions and sees itself as consultants rather than salespeople. Price is a very low concern, as they believe their role is to create people's dreams. Many horticultural retailers have a problem developing this concept but are exposed to this style of retailing every day in upscale furniture and clothing stores.

What is happening in the market place is polarization. The market is growing for price-led retailers, and a drive around any American city will soon show you how many box stores have developed in the last few years.

At the other end of the market, the lifestyle centers are finding a market niche. These are often independently owned operations or franchised. It is the retailers in the middle that have found it difficult to survive, as they have been perceived by the customer to be neither one thing nor the other. Ken Allen, a consultant to Jardinere/Blooms Ltd. in the United Kingdom, has been telling traditional garden centers for a number of years that unless they change, their future is short lived. He took his company from a more traditional retail offer to a contemporary offer and has proved that there is a profitable future for lifestyle-led horticultural retailers.

Sigmoid Curve

It all depends where you are on the sigmoid curve. Every business is situated somewhere on the curve, and an astute business knows where that is. Let me explain the curve, and then you can make a decision where you fit.

A sigmoid curve represents the life span of anything—a person, business, industry, nation, or empire. In the beginning we start slowly, learning and experimenting. Then we progress and prosper, getting stronger and wiser as we move up the curve. At some point we hit the high-water mark, and then, as the saying goes, it's all downhill from there.

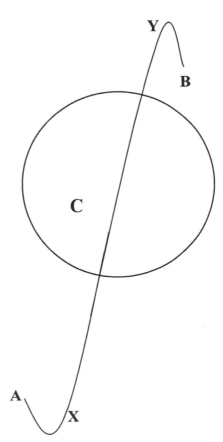

We shall use the illustration here to represent the life cycle of a garden center. We start at point A and decide, for example, to open a garden center. This costs time, money, and energy. And when we launch into the project, we tend to lose money. But, based on your concept and business plan being sound, there comes a turning point, X, where you start making money. Your business is now a success, but if you keep doing what you have always done and never change. You get to Y, the top of

Photos 1-2 and 1-3. Jardinere was revolutionary in garden center positioning. The shop and the outdoor plant areas both speak to a lifestyle rich with plants and flowers.

the sigmoid curve, and from there is only a matter of time until you shut your doors for good. Remember, there is no time frame to the curve. A British retailer recently went over the top of the curve after over one hundred years of profitable trading!

The key to success is to know when you are near the top of you're growth period on the curve. The key is to creatively destroy the business in the C zone. At this point you have the resources to reinvent your business and to create a new sigmoid curve. A lot of businesses fail because they do not fix the problem when it is working. If you wait too long, you may never be able to fix it.

This means you must constantly work on your business and make changes when they should be made. Ken Allen of Jardinere/Blooms garden centers in the United Kingdom claimed garden centers were dying in the late 1990s. He then went about reinventing his garden centers into contemporary lifestyle outlets revolving around the garden. He has proved this to be a winning formula in the United Kingdom, and we will see similar revolutions take place in other parts of the world as more and more retailers meet their customers' needs.

Understanding Today's Consumer

Consumers today—you and I—are changing in the way shops do business. Ten years ago we would not have had a computer in our homes and we would be relying on independent garden centers for our gardening products.

The guru on how you and I are changing our consumer habits is Faith Popcorn, a "trend forecaster" and the author of several books on the subject. According to Faith, there are some trends we all need to be aware of as they affect how we do business.

1. We are cocooning, or spending more time at home. This is a plus for the garden industry, as we are selling the right products at the right time. According to Li Edelkoor, the French futurologist, gardening is the retail business of the future. Research carried out in Germany by Prof. Houst Opaschowski in 1999 highlights the cocooning effect with 52% of Germans preferring to stay at home and garden.

2. Fantasy adventures. Yes, we do venture out and spend our leisure money, but when we do, we want to spend it at exciting places. Whether that is a themed restaurant, Disneyland, or your garden center, we are looking for somewhere that stimulates all our senses.

3. Small indulgences. Historically, if we were affluent we would spend on big-ticket items, such as exotic holidays, expensive cars or second homes. Now the trend is for smaller luxuries, such as Belgian chocolates, garden improvements, and weekends away.

4. Egonomics. Individuals feel they are important and want to be treated as someone special. Ignore the customer at your peril. Today the customer is truly king.

5. Cashing out. Many of us so-called baby boomers have paid of the mortgage and don't want to get into the same type of debt again .We now plan to enjoy our wealth rather than worry about more debt.

6. Down aging. Ask most fifty year olds how old they feel, and they will tell you they feel the same way as they did ten years ago. Today people are living longer and feeling younger than previous generations.

7. Being alive. This brings us on to the next part of what Faith Popcorn is predicting: a growth in products that help us stay alive. We are seeing this in the proliferation of sports facilities and vitamin and herb sales. Gardening is one of the being alive industries.

8. Vigilante consumers. In recent years, we have seen demonstrations against globalization around the world—this is an example of us being vigilantes. It happened in Europe over the cost of gasoline, and it could happen to your business if the customer base feels what you're doing is against the environment or the good of the world. In the U.K., we have seen a negative reaction to peat-based products, and I'm sure there are

other products in garden centers that will face similar backlashes in the future.

9. Ninety-nine lives. We are a time-poor society, as we try and cram as many things as possible into the day. This has huge opportunities for the garden industry. We all want a beautiful garden, and we used to do it ourselves. Retailers were geared up for the DIY market. That is changing rapidly as we now enter the DIM (do it for me) market. This means that the more finished product you can supply, the more in tune with your customers you will be. For example, Blooms in the U.K. now provide Gardens To Go as well as selling individual plants.

10. Save our society (SOS). We want to save our society; we are joining clubs and groups that will help us preserve what we believe are important to us. We are also supporting retailers who believe in what we believe in. The Body Shop has used this to their advantage, and there is no reason why you should not do the same. The key is to look at your customer base and supply to their needs. There are global trends in the marketplace, but the customers' needs in Des Moines will be different from those in New York, San Diego, and Little Rock.

11. Anchoring. We are becoming more in tune with our past and spiritual roots, hence the increase in retail outlets selling natural remedies and New Age products. This can be reflected in the type of products now being sold in gift shops within garden centers, especially in Europe.

12. Atmosfear. The public is becoming more concerned about air and water pollution and, as a result, is even rebelling against companies perceived as polluters. This is an ideal opportunity for a horticultural retailer to be perceived as an environmentally friendly company.

13. Clanning. We want to form groups of like-minded people. This is an opportunity that has been taken by many retailers to form in-house clubs, such as a garden club for experienced gardeners, beginners, or a kids' garden club.

14. Eveolution. One of the more recent trends Faith has written about is that women think and buy differently to men. As a result, we are now seeing suppliers package and present products in different ways. An example of this can be found in the power tool department in your local hardware store, where products such as power drills are being packaged with either women or men in mind.

15. Icon toppling. The pillars of society are now being brought in to question, as can be seen in the politics of the U.S. in recent years. As far

as we are concerned as retailers, this means that the local garden center can still play a positive role, even when in competition with national or multinational horticultural retailers.

16. Pleasure revenge. You and I are starting to enjoy ourselves and are less politically correct. In gardening, that means we are becoming more individualistic and our gardens are beginning to reflect our character rather than conforming to the neighborhood expectations.

And finally, one of my own:

17. Futuretense. Consumers are getting more frustrated with modern technology that does not live up to its expectations. As a result, old-fashioned service and services still have a role in modern retailing, but you still need to ensure you can exceed the promise you gave to the customer.

Don't Fall into the Failure Trap!

Starting a business is a real challenge. If you look at the statistics, they will show you that you will probably fail. Yet our aim in starting a business is to create profit and to develop an asset to either sell later on or to develop for future generations.

Jay Abraham, a management consultant, has studied many small businesses and has come up with a formula why most businesses fail or succeed. His theories are well researched and worth sharing with you prior to developing your business via ideas in this book. Jay calls his theories the ten steps to business failure or success.

1-4. How's this for fun? A display such as this lets your customers know you have a sense of humor and that gardening should be *fun*. Carry this feeling throughout your center, and your customers will be telling their friends about you.

1. Testing. Before you introduce any new development in your business, you must test prior to introduction. How many businesses do you know who will not make any changes because they might fail or who introduce change and then realize it is a mistake. The key is you always test before introducing any change into your business.

2. Run client-response advertising rather than institutional advertising. In a future chapter we will discuss advertising in great depth. At this point I just want to stress that target advertising will always be more effective than mass advertising.

3. Not knowing your USP and not communicating it to your customers. When you go into business, you have to be famous for something and you have to tell your customers what you're famous for. This is your unique selling proposition, or USP. If you cannot identify what you're famous for, then neither can your customers. In my experience, a lot of garden centers know what their USP is but fail to communicate it to their customers. They assume their customers will know. This is a dangerous situation to be in if you plan to grow your business.

4. You must backend. I often say that you should sell something and then sell something else, which is called backending. The key is that in the plant retailing industry there is always a backend that shows you care about the customer. Backending is more than "would you like fries with that," which we have all experienced in our local fast food outlet. Backending is offering advice or a product that will enrich the customers' experience once they have purchased the core product. In our industry, that could include fertilizer, snail control, growing media, or a tree stake. Unfortunately, in my experience not many team members are trained in this valuable skill.

5. Address your customers' needs. You must know your customers and address their needs. Failure to do so will translate into a short life for your business. This is why customer focus groups, mystery shopper surveys, and customer questionnaires are a vital part of your business tool kit.

6. Don't sell your way out of a problem; educate your way out of a problem. How often have you seen companies have a sale when they have product they have overpurchased or is not selling. Prior to getting to this stage, you need to see how else you can move the product. Can it be grouped with other products or displayed in another way. Far too often we start by reducing the price when this should be the last measure.

7. Make business fun. If our customers don't enjoy the experience, they will not come back. This may sound obvious, but how many business do you know where the experience is forgettable. Many just go through the process rather than making it a fun and memorable experience.

8. Always tell customers why. Retailing is not always a smooth journey; things will go wrong. The key is to be honest with your customers. If you don't tell them why, then you will loose loyalty. If you do tell them the truth, you will still loose some customers, but the majority will respect your honesty and stay with you.

9. Stick to marketing campaigns that are working. Too often retailers change marketing campaigns too early. They get bored before their customers do. The key is to change your marketing campaign when the customer is feeling it's time to change, not when you feel it's time.

10. Always focus on your customers and nobody else. Companies often tell me what their competition is doing and how it is affecting business. On closer scrutiny I find that the problem is often in-house. They are not focused on their own customers. When you loose focus, you loose customers. Yes, you need to be aware of what your competitors are doing, but you should not become so obsessed with what they are doing that you ignore what you do. Concentrate on your business and what you have control over.

Keys to Success
Most new businesses fail. Why? Because of lack of planning. Enthusiastic technicians often start businesses when what are needed are sharp business operators. How many people have you met that want to start a garden center because they enjoy working with plants and have visited a garden center on a Saturday in spring and think it is the best business in the world to make money at?

To be successful, you need to be aware of four critical aspects that will control your business destiny.

Location, Location, Location
Many retail gurus will tell you that the real key to success is location. Yes, location is important, but it is only part of the story.

You do need to be located near to your market, and you will need to understand the demographics of your vicinity. You will need enough local customers to generate a profit for your business.

But location is more than just being near to potential customers. You also need to consider the following:

• The existing competition within the catchment area in the

gardening market, where they are located and their distance from the customers and your proposed retail outlet. There are two options to consider. Some retailers prefer cluster retailing. This is where retailers offering similar products cluster together in the belief that they will get a bigger slice of the market. An example of this is the fast food market, where retailers prefer clusters to generate business. The alternative option is to position your business well away from the competition, to enable you to have the market to yourself. You will need to consider which option is best suited to your selected location.

- The position of other leisure retail outlets in the vicinity. I advise you to locate your center next to other suitable leisure retail outlets. For example, it may be next to leisure furniture businesses, pet stores, and toy shops.

- Remember, historically humans have disliked crossing rivers or hills. Things have changed very little with today's hi-tech consumers. When leisure shopping, they still look at hills, rivers, and freeways as subconscious barriers to travel.

- Road exposure—it is critical to your success. You need passersby to know you exist. Therefore, theoretically, the busier the road, the more passing traffic you will attract. The theory sounds fine, but in practice very busy roads can be a disadvantage. If possible, avoid roads with median strips, areas near major traffic junctions, or speed acceleration zones. Often these locations will deter potential customers from driving into your entrance.

Merchandising Strategy

I discuss merchandising strategies in more depth in chapter 6. For our purposes here, let's simply say that even if you are in the right location, you may still fail because your merchandising strategy is wrong. Your aim is to get 100% of the people to see 100% of your product, and you need a customer flow plan that achieves this objective. You also need to place purpose products in the right location to encourage customers to visit all parts of your store. As part of your merchandise strategy, you will also need to consider signage and planograms of product placement to maximize sales per square foot.

Communications Strategy

Every business has internal and external customers, and you need an effective communications strategy to ensure your business runs as smoothly as it can. This means you need an effective recruitment policy, team training program, team meetings, and customer communications strategies. We will discuss these further in future chapters.

Size of Your Retail Outlet

The key is sales per square foot. If your garden center is too large or too small for the size of your market, then the business will find it will not achieve its full potential. Every site is different, and there are no fast rules one can offer. But, in my experience, many retail areas are too large and the results are low stock turn and higher running costs. The key is to have a compact center and maximize stock turns.

Get these four strategies right, and you may have a successful business. But a lot still relies on available capital, sourcing of product, and your own attitude to business and customers.

Book List

Abraham, Jay. *Secrets of a Marketing Genius.* Abraham Publishing.

Downes, Larry and Chunka Mui. 1998. *Unleashing the Killer App: Digital Strategies for Market Dominance.* Boston: Harvard Business School Publishing.

Johnson, Richard. "Who is Faith Popcorn?" *The London Sunday Times Magazine.* 24 December 2000.

Popcorn, Faith. 1991. *The Popcorn Report.* New York: Random House.

Ries, Alan and Jack Trout. 1994. *The 22 Immutable Laws of Branding.* New York: HarperBusiness.

Chapter 2

Location, Location, Location

In this chapter we will concentrate on the physical considerations when building a garden center. You should have a business plan in hand by the time you are buying or leasing your property and designing your retail operation.

You will need to find a piece of land that is in the right location and is the right size and shape. Not an easy task when you actually start looking. In the ideal world, you are searching for a square piece of land that is well drained, facing a major road, is the right size and allows for expansion, and has the correct planning permission with access from the highway. Local planning laws will vary depending on your location, and the size will vary depending on your local market. You will need to do your research, as each situation is unique.

We shall examine the main considerations as you select a location and a layout for your center. While the aesthetics are up to you, the basic logic and structure of the recommendations are sound and are present in almost all successful garden centers.

Entrance to Your Garden Center

You grow your business by getting existing customers to buy more and new customers to enter your store. How often have you driven to a new

Photo 2-1. This sign in California is very attractive, and it plays to the lifestyle aspect of garden centers.

location only to shoot past the entrance?

About 60% of customers will discover you when driving, and you need to get them into your center safely. You therefore need to be visible from well down the road so that vehicles can see you and have plenty of time to safely enter your parking lot.

Prior to purchasing a site, stand outside and count how many cars pass an hour, at what times, and at what speed. You can then judge whether you have the viable volume of traffic to set up a business.

To get your customers'—and potential customers'—attention, you will need an attractive entrance and a clear sign. Planning laws vary around the country, and you will need to check on these before putting a sign up. Unfortunately, in many commercial zones there is already "signage pollution" and your sign could get lost in the confusion of signage.

To get your sign read, there are some important considerations:
- Keep it simple
- State that you are a garden center
- Use colors that stand out, i.e., green and yellow or red and yellow
- Use lowercase words, as they are more easily read
- Letters should be at least a fifth as wide as they are tall
- Use flowering plants en masse around your sign in company colors, as this will give your sign more emphasis.

You are building a gardening center of excellence: First impressions are critical. You must provide an image of being a professional gardener. The exterior should provide a high quality landscape appearance. At the same time, remember that the more elaborate the landscape design, the higher the maintenance costs. Keep it simple and professional—this will keep your maintenance costs under control.

Be sure to use low-growing plants so customers have a clear view of your signage and the garden center building.

Stopping Time

According to the British Department of Transport, the distance to a driveway at 30 mph should be twenty-five yards. This allows for ten yards of thinking time and fifteen yards of braking time. If you are located in an area where vehicles are travelling at 60 mph, then you will require seventy-five yards-twenty yards for thinking time and fifty-five yards for braking time.

Access

You will need the store to be highly visible from the road. The main access will have to accommodate cars and large trucks. You may need to consider a separate entrance and exit, depending on your site.

In the Garden Centre Manual, which I wrote with Ian Baldwin, we set out a garden center vehicle access plan that still applies today.

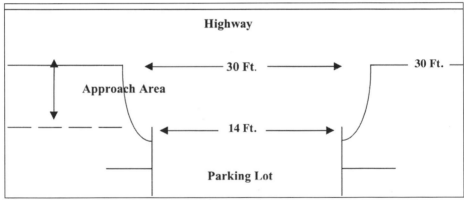

Figure 2-1. Entrance to parking lot from road.

The approach area between the road and the drive should "bulge" outward to allow vehicles to turn easily off the road.

Parking

You need a solid surface for customers to park their vehicles, especially as spring and fall are busy seasons and often not the ideal weather conditions to park on grass.

The amount of parking you provide will depend on the size of your center, whether you have a coffee shop or not (people will stay longer if you do), and other parking facilities that are available around your center. Remember, too small a parking lot or too big could affect your sales. Too few spaces will drive customers away when they cannot find parking, and too many spaces will give the impression that you are never busy. We will discuss design of parking lots at greater detail in chapter 4.

Provide Windbreaks

Customers will buy more in a sheltered site. Plus, in an exposed, windy site, your cost of exterior plant maintenance will increase.

Ideally, a natural shelterbelt of trees will look a lot more aesthetic than an artificial shelterbelt. Provide shelter and you will improve the quality of your plants, have less heat loss from buildings, less labor in picking plants up that have blown over, and a more comfortable shopping environment that should increase your average sale per customer.

Your aim is to reduce wind speed using a semi-permeable windbreak with 40 to 50% permeability. A solid wall will create turbulence on the leeward side, which could increase your problems.

The type of plant used for windbreaks depends on the climatic zone you are located in. Do not select a plant that is a major host of a pest that could damage your plants or the windbreak. Commonly used coniferous hedges include *Pinus nigra, Pinus nigra* 'Maritima', *Pinus radiata, Picea sitchensis*, and × *Cupressocyparis leylandii* (this plant has received bad publicity in recent years and, therefore, I would not plant this hedge near to a neighbor who may find it to be a problem weed). As an alternative to a conifer, you can use a hardwood species. Again, commonly used species include *Acer pseudoplatanus, Acer platanoides, Populus alba, Salix alba, Quercus* species, *Eucalyptus* species, *Alnus cordata*, and *Alnus incana*.

Buildings and Structures

Buildings will be required to retail dry goods, gifts, indoor plants, and to house coffee shops, storage, and offices. You can spend hundreds of thousands of dollars on buildings, but the key to remember is that you need a return on your investment. Do not over-invest in expensive buildings.

At the same time you will need a building that will reflect your image; is flexible in use and will withstand the climatic conditions. In

Europe, traditionally they have used converted greenhouses, whilst in Australia purpose-built brick or wooden buildings are the norm.

In general select from one of the following, but do analyze the pros and cons very carefully.

Greenhouses

Greenhouse structures are ideal for indoor plant displays and are in keeping with the industry we are in. They feel spacious and light and therefore can create the correct ambience for both product and consumer.

Greenhouses can also make a strong image statement that is completely different from other retail outlets. You can therefore make a strong statement from the road.

Companies such as Thermoflor in Holland and Private Garden in Massachusetts now make purpose-built glasshouses for retailers. These can come with adjustable roofs or sidewalls to provide complete flexibility. Many Dutch experts believe that within the next decade, Dutch garden centers will be completely covered to allow a year-round shopping experience. On the downside, greenhouse structures are expensive to heat, and many local planning authorities require so many structural alterations to make them comply with retail requirements that they can become very expensive to construct.

Photo 2-2. Lanoha Nursery in Nebraska makes it very clear they are a garden center and provide a bright, clean environment for their customers.

In high-light locations, dry goods packaging can fade very quickly in the intense light, which makes products look stale very quickly. Plus, if you are not careful, condensation on the glass can also spoil products.

Photo 2-3. Ugly greenhouse support poles can be made to look attractive using rope to soften the view.

Plus, there is the extra concern of leaks occurring between panes of glass in heavy rainstorms.

Wooden Buildings

Some retailers may select "off the shelf" wooden buildings as they are relatively cheap to purchase and construct. Gardening is a natural industry, and wood fits into the image you are aiming to create. These buildings are flexible and easy to alter as your business develops.

But, wooden buildings have to be cared for and maintained. If you do not, you will find your visual image can deteriorate rapidly. Depending on the size of the structure and geographic location, they can be cold and drafty. Plus, you have a more serious fire hazard than with some other types of buildings. Do check with local planners before you construct a wooden building to ensure you are within local regulations.

Designed Garden Center Buildings

The most common approach is to work with a consultant to develop a design-built building for your garden center. This should ensure you have an eye-catching building that meets all your needs to retail efficiently. The advantage is it is purpose built, whilst the disadvantage is that it is more expensive and often it is less flexible in its use for other retail functions, if you decide to get out of horticultural retailing.

The range of buildings is enormous. At one extreme, you may select an earth-covered building using geotecture (conservation-based method of building that conserves land, surface, and thermal energy). This style of building is one of the oldest styles (e.g. Montezuma's Castle, Arizona), but is now back in vogue and could well be used to develop a futuristic garden center.

In areas where snow is a factor, the pitch of a building's roof is critical. As a rule, work on one inch of height to every inch of width. If heavy snow is common, the ratio will need to be increased to shed snow from the roof.

In a hot region, air movement is the critical factor. You may need a building with wide doors or removable walls to ensure customers feel comfortable when they shop.

It is important to have some idea on what type of building you would prefer before employing an architect. You are going to have to run your business out of this building for a long time to come, so be sure it is what you and your customers will like.

Shade Structures

Customers will require some shade or shelter, as will some of your plants. From the consumers' perspective, they prefer a "transition zone" between the building and outdoors. A shade structure attached to your main building will encourage customers to leave the building and start shopping outdoors.

Many businesses now provide cover for the consumer along the outdoor "racetrack," the main traffic route; this encourages the customer to shop the whole outdoor retail area in comfort. To help ensure customers shop the whole area, many businesses place bedding plants (a prime purpose product) and the coffee shop (a prime leisure destination) at the farthest point away from the shop.

Photo 2-4. Shade structures protect sensitive plants and keep customers safe from the elements.

Facilities

It is worth listing the facilities you will need so you can logically go through them with your consultant, architect, and planners. Some of the more common elements not to overlook are:

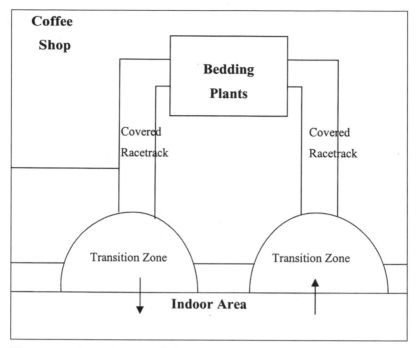

Figure 2-2. Organization of shopping area outside of main retail building.

- Services
  - ☐ Electricity
  - ☐ Telephone
  - ☐ Water
  - ☐ Sewage
  - ☐ Parking lot
  - ☐ Hard service
  - ☐ Handicapped parking
  - ☐ Loading area
  - ☐ Unloading area
- Building
  - ☐ Air conditioning
  - ☐ Heating
  - ☐ Lighting
  - ☐ Office for owner
  - ☐ Office for manager
  - ☐ Staff room
  - ☐ Restrooms

☐ Storage area(s)
☐ Retail area
☐ Checkout facilities
• Coffee shop
  ☐ Preparation area
  ☐ Seating area, indoors
  ☐ Seating area, outdoors
  ☐ Office
• Live goods area
  ☐ Watering system
  ☐ Display gardens
  ☐ Retail area
  ☐ Race track (main customer flow and materials used to identify it)
  ☐ Shade hall
  ☐ Information zone
  ☐ Promotional sales area

Build Your Own or Buy an Existing Business

We have thus far focused on building your own center, but it may be more viable to buy an existing business. Garden centers often become available, and this could be the opportunity you have been waiting for.

Before you rush in, find out why the business is for sale. It may be because the owner has reached retirement, lost interest, or is looking for a change of direction. It may be because it is a badly designed center or has been badly managed. It could be that the existing owners have done everything correctly, but a center is not viable on this site. You will need to make your own decision.

An ideal time to buy is when the company and stock has been run down but is still salvageable. Timing is critical when buying an existing business.

Before you purchase, you must obtain the financial figures for the business. You will need figures for when the business was at its peak as well as for the last twelve months. Find out the existing customer count, average sale per customer, and sales per square foot. You can then work out the true potential of the site.

Have an expert inspect the buildings. You need to be confident that they are stable and safe. If they are, this means you can start trading the day you move in.

The disadvantages of buying an existing business is that in the majority of cases the layout and buildings will need revamping and you will need to calculate how much capital injection is required.

Talk to a few locals before you purchase. You need to know what the recent reputation of the business is like. It is exceedingly hard work turning a business around when the previous owner has been negative in their customer relationships.

The contentious issues are always the value of stock and goodwill. A stock take is essential; only pay for salable product at wholesale value. Do not buy the previous owner's rubbish.

Goodwill is the real challenge. Is it really worth anything? The seller will convince you it is often worth considerably more than you are prepared to pay. In most situations I have come across, you will need to negotiate and both parties will need to give a bit to reach a compromise situation.

If you are looking to purchase an existing garden center, do provide your agent with precise information concerning catchment population within a set radius, site size, frontage specifications, and minimum size of the parking lot.

It is my opinion that in the next few years, a number of excellent sites could become available as more traditional garden center owners identify the trends in the marketplace and feel that they would rather retire than invest in a new challenge.

Get the Layout Right

When designing or buying a site, take into consideration the operation of the business. Your aim is to maximize sales and minimize costs. Costs can often increase due to bad design and layout. Before you build or buy anything, consider the following:
- Stock access. Are there separate entrances for stock and for customers? Is it easy to get goods to the shop, the live goods, and coffee shop? Are pathways wide enough to move products quickly and easily to all part of your retail site?
- Are the office, staff facilities, and checkout facilities located close together? The last thing you want are team members walking

great distances across your garden center just to get to key stations in the business.

- You need a clear racetrack to get customers around the store, but are there adequate escape routes to allow team members and customers to take shortcuts if required.

Book List

Baldwin, Ian, and John Stanley. 1982. *The Garden Centre Manual.* London: Grower Books.

Baggs, Sydney A., Joan C. Baggs, and David W. Baggs. 1985. *Australian Earth Covered Buildings,* Sydney: New South Wales University Press.

Saxtan, John H. 1994. *GrowerTalks on Retailing.* Batavia, Illinois: Ball Publishing.

Snook, Chris and Ken Crafer. 1999. *Grower Manual No. 4: Garden Center Manager.* London: Nexus Media Limited.

Chapter 3

Work *on* Your Business Plan, Not *in* Your Business

Going into business takes courage, especially when the statistics tell you that the chances are that you will fail within the first three years. This means you need to arm yourself with as much homework as possible, prior to opening the doors.

Owning a successful business is a rewarding experience—that is why so many of us set up our own business each year. But before even considering a business plan, the first priority is to look carefully at yourself and ask whether you are a suitable person to start a business. The questions you need to be asking yourself are:

- Are you a self-starter?
- Can you start and follow through long projects?
- Can you accept the responsibility?
- Are you prepared to work long days, seven days a week?
- Do you have sound health?
- Is there someone to take over if you get sick?
- Do you have leadership qualities?
- Are you organized?
- Are you a logical thinker?

Types of Financing and Sources Available for Starting Your Business			
Type	**Source**	**Description**	**Comments**
Overdrafts	Trading banks	Provides essentially short-term finance for such requirements as working capital, especially where seasonal fluctuations occur.	Should not be used for long-term purposes. Can be recalled at short notice.
Term loans	Trading banks	Generally available for the purchase of land, buildings, and equipment for fixed period ranging from three to eight years. Development loans for medium to long term.	Repaid with interest installments over the period of the loan.
Mortgage loans	Saving banks, trading banks, building societies, trustee companies	For purchase of land, buildings, and equipment.	Usually secured on a first charge on land and buildings.
Leasing finance	Trading banks, finance companies, merchant banks	Available for lease of equipment. Generally for the "economic" life of the leased goods.	Allows lessee use of productive equipment without capital outlay. Interest tends to be above medium- and short-term loans, but payments may be fully deductible from pretax income.
Hire purchase	Finance companies	Used for financing the purchase of equipment.	Ownership is vested with the lender until final payments are made. Interest usually charged as a flat rate over the life of the loan. The borrower is required to place a deposit on purchased goods.
Bridging finance	Finance companies, trading banks, merchant banks	Provided as an interim form of finance.	Useful only for short-term periods. Interest rates tend to be above other medium- to short-term loans.
Personal loans	Savings and trading banks, finance companies	Secured by the borrower's assets or by an income stream, these loans have a wide variety of applications	Interest usually charged at a flat rate over the medium-term length of the loan.
Equity and venture capital	Financial companies, merchant banks, friends, relatives	Source of equity funds or medium- to long-term debt capital, usually with provision for conversion into equity.	Generally available to sound, fast-growing businesses and for the launching of new ventures. Usually sought by businesses that have been unable to obtain low-risk funds from other sources.

Source: Planning and Starting a Small Business, *National Training Council, Australia.*

- Can you work easily with other people?
- Can you compromise?
- Are you a good listener?
- Are you a good communicator?
- Do you have experience in horticultural retailing?
- Do you have the knowledge to start a business?
- Are you sensitive to the needs of customers?
- Can you cope with crisis situations?

I would not expect you to answer yes to all the questions, but you need to know your strengths and weaknesses prior to starting on a business venture. (This list was adapted from a checklist in *Planning and Starting a Small Business*, Department of Industry and Commerce, National Training Council, Australia, 1983).

Having made a decision to proceed, it is now worth considering your personal financial worth. You will need immediate money to pay the initial rent, legal expenses, operating costs, and to support yourself. Consider what you own (cash, stocks, property, car, insurance policies, etc.), what you owe (bills, mortgages, loans, etc.), and work out what your personal worth is. Having calculated your worth, you can then start calculating your personal needs for each month and how much you need to generate to maintain the lifestyle you require.

Seed Capital

To start our garden center, you will need an initial sum of money, often called seed capital.

Financing is available as short term (less than three years), medium term (three to ten years) and long term (over ten years). You will need to consider how big and long a loan you will require, plus what type of loan.

Business Plan

There is no point approaching a finance house until you have a business plan. Remember, financial managers lend to people, not businesses. They do not know anything about garden centers. They expect you to provide a business plan with all the details.

The business plan serves a number of roles. First, it provides a pro-grammed set of activities in order to achieve defined objectives within your business. It is also a valuable communications tool, as it allows a third party to look at your business and consider whether they will support you financially. Finally, it allows everyone inside the business to know where the business is heading and their role in the overall picture.

A business plan should consist of:

Executive Summary

Although it comes at the beginning of your business plan, it's the last thing you actually write. Its aim is to provide an overview of your business that can be read in less than five minutes by a third party. The executive plan is made up of:

- Overall objectives of the business
- The competitive advantages your business has
- What products and services you will sell and to what target consumer
- A profile of the first three years projected sales and how you feel you will achieve this
- A summary on your marketing, retail, personnel, and financial strategies

Once you have whetted the reader's appetite, he will then venture to the next stage of your business plan.

Business Introduction

Having read the executive summary, the reader should be introduced to your business. This section should include your mission statement and business objectives.

The mission statement

Your mission statement is a simple, descriptive statement of exactly what your business will do. It also explains your business concept to people outside your business. Mission statements may sound simple, but can take a lot of time and effort to produce.

Leaders of today's garden centers are faced with the challenge of trying to transform their companies, to adapt to increased competition, downsizing, and the globalization of the industry. The starting point for dealing effectively with such issues is the organization's mission statement. By considering the following guidelines, you too can develop a mission statement that instills inspiration among your team and truly reflects their dreams, hopes, aspirations, and reasons for being.

Mission statements are not simply slogans or mottoes. They are the operational, ethical, and financial guiding lights for organizations. They articulate the goals, dreams, behavior, culture, and desired future of companies. A mission statement is a key component in an organization's entire planning process. Strategically, it is a tool that defines a company's business and target market. Culturally, it serves as the glue that binds the company together through shared values and standards of behavior. It must inspire and stretch staff to higher levels of performance.

Gathering the right words, setting the tone, and finding the main theme should involve individuals whose commitment to the final statement is expected. Establish a working party comprising representatives from various departments. Select wisely, for people's hearts as well as their heads are required.

Conduct a situation or SWOT (strengths, weaknesses, opportunities, threats) analysis to identify what your organization will stand for, what external forces will probably influence its future, and what it hopes to become. Be sure to get input from the owners and other senior people. With this background, the working group can brainstorm to compile a collection of ideas that can be synthesized into a draft statement.

In preparing a first draft, bear in mind the following cardinal rules for writing a mission statement:

- It can vary in length. It can be very short ("Total customer satisfaction"—Motorola) or several paragraphs long, where the mission is supported by vision statements, values, objectives, principles, or philosophies to provide guidance. Most would average twenty-five words in length.
- It must be clearly articulated. It should be easily understood, pithy, and to the point, free of empty phrases and complex terms or jargon, and should espouse principles and values that will guide the stakeholders in their day-to-day and future activities. The mission of this airline was succinct and readily understood: "The mission of Southwest Airlines is dedication to the highest quality of customer service delivered with a sense of warmth, friendliness, individual pride and company spirit."
- It should be written in an inspiring tone. It should encourage

commitment and energize all staff towards achieving the mission. It should be elegant, positive, colorful, and inspiring. Consider Intel Corporation's mission: "Do a great job for our customers, employees, and stockholders by being the preeminent building block supplier to the computing industry."

- It must be relevant and current. It should echo your organization's history, culture, and shared values, and should focus on the present but look to an attainable future. But in an ever-changing, competitive environment, the mission should be regularly reviewed and subject to revision to retain your company's current focus and direction.

- It must reflect your organization's uniqueness. It should set your company apart from others, establishing your individuality. Consider the mission statement of Celestial Seasonings: "Our mission is to grow and dominate the U.S. specialty tea market by exceeding consumer expectations with the best tasting, 100% natural hot and iced teas, packaged with Celestial art and philosophy, creating the most valued tea experience. . . ."

- It must be enduring. Mission statements should guide and inspire for many years. They should be challenging, yet just short of total achievement. Disneyland's mission, for example, will be forever, provided there is "imagination" left in the world.

- It must cater for all audiences. The statement must convey your message clearly, concisely, and strikingly to all your stakeholders, who must universally understand and accept its meaning.

A statement that is hurried or does not reflect the input of those who must carry it as their standard into the community will rarely inspire nor involve those whose input matters most. The process may take a few weeks, a few months—even a year. During that time, you should circulate drafts to any who were not present at drafting meetings and whose commitment is required and display the mission statement for employees to see, inviting them to add any minor finishing touches.

When you are confident that the mission statement has received and benefited from stakeholders' input, produce a final version. Hold meetings to gain commitment to the mission and to turn its message into reality. Agree on the other uses to be made of the mission—on posters, publications, business cards, T-shirts, coffee mugs, products, calendars, etc.

Developing a mission statement is just the beginning. It must continue to have meaning for all employees. So, periodically refer to it on the agenda at meetings of staff, board, and other groups. An annual revisit should occur as part of the review of your organization's strategic plan.

(Note: The section on mission statements is adapted from *Just about Everything a Manager Needs to Know*, by Neil Flanagan and Jarvis Finger, Brisbane, Australia: Plum Press, 1998.)

Business objectives

Having spent time on your mission statement, it is now time to move set your objectives. Your business objectives allow you to measure your performance. Your objectives could be sales targets for a twelve-month period, average sale per customer, or average sale per square foot.

Since you are starting off in business, you may also wish to include your personal objectives. To write these, include your partner and make sure you both agree on these objectives. Personal objectives could include days and hours a week you will work, vacation objectives, hobby objectives, or domestic objectives.

Finally, in this portion of your business plan you should include a section on your competitive advantage. This should include what makes you unique in product and services, how you plan to manage your unique niches, desirability of your location, service, and quality strategies.

Horticultural Retail Industry Analysis

The reader of your business plan needs to feel confident that you understand the horticultural retail industry. They need to know you have analyzed it and are aware of the trends and where your business will fit into the overall picture.

Explain how the industry is structured nationally (peak body and its role) plus how it is structured within your state. At a state level, provide a total retail value for horticulture goods and who are the dominant players in the industry. Also, provide a total number of horticultural retail outlets within your catchment area. Follow this with a summary of the industry—is it in a growth phase, declining, or static? Give your reasons for this and provide some future projections.

Analyze customer buying habits and discuss the changes in consumer buying habits. How lifestyle changes effecting the gardening industry locally and how you will address this in your own garden center.

Finally, provide a paragraph on the opportunities and concerns for the garden industry in your state.

Introduce Your Business

Now is the time to introduce yourself and your business. You should include basic facts on your skills, work history, education, and training as it relates to the project and your aims. Also, provide information on your business advisors, especially your accountant, lawyer, banker, and consultant.

You will also need to assure a financier that you will comply with the laws and regulations in your state when operating a garden center. These may include registrations, permits, trading hours, fire prevention, safety regulations, and licenses.

As far as the premises are concerned, you will need to provide details on the duration and cost of the lease or rent per week and square foot (plus when and how often rent reviews are). Provide details about the owners of the premises and the managing agent. Be honest; discuss the current strengths and weaknesses of the business and what you see as the business opportunities.

Having set the scene for the business, it is now time to go into depth in the following specific areas:

Marketing Strategy

Someone once defined marketing as "selling products and services that do not come back . . . to people who do." Marketing involves your pricing, promotions, sales, advertising, and product distribution.

As far as financiers are concerned, they want to know your product and competitive advantage, your market segment, barriers, and strategies. They want to know what you believe will be your market share and how you will achieve that.

I am a great believer that it is your business, not your product, that is your brand, and your objective should be to promote your brand (garden center), not your products. Success is based on differentiating your garden center from other garden centers, and to be successful, you need to spend time on developing a unique brand within your catchment area. To achieve this you need to be very clear on knowing your competitive space (catchment area) and your target consumer. You need to understand the benefits they need and want in the future from your garden center. Make a list of all the values you could offer these customers. This may include a mowing service, garden care service, delivery service, and so on.

Once you have listed the values you can offer, you should then identify how you can create a profitable, competitive advantage from the list you have drawn up. You may not be able to service all the value needs of the customer, although you may be able to network with other businesses to provide a value package to your customers. For example, you may be able to network with a garden designer to create a win-win situation for all concerned. Look at your customers' needs and build your brand around those, even if it means creating new and unique business associations.

Once you have developed to this stage, you can then decide how to communicate this to your target customers. Define your real brand core and keep evolving, as time and change never stand still.

In defining your brand, you have one major problem—brand differentiation in the consumer's mind is on the decline. Twenty years ago, consumers knew where to go for brand specialists in meat, fish, gas, gardening, and so on. Today, many retailers are trying to be a one-stop shop. For example, at my local gas station I can buy ready-cooked food, do my banking, rent a video, buy my weekly groceries—oh, and get gasoline.

I believe this is an opportunity—consumers are looking for clearly differentiated brands that stand out. Your role is to make your garden center stand out from the crowd.

Other chapters in this book discuss various marketing strategies, so I will not cover them in this section. But I must stress that your marketing strategy is an important section of your business plan.

Pricing Strategy

Financiers will need to feel comfortable about how you price your products. Their concern is, Will they get a return on the capital employed and what are the safety margins for the business? They are interested in the *minimum* profit you will make as a retailer.

Retail Strategy

Your garden center's lifeblood is its customers. You will need to show what your service standards are and what training program you will use

Management Memo

Target setting could include:
• Staff retention: Of my five current staff, at least four will still be with me at the end of the year
• Stock turn: Achieve an average stock turn of 4.8 times per year
• Margin achieved: Achieve an actual margin (after discounts and stock losses) of 36%
• Sales per staff member per hour: My annual sales target is $700,000. My average sale is $40 per transaction. Therefore, I need 17,500 transactions per year, or 56 per day (for a six-day week). With four of us on the floor, we need to average 14 sales each per day or two per hour. (Two sales per hour each sounds a lot more achievable than $700,000 per year!)
• Proportion of customers making a purchase: For every ten customers coming into the store, we want to sell something to seven of them. This can be measured by counting customers coming in via a counter and comparing this against the transaction numbers on the cash register.
—John Albertson

to maintain the consistency level you aim to achieve.

Personnel Strategy

The people you employ will often determine success or failure. Therefore, financiers will want to see your company personnel structure, job titles, and job descriptions. You should also include your wage rates and your incentive program. Include in this section the performance measure for your team (average sale per customer) and how the incentive program will kick in.

Financial Strategy

At the final crunch, it is the financial strategy that a financier will be interested in. Remember, this is their comfort zone, and the more details you can provide in this section, the happier they will be. This also means you will probably need your accountant to help you.

You will need to provide details on resources and assets you require and forecasts and budgets on sales, expenses, purchases, profit, and cash flow. It pays to be conservative when doing forecasts, as you cannot forecast the weather, economic trends, or changing consumer habits.

Chapter 8 concentrates on financial strategies, and you should refer to this chapter for the details you require to compile your financial details.

Finishing Your Business Plan

Having done all your homework, it is time to finalize your business plan. Once it is all typed up, I recommend you give it to a colleague who has not been involved with the construction of the document. Ask him or her to read it and check it for spelling mistakes, punctuation, and arithmetic errors. The last thing you want is these mistakes being picked up at your presentation.

You should add on appendices with photographs and support documentation and then bind the document. The more professional the document, the more likely you will get the support you will need.

Talking to the Bank Manager

Once you have completed your business plan, you will most likely need to talk to the bank manager. The objective is to get the bank manager to say yes. But, what do you have to do to get to a yes?

Moneylenders in banks are guided by bank policies, lending manuals, and textbooks written by bank managers, not garden center managers. They do not understand our industry, and their thinking process is completely different than yours.

There is a large gap in financial thinking between the entrepreneur and the bank manager. Remember, bank managers will be cautious—they are lending money to a risk venture. A manager's major fear is lending to a loser. This is a far more important driving factor than lending to a winner. You therefore need to consider your project from a bank manager's perspective and prompt the manager by helping along the decision making process.

As a bank manager, you would consider:
- The purpose of the financing.
- The business risk of the venture.
- The timing of the financing. The bank manager knows the average life of a small business is three years. Do not ask for the financing of a new business to span six years—it's not worth the risk.
- The lender's knowledge of the business. Have you done your homework on the competition, the financing, cash flow, marketing, merchandising, and so on?
- What references the lender can provide. Your accountant should be a reference to the viability of the project. Plus, garden center and retail consultants!
- The size of the enterprise the lender is planning. Bank managers know that small businesses, to keep families employed, are a greater risk than medium to large projects.

Having prepared yourself prior to meeting the bank manager, you can then submit your loan application. Be specific in your requirements. Submit your business plan, but also submit a separate document. The business plan should supplement the document the manager wants to see.

Set out a document for the bank using the following headings:

1. Amount sought
2. Term period sought
3. Interest rate sought
4. Purpose of financing
5. Background of the management team
6. Management reporting systems
7. Industry risk
8. Business risk
9. Financial risk
10. Historical information on management team and previous projects
11. Cash flow and financial performance forecasts
12. Security available, with independent valuations that you are offering
13. Summary of the business plan

The more thorough you are, the more confident your manager will be. It is a matter of convincing the manager that you are not a loser.

Now Become a Winner

At the beginning of this chapter, I mentioned that most businesses start and fail within a three-year period. Perhaps it's now time to reflect why this happens and what you can do about it. Michael Gerber in his excellent book *The E-Myth* explains that most people go into business as technicians rather than entrepreneurs. How often do we see that in our industry?

I recently worked with a young couple who wanted to start a garden center. Both worked in a garden center and felt they knew enough about plants and customer service to start their own business. They felt they could take a wage out of the business to survive. But their knowledge of retail concepts, business and financial planning, and market trends was practically nonexistent. This is a classic example of a technician wanting to be an entrepreneur.

Your objective is to produce a business plan for a company that works rather than to create a job for yourself. To achieve that, your business plan should be based on what you want the company to look like when it is finished so you can then work toward those set goals.

You will be successful if you have a vision and set out a business plan to achieve that vision. Success is not about luck; it is about vision, business planning and implementation. Enjoy the journey!

Book List

Gerber, Michael. 1985. *The E Myth: Why Most Businesses Don't Work and What to Do about It.* Cambridge, Mass.: Ballinger.

Step-by-Step Business Plan. 1995. Perth, Australia: Business Enterprise Center.

Planning and Starting a Small Business. 1983. Canberra, Australia: Commonwealth of Australia Publication.

Chapter 4

Get 100% of Customers to See 100% of Your Product

The objective of opening a garden center is to expose customers to your products so that they are inspired enough to buy them. It may seem obvious, but if the consumer cannot see the product, they cannot buy it. Therefore, one of the main goals is to ensure that 100% of your customers see 100% of your product.

This is logical, but, alas, the majority of consumers in most retail establishments don't see the majority of products. In fact, research carried out by Eve Tigwell (Eve Tigwell Consultancy UK) in 1998 in British garden centers found that 80% of consumers only saw 20% of products. Why is this?

The golden rule to remember that is you, the retailer, decide where I, the consumer, will go in your garden center. If you do not understand how the consumer shops, then you could well fail to maximize the sales per square foot in your store.

Paco Underhill is viewed as the guru on the psychology of shopping and his book *Why We Buy* is, I believe, essential reading for anyone in retailing.

Management Memo

Working with a Store Designer

The relationship between you and the designer must be a smooth partnership from the outset. The brief you should give the designer must contain the following:

• Target customer profile and all available market research information. The spending patterns of your customers and products that must be stocked.
• Planned product mix and stocking policy
• Proposed departments and adjacent categories (e.g., coffee shop)
• Display policies
• Back room facilities required (e.g., stockroom, staff room, offices, etc.)
• Requirements for the checkouts, telephones, and security
• The capital available to develop the total concept

—Malcolm H. B. Macdonald and Christopher C. S. Tideman

Before we can design a garden center, we need to understand how a customer shops a garden center. Garden center retailing has the added complication of indoor and outdoor retail departments, whilst the majority of other retailers only have to deal with one environment.

Climate Zones

One of the biggest challenges a garden center consumer has is adjusting to different climatic zones and lighting zones within the same retail environment. Let us look at the shopper's environmental experiences when shopping a garden center. She exits her car and steps into your parking lot. Outdoors, it could be wet or dry, hot or cold, dark or light. When she enters the shop, the environment changes. Indoors can be warmer or colder than the outdoors and either lighter or darker. When she walks to the plant area, she shifts back to the outdoor conditions again. After finding the plants she wants, our shopper must return inside to indoor conditions, before returning to the parking lot and dealing with the conditions there again, this time though with merchandise in hand or in tow.

Consumers may or may not be prepared for the variations in environmental conditions, and if you do not help them, they may not make the complete journey through your center. You cannot eliminate all the variables on the journey, but you can reduce the consumers' stress.

Let us take the journey again and look at some options you need to consider:

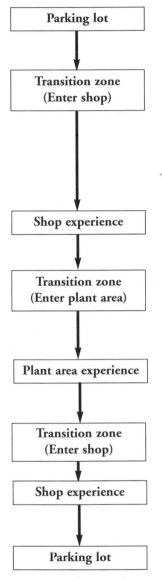

Weather protection from the car to the entrance needs to be considered, e.g., complimentary umbrellas, shade trees, shaded parking, covered walkways.

This is the area at the entrance where the consumers have to adjust to entering your store. They have to cope with light differences, temperature differences, and entering a new environment. Help them adjust. Give them space to relax, and do not try and sell them product until they are ready to buy. The transition zone could be ten feet or larger, depending on the size of your store.

Customers need direction and space to browse your shop. If you confuse them or overcrowd your store with product, you will reduce your average sale.

The emotion is the same as entering the shop, but in reverse. The shock in environmental change can be greater, especially in extreme weather conditions. Consider entry via a shaded hall, covered walkways, or with umbrellas.

The criteria are the same as in the shop, but, alas, this is where many garden centers lose the customers and they wander around in confusion.

The same rules apply as when they entered the shop.

Again, the consumers experience the same emotions as previously discussed, and the considerations you make will be the same.

Again, same considerations as when they first came to your center, though now they will also have to contend with an armload or cartload of purchases.

Parking

The consumers' journey, once on your plot, starts in the parking lot. This is where they have their first internal image of your business. All the research indicates that good parking facilities rank as important elements in attracting customers, but what are "good" parking facilities.

You need the right number of parking spaces for the customers you

Management Memo

What Makes Shoppers Stressed?
1. Congested streets and shopping aisles
2. Delays in parking lots and checkout lines
3. Difficulty in finding items in the store
4. Loud music
5. Too hot or too cold
6. Lighting too bright or dim
7. Public announcements over loudspeakers
8. Confusing store layout
9. Inefficient signage
10. Bad labeling
   —David Lewis and Darren Bridger

attract. An overcrowded or an empty parking lot will turn customers away. According to Louis Berninger in his book *Profitable Garden Center Management*, you should work on a ratio of fifteen spaces per hundred cars expected on an average day. The only caveat I would mention is spring business. I would look for overflow parking facilities if they are available. Plus, in some parts of the world, the planners will make the decision for you.

You must also provide enough space for customer parking. The last thing you want is customers damaging each other's cars due to tight parking. This will soon put off return visits.

As with almost everything else you'll be designing and building, parking lots are subject to your local zoning commission. You should check with them about specific rules for parking space size and the width of aisles. Typically, each space should be about nine feet wide and about twenty feet long, which is large enough to accommodate today's vehicles. Aisles should be wide enough to allow traffic to flow easily and for people to back out of spaces without hitting other parked cars. Parking angles of 70° or more should allow for two-way traffic down each aisle. The following chart lists some simple guidelines to determine parking lot size.

Parking Lot Requirements			
Number of Rows	**Width of Lot Required**		
	90°	60°	45°
1	43'	39'	32' 10"
2	62'	60'	49' 5"
3	105'	99'	79'
4	124'	120'	98' 10"

* From Louis Berninger, Profitable Garden Center Management *(Reston, 1982).*

You will need wider handicapped parking spaces (twelve feet) near the entrance to your garden center. The number of spaces required is dependent upon local, state, or federal law. Your local zoning commission should tell you how many are needed. For information about these spaces and other requirements, contact Office on the Americans with Disabilities Act, Civil Rights Division, U.S. Department of Justice, P.O. Box 66118, Washington, DC 20035-6118; (800) 541-0301.

A few other recommendations are:

- Painted spaces will allow for better flow and a more organized parking lot, resulting in more vehicles being able to park at any given time.
- Do not design your parking lot so that cars are reversing into the road.
- Keep the parking lot near the center and within easy access of the exit. Customers need to load their cars with ease.
- Make sure that the parking lot is well drained and you can take a cart across the lot with ease. You do not want to make a bad first impression by having your customer step in a puddle getting out of her car, nor do you want her struggling to push a cartful of merchandise across a bumpy lot.
- If you plan late-night shopping, you will need lighting in the parking lot.

A well-designed lot will be easy for the customers to enter, park, and find your center's entrance. You want to make everything as easy as possible for them to get to your front door. You want them in a good mood so they'll spend and return to you business again and again.

Foot Traffic

Consumers go where we tell them to go. We either make a conscious decision to direct them, or it occurs by accident.

Research by Paco Underhill, carried out around the world in various types of retail environments, confirms two important facts: If you drive on the right-hand side of the road, you want to enter a store on

> *Management Memo*
>
> Retailers are missing a great opportunity to increase their sales simply by having people visit more square footage and spend more time in the store.
>
> —Thomas Huff

the right and shop it in an counterclockwise direction, and if you drive on the left-hand side of the road, you want to enter a store on the left and shop it in a clockwise direction.

The position of your entrances, exits, and cash points is vital to your success and sales per square foot of retail space. Let me give you some examples based on American (right-handed) retail situations.

Pig Trough Retailing Style

This is called pig trough retailing because the checkout is situated in the center of the shop clearly visible from the entrance and exit in the first third of the building, like a trough in the middle of a barnyard.

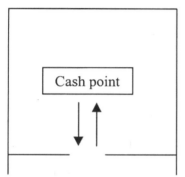

Figure 4-1. Pig trough design.

The result is a large percentage of consumers enter and only shop in front of the cash point and neglect products behind the cash point. By moving the cash point to the left-hand side of the store you could increase sales threefold (some businesses have).

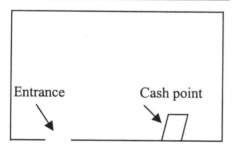

Figure 4-2. Reversed layout, which disorients the customer.

Confusing the Customer

The consumer wants to enter on the right and expects to see the cash point on the left. When you reverse this you confuse the customer. They feel disoriented, and the result is that they will often not shop the shop to the level you desire.

The Ideal Garden Center Layout

I appreciate that every garden center is different and has its own restrictions due to geographic, structural, and legislative restraints, but you need to start with a model and adapt it to your own requirements. The following model is how I would tackle the situation.

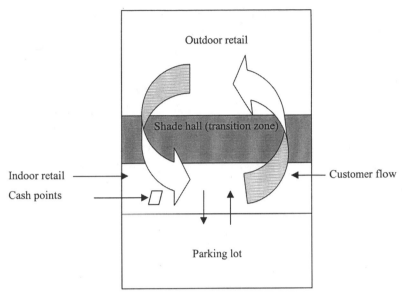

Figure 4-3. Ideal layout provides good customer flow and a shaded transition area.

Obviously to make any customer flow work, you need to ensure the right product categories are placed in the right positions on the route the consumers take. We will discuss that later in chapter 5.

In my opinion, one of the most effective customer flows in retailing has been devised by IKEA, the Swedish furniture company. Their customer flow layout ensures you "shop the shop" and could easily be adopted by a garden center. At IKEA, you enter the store and walk along a well-defined racetrack through "boutique" rooms that display lifestyle statements. The customer is encouraged by stimulating merchandising to visit all parts of the store.

> *Management Memo*
>
> You create traffic flow in a layout by the placement of cash registers, fixtures and fittings, aisle patterns and merchandise displays.
> —Lorraine Thornton

Create a Layout to Reflect Your Needs

Garden center design is the province of the professional garden center designer. Reputable designers exist in the U.S., Europe, and Australia. They understand layout and can determine the way customers should flow through a garden center.

The layout should reflect the needs of the particular retail sector and the image the owners hope to achieve. There are two extremes in styles of layout:

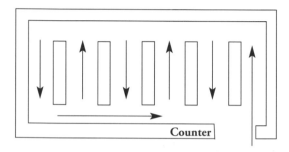

Figure 4-4. A grid layout guides consumers through each aisle of your shop.

The Grid Layout

"Box" stores are the experts at implementing this design, as are supermarkets. It is a simple layout that aims to ensure 100% of customers see 100% of product. Shoppers enter one end of the store and go up and down long, straight aisles until they reach the opposite end.

Photo 4-1. Informal store layout is relaxed and inviting.

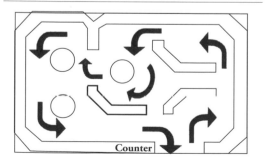

The Informal or Boutique Layout

This design is ideal for smaller garden centers. The leading boutique retailers are very skilled at getting their consumers to flow around an informal layout. A well-designed store will lead the customers through the shop while letting them enjoy their surroundings.

Between these two extremes there are a range of variations in layout, all of which work for different garden centers.

Figure 4-5. An informal layout lets customers flow through the shop in a much more meandering route.

Bounce Customers around Your Garden Center

Your aim should be to encourage movement of customers throughout your entire garden center. The placement of products or departments is the key to doing this. Here is how.

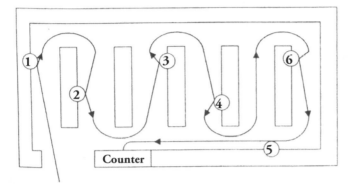

1. Shade trees (seedlings)
2. Garden care
3. Growing media (potting soil)
4. Bedding plants
5. Roses
6. Turf (sod)

Figure 4-6. Strategic placement of these anchor products ensures that customers will walk your entire store.

Review your customers' shopping lists—what are the most common items purchased? It is these that you should place at regular intervals around the garden center. In this way you force customers to visit all parts of the site. For example, consider the strategic placement of the following basic shopping list items, often referred to as anchor products:

Maximize the Use of Sight Lines

Sight lines are essential in all styles of layout, but are far more important in a boutique layout than in a grid design. Positive, appealing sight lines will draw customers around your center. Sight lines should use color, lighting, and product to attract the customer throughout the center, piquing their curiosity or revealing intriguing items and signage.

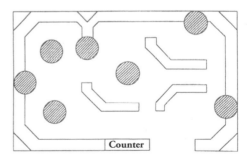

Critical sight lines throughout the store—

Figure 4-7. Sight lines draw your customers through your shop.

4-2. Tilted displays "throw" the product into the sight line of your customers, creating interest and leading them forward.

Develop Destination Departments

Entice customers to various parts of your garden center by developing and strategically placing destination departments in the corners of your garden center and at the farthest points from the entrance and exit. Promote these departments and become famous for them.

Examples that garden centers have established are: bedding plant departments, florist departments, coffee shops, cacti/succulent departments, rose gardens, and mazes (Van Hages Garden Company in the U.K. have an excellent maze using maize).

Management Memo

Layout Tips
• Gondolas at right angles to main aisle opens up the walls and brings all the classification into focus.
• Register at the front eliminates dead area and all merchandise is seen prior to reaching the cash desk.
• Space for strong promotional activity at the front of the store creates ideal impulse lines opportunities, but double-position them in their category as well.

—Peter Latchford

Remember "Butt Brush"

Paco Underhill coined the term "butt brush." It basically means that if you want consumers to browse your shop, you need to give them space. As retailers, we tend to get hung up on product rather than space, but if we restrict space by placing too many products in front of the customers, they end up leaving because they feel threatened by the lack of space.

When considering how to use retail space, take the following into consideration:
• To maximize your sales per square foot, about 40% of floor space should be allocated to product and 60% to browsing space.

- Some product categories require more space, as they are browse products. Provide more space for products such as gardening books, herbs, seeds, trees, and perennials.
- The main "racetrack," or traffic route, around your garden center should be at least nine feet wide if you are going to encourage the consumer around the whole garden center.

Book List

Lewis, David and Darren Bridger. 2000. *The Soul of the New Consumer.* London: Nicholas Brealey.

MacDonald, Malcolm H. B. and Christopher C. S. Tideman. 1993. *Retail Marketing Plans.* Woburn, Mass.: Butterworth-Heinemann.

Stanley, John. 1999. *Just about Everything a Retail Manager Needs to Know.* Brisbane, Australia: Plum Press.

Thornton, Lorraine. 1996. *Retailing: How to Lift Sales and Profits.* Adelaide, Australia: Stirling Press.

Underhill, Paco. 1999. *Why We Buy: The Science of Shopping.* New York: Simon & Schuster.

Chapter 5

Product Classification
and Product Placement

Part of the success of merchandising is placing the right product in the right place at the right time. To achieve this, you will need to understand the classification of products, as this will help you place the product in the correct position in the garden center.

Products can be classified in a number of ways and one product may fit into more than one classification. First, let us look at the classifications products fit into:

Known-Value Products (K.V. lines)

These are products that are purchased on price rather than their benefits, as the consumer perceives they know the exact price of these products. In general, K.V. lines include gasoline, cigarettes, hamburgers, milk, bread, and toilet paper. These products are sold on price, and even a five-cent increase in price is criticized by consumers (think about the global discussions on the price of a barrel of oil in recent years), but the reverse is that a five-cent reduction in price can result in a buying frenzy.

In our industry, very few products traditionally fit into this category. Consumers will tell you the list is narrow, although, it varies slightly around the world. In my part of the globe, known-value products are potting soil, slug and snail control, a common red rose, six packs of petunias and impatiens, and that is it. In some countries, they may add a pot chrysanthemum. The list is very small, although some growers and retailers will argue that K.V. lines include a larger range than I have given, but I believe that the maximum number of K.V. lines is twelve in any retail market.

When planning your strategies for K.V. product lines, consider the following:

- Do not be cheaper than anyone else on K.V. products; it will not help your bottom line. I do believe that a sound business decision could be to match your competitor's price, but do not be cheaper.
- Consumers will judge your whole product price strategy based on a few known-value lines. Make sure you are aware of the price structure adopted by your competitors on these lines. Mystery shop your competitors on a regular basis to ensure you are in tune with what they are doing.
- Research proves that you can be more expensive on known-value lines than your competitors. If you are, you must provide better quality, service, and services as perceived by your customers. But if you are more than 10% more expensive than the price leader, you will be perceived as being too expensive on your whole product range.
- The placing of the K.V. lines in your store is critical to how the consumer judges your image. If you want a perception of being product-driven, then place your K.V. products in your primary selling positions. If you want the perception of being lifestyle

Figure 5-1. Proper signage proportions for known-value products.

driven, then I would never place K.V. products in primary positions. I would use those positions for lifestyle statements and place the K.V. products in secondary positions.

- When merchandising K.V. products, you need your product signage to give the right message. K.V. product signage should, ideally, be written as in figure 5-1.

Non-Known-Value Products (Non-K.V. lines)

As you have already probably gathered, this includes the 98% of products you sell where the consumer does not know the exact price. They will have some perception of price bands, but they will not argue over the cents. These products will reflect your image and should be of the highest quality, something we will discuss in another chapter.

Photo 5-1. These known-value petunias are featured in a shaped display and highlighted with signage in the proper proportion.

Box store retailers rely on K.V. products to promote their business. In independent garden centers, I would rely on non–K.V. lines to grow my business, and it would be these I would promote when doing product-driven promotions.

Many retailers miss the opportunity to promote non–K.V. lines in the most effective way. The key is to promote the benefits prior to the price and to use these products in primary locations.

The key to success is how you manage your (non-price-sensitive products). Surprisingly, price is not always the major reason people purchase a product. A recent survey of customers at a Melbourne, Australia, garden center found that their priorities for purchase related to, in order of importance—name of plant, its height, the color of its flowers, the scent, its non-poisonous nature, and, finally, price. Indeed, the majority of products sold today are not price-sensitive products. Understand the special nature of such items, and you can improve your profit line.

Be Aware of Your Non-Price-Sensitive Products

Non-price-sensitive lines are normally purchased on impulse. They are often a want rather than a need and are normally not purchased with price being a major initial motivator. These are the items that can grow your bottom line since they should have a larger gross profit than price-sensitive product lines. In the majority of retail situations more than 80% of products stocked will fall into this category.

Position Non-Price-Sensitive Lines Carefully

Positioning is based on image. If your customers come to your store because price is a major motivator, then price-sensitive products should be displayed in major sight lines. However, if they come because of your range, quality, and service, then non-price-sensitive products should be displayed in those key positions.

Obviously you cannot display all your products in prime selling positions, so you will need to adopt a procedure where you rotate products in sight lines.

Figure 5-2. Format for non-known-value merchandise.

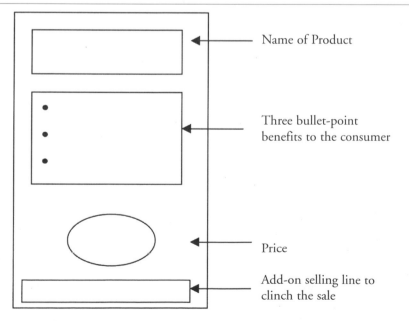

Name of Product

Three bullet-point benefits to the consumer

Price

Add-on selling line to clinch the sale

Produce Special Signs for Non-Price-Sensitive Lines

Customers purchase non-price-sensitive products for reasons other than price and so, to maximize sales of such items, you will need carefully constructed signage to emphasize qualities other than price.

Research tells us that we remember facts in groups of three, and this is a valuable guide when preparing your signs. Figure 5-2 illustrates a proven format for non-price-sensitive signs:

Understand Needs and Sell Benefits

Price may be an issue for your sales team, but it is normally not an issue to the consumer in terms of non-price-sensitive products. For this reason, sales people should listen to the shopper, identify the real benefits to that customer, explain these benefits—and finally get around to price. Training programs should include product benefits training and its importance in the role of selling.

Sales team members should:

Offer assurance. Your signs and selling techniques should erase any doubts customers have. "Stroke" them so that they will feel like winners by making this buying decision.

Project quality. Be ruthless with your standards because, in today's retail world, quality is expected.

Inspire customers to buy. Group products in themes, suggest uses for the products, show how easy they are to use, and demonstrate the benefits.

Offer a complete package. Always think "link" and offer a complete package. Customers have come shopping for enjoyment and expect you to provide everything they need—including related items.

Display Products to Maximize Sales

The aim is to encourage customers to shop the non-price-sensitive lines and search for the price-sensitive lines. You may need to reorganize your merchandising to achieve this objective.

By placing the appropriate non-price-sensitive lines at the gondola ends and the budget lines in the center, you can achieve extra sales along the whole gondola.

Figure 5-3. Proper merchandising of gondolas.

End of gondola   Middle of gondola   End of gondola

Non-price-sensitive products	Price-sensitive products	Non-price-sensitive products

Note these key points in managing non-price-sensitive product displays:
- Ensure the display is striking, yet in keeping with the style of the retail outlet.
- Communicate with your customers by providing information via leaflets, advertisements in newspapers, recorded messages in the store, literature near the cash register, promotions on cash register receipts, and promotions on carts and baskets.
- Let the display promotion spread into a storewide promotion. This is easily achieved with theme selling for spring, fall, Halloween, and Christmas promotions, but more difficult with generic promotions by an individual company.
- Prepare a promotion plan and record all activities. You need to measure the success and failures of any activity so you know if it's one that you wish to repeat or need to improve on before trying again.

Purpose Products

Sixty percent or more of purchases in garden centers are made on impulse, but many consumers come for a reason—they plan to purchase specific products. These are their "purpose products." Many of us will have the same purpose products on our mind or on a shopping list, and these are the products I want to discuss here.

It's the common purpose products that are the key products. These include bedding plants, potting soil, roses, flowering perennials, slug and

snail control, and Christmas trees (in season). These products are often
called anchor products—their role is to bounce the consumer around the
garden center. Let me explain: If you placed all the purpose products in
the front half of the garden center, the consumers may not feel the need
to visit the rear of your garden center. The result would be lower sales
over the whole sales footage. By spacing the anchor products equally
around the garden center, you encourage your customers to walk the
store and expose them to more products and raise your average sale per
customer.

Figure 5-4. Placement of Purpose Products

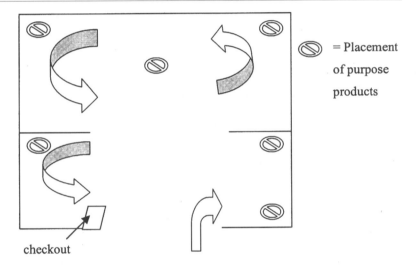

= Placement
of purpose
products

checkout

Impulse Lines

The opposite of a purpose product is an impulse product, an unplanned
purchase when the consumer enters your garden center. These are the
products you should display in primary locations to inspire the consumer
to buy.

Impulse products fall into a number of categories: plants in flower,
products that have become fashionable (a trend product), fad products (a
craze rather than a fashion), products recently promoted in the media,
and products being promoted by suppliers with promotional material
supplied.

Impulse items create the interest in your garden center. These lines
should be displayed in prominent positions in the garden center, and the

displays should be changed. The change should be based on how often customers come into your center. If the average customer visits once a month, then change your impulse displays once a month. You do not need to change all your displays at the same time. Have a revolving plan to change a percentage of display positions once a week. This will ensure you have a system that is easily manageable.

Browse Products

These products were mentioned briefly in the last chapter when we discussed "butt brush." To recap, these are products that customers need to browse shop and hence need more space whilst they make buying decisions. Browse products include seeds, perennials, herbs, and fruit trees.

Figure 5-5. Suggested browse category positions.

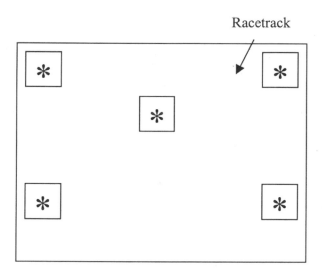

These categories should not be positioned on or near the racetrack. Ideally, they should be positioned off the racetrack where you can provide the customer with space to browse. This means the departmental signage is critical. The consumer needs to be able to easily find the department from the racetrack.

Link or Tie-in Products

One of your objectives is to create add-on sales when customers enter your center. One of the easiest ways of achieving this is by linking products together that are perceived as natural tie-in products by the consumer. If these products can be visually linked at the point of purchase, sales will automatically increase.

This may seem obvious, but it still surprises me how often this does not occur. The main reason is often because the "green" buyer and merchandiser deals with different product categories to the "dry" goods buyer and merchandiser, and they often do not communicate with each other. It is important that you think for your customer and display products where the customers expect them to be.

For example, from the consumer's perspective, the following products should be linked together when merchandising:

- Trees and tree stakes
- Pots and potting soil
- Vines and vine supports (climbers)
- Bedding plants and slug and snail control
- Orchids and orchid potting mix

Photo 5-2. Mix green and dry goods to help the customer. Chrysanthemums and slug control were an ideal combination. Be bold and use a minimum facing of three of each product to make sure the customer gets the message.

Photo 5-3. Trees can be awkward products to display. At Jardinere/Blooms in the U.K., trees are displayed in purpose-built fixtures with end displays used to cross-merchandise tree stakes, ties, and guards. Everything the homeowner needs is in one location.

Dump Bins

A dump bin is a display unit located in the race track that is used to promote one product by displaying it in a "dump" arrangement to give the impression that it is a price-motivated promotion. Only position them in a racetrack and only when you have six-foot path clearance all around the dump bin.

To merchandise your dump bin, allocate only one product type per bin, and display the product as if it was all just dumped into the bin. Dump bins will have a price sign in the bin to highlight the special price, and they must look full all the time. The life of a dump bin will be a maximum of one month.

While you may not like the way it looks, sales will increase by a minimum of 30% for the specified product.

Male and Female Products

Yes, I am a firm believer that some product purchases are female led whilst others are male led. Also, all the research shows that women are the predominant buyers in garden centers, especially as those establishments become more lifestyle orientated. It is women that have grown the sales of cut flowers, perennials, annuals, and herbs and have urged retailers to introduce coffee shops. The more attractive your garden center looks to women, the more successful you will be.

But, a word of warning: Men garden too, and they need zones in your garden center where they feel comfortable. Men are the major purchasers of fruit trees, orchids, large garden tools, riding lawn mowers, and gardening power tools.

In my experience, I have found it most appropriate to clearly define the male shopping zones. This encourages the male shopper to browse shop in comfort. Once relaxed, men tend to spend more money; hence, the male browse departments could be critical to your success.

Retailing Styles

Having reviewed the classification of products and their placement in your garden center, it's now time to consider your retail style.

There are six styles of retail outlets, and the consumer judges them based on the product assortment. Your decision is what type of retailer do you want to be.

Convenience Retailer

This type of retailer attracts a broad base of customers. Prices tend to be slightly higher than some other stores selling the same product, as customers will pay for convenience. As far as garden centers are concerned, a convenience garden center would be a general "middle of the road" independent garden center found in your typical suburban area. Be warned though—this type of garden center is on the decline because you cannot please everyone.

Competitive Retailer

This type of retailer again has a large inventory but is more competitively priced than the above and hence tends to take market share. In general retailing, they are often franchises, but in the garden center industry they tend to be chain operators, although perceived as independent centers by the public.

Focused Retailers

These businesses target specific customers. They select one range of products and do it well. For many consumers, retailing can be a boring experience with so many garden centers selling the same things in the same way. At the same time, new garden centers are opening and reducing the opportunities for many retailers to increase their market share. The secret is to become the customer's favored store—but first you have to be noticed.

According to Donald Cooper, the Canadian fashion retailer and consultant, the key to success is that you have to become, in sequence: noticed, remembered, preferred, and then trusted. This means that you must work on a strategy aimed at having you stand out from the crowd.

Perth, Australia–based consultant Barry Urquhart emphasizes that in the future, you will have to dare to be different. You will have to think and act outside the box so your garden center will be noticed by the consumer—in a positive way, of course. This means creating adventurous services, displays, staff costumes, and total experiences for your potential customers. Being different and famous takes team commitment. Brainstorm ideas with your team, and involve all team members. And believe in the concept you come up with.

To be a destination, you have to provide your customers with a destination product range. Research your market and find out where other

5-4. **M. T. Pots in New Zealand create added-value pots. To be a destination, you need unique products, so source out custom-made products so your customers will keep coming back to see what's new.**

garden center retailers are not providing the full width and depth of product range and associated services. Then set about developing this product range and gain a reputation locally as the expert and the most comprehensive supplier of this product. It could be that you have the best selection of perennials, water plants, bonsai, or camellias. Whatever it is, do it the best.

Do not be shy about your strengths. Too often, garden center retailers establish the range that they are famous for but fail to let the customer know. Assumption is one of the leading failures in business. Never assume your customers know what you do.

Dominant Product Retailers

These are the category killers of retailing. They dominate the sector they are in. I know of one example where a dominant retailer went from zero to 54% of a gardening market in three years—that is a category killer!

Opportunity Retailers

These are the companies that came into a category when it is in vogue and then leave it when it is out of fashion. A supermarket that only comes into gardening for spring would fit into this category.

Velocity Retailers

These are the warehouse retailers that offer no choice, but move product quickly. One that comes to mind is a company that only sells the top ten roses and only when they are in season.

Chapter 6

Furniture Requirements
for Successful Retailing

Retailing is about putting the right product in the right place at the right time. Putting the product in the right place means making sure you have the right fixtures to enable you to maximize the right place. Fixtures or retail furniture should show off the product to its maximum effect, enhance the image of your business, and be cost effective.

When building a garden center, you will need a budget for fixtures and furniture. Many retailers often underestimate the cost of such items, and the result is that they do not maximize their sales. Fixtures come in all price brackets, your aim should be to obtain shop fixtures that do the job you require and maintain your image, but do not overspend on the fixtures. You do not make more sales if the fixtures look expensive; you make more sales by optimizing the position of the product.

As a general rule, keep the following in mind:
- Fixtures that are light and easy to move will allow you to change the layout of your garden center more easily.
- Purchase adjustable shelving. Not all products are the same size, and you will need flexibility in your shelving.

- Be consistent in what you buy. Standardization on the style of store fixtures will enhance your image.
- Review what is available before you select which system to use in your garden center.
- Make sure the fixtures are safe and robust; garden center fittings get more wear and tear than department store fixtures.

Before you purchase, ask yourself whether you need to buy new fixtures. Store fixtures are available secondhand and at auctions, and these may suffice your needs. Also consider whether suppliers will help finance such fixtures if they can see the benefits to them.

At this point, it is worth discussing supplier fixtures, or POP displays. Many suppliers will supply them. Some of these fixtures are excellent and enhance the product and your center. Others may conflict with the image you are aiming to create and would not be suitable. You will need to make a decision based on each situation. In some horticultural categories, such as seeds, the seed houses are providing excellent stands that enhance the product and the store.

Interior Fixtures

When it comes to interior fixtures, the choice is enormous and the decision-making process is difficult.

First, the trend is to use fixtures against the walls up to a height of seven feet or to the ceiling to maximize wall space. In the center of the store, the trend is to keep fixtures to a height of five feet to enable you and the customer to look over them. This is done for two reasons: It will make your shop feel more open, and it will reduce pilfering, as you can keep an eye on customers and vice versa.

Your fixtures must be strong enough to take heavy items such as large pots, growing media, and heavy ornaments, but they must be adjustable to enable you to maximize the use of your vertical space.

At the cheaper end of the price scale are pegboard-backed fixtures, whilst slatwall displays would be considered to be more durable and expensive.

When designing the shop fittings for the interior of your business, you will need:

Linear Wall Units

These can go to a height of seven feet and must have adjustable shelving. You may wish to place a company fascia at the top of the fitting. This will enhance the image of your garden center and will stop the customers' eye wandering into the ceiling area.

Linear Island Units

Ideally, these should not exceed five feet in height. They should be double sided, have adjustable shelving and be easily moveable. Many of my clients put them on industrial wheels (with brake locks) so that they can move them around the store easily.

Endcaps

Endcap displays are critically important areas for promotional displays. You therefore need to invest in end display units that are the same height as your linear units in the center of your store. These units again need adjustable shelves and need to be moved easily.

Island Displays

Your island promotions are critically important. I recommend you invest in small plinths you can use for displays. Ideally, select three sizes to enable you to introduce a variation in height to your promotions.

Photo 6-1. These linear units at Lifestyle Family Garden Center (South Africa) make an effective frame to the seed department. The image boards on top keep the customers focused on the shop, not the ceiling.

Photo 6-2. This linear unit is curved, to create customer interest.

Checkout Your Checkout

Of all the areas of a garden center, it is often the checkout that causes the most concern. As far as the customers are concerned, it can be a major point of stress. Research shows customers start getting stressed when the line is longer than three-people deep. This can be a major problem during the spring months.

Business is always looking at a checkout that is efficient and ergonomically correct for team members. Plus, do you design a full service desk, double-belt checkouts, left hand/right hand passage, or tandem layout systems? To add to the confusion, technological changes are taking place. Whilst some garden centers are introducing scanning systems, others are already developing new data fills, customer scanning, and cashless payment systems.

Suppliers also look at the checkout as a profit center and see opportunities to expose their product as the last product the customers see prior to paying for their goods. With all these challenges, you need to try and please everyone—team, customers, suppliers, and management.

Design a Checkout That Works

The checkout must be functional. Basically, a checkout is a platform or conveyor belt on a box. You need to make some design decisions:

What materials should it be made out of so that it fits your store's image? Remember, everyone goes to this part of your store, so it is a major point to reflect your image. Materials that may be suitable include sheet metal, corrugated metal, stainless steel, wood, plastic, glass, or aluminum.

What size should the checkout be? The more upscale your store, the smaller the checkout. If you are a discount store, you may need up to nine feet of conveyor belt. As a general rule, make sure your counter can accommodate products from one and a half shopping carts. Before building a checkout, it is well worth studying the system at your local supermarket. They are the retail experts at processing people and product. Most work on a five-foot feeder belt and a large packing area.

In garden centers, the team often needs to exit the checkout using a hand scanner to scan large products in shopping carts. If this is the case in your store, make sure you design an exit at the front of the checkout.

As already discussed, your team's health and work efficiency is critical and therefore the ergonomics of the checkout is important. Your objective is to position a number of different pieces of equipment in a tight space, whilst ensuring the team can use this equipment without getting fatigued. In countries like Sweden and Germany, there are now legal regulations to ensure the design of checkouts minimizes stress.

The key points are that team members have enough legroom, a chair, and a correct layout of the keypads. Remember, get it right for the team and you will have fewer errors at the till.

The most intensive research in this area has been carried out by the Fraunhoter Institute in Stuttgart, Germany. According to their research the layout should be as illustrated in figure 6-1.

Figure 6-1. Ideal checkout station design.

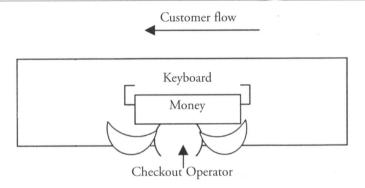

Register Rage

Customer rage at the counter is becoming an increasingly important consideration at checkouts. As a result of this, stores such as Wal-Mart and Kmart are investing millions on futuristic ideas to overcome this problem.

In the future, super-fast checkouts will be the norm. To achieve this, "smart packing" of products will need to evolve. Future products will have a tag that emits a radio signal, which is picked up by a computer at the exit. This computer will add up your bill and take the money out of your account.

Management Memo

Eighty-three percent of women and 91% of men say long lines will make them stop patronizing a particular store.

—American research group
Retail Asia, September 2000

In the meantime, ensure you have a policy to manage the checkouts. Make sure all checkouts are operating during busy periods. When the line of customers gets too long, get team members to acknowledge the problem and show some empathy to the customers. If you don't, they may be one-time shoppers!

Product Placement

View the checkout as a separate profit center. Recognize it as one of the most important departments in the store. Assign one person to the responsibility of maintaining the checkout area.

The checkout should be used for a maximum of two impulse products aimed at increasing the average sale per customer. Products should not exceed the ten-dollar price point and ideally should be below five dollars. The products must be topical and natural add-on products for the majority of your customers. Staff must verbally promote these products to the consumer where it is appropriate. And a point-of-purchase sign must be positioned next to these products to further entice your customers. Last, do not let the display get below half full.

Photo 6-3. Keep your checkouts clean and professional. They are the last impression your customers will have of your center.

Maintaining the Checkout

Last impressions are lasting impressions. It is critical that the checkout is kept clean and tidy at all times.

Check at least three times a day to make sure the area is clean and uncluttered. Dust every day, and do not clutter with coffee cups, garbage, or irrelevant products. Do not store products at the checkout; it clutters the area and makes it look like a stockroom. And never eat at the checkout or in view of customers—it is highly unprofessional.

Plant Fixtures

Traditionally, nurseries have placed plants on the floor, making the customers bend to select products. Retail research has shown that this dramatically reduces sales per square foot of retail space, and retailers now place plants at the correct shopping height to maximize sales.

It is surprising it took so long to raise plants off the ground when you consider that for every hundred units you sell at the correct shopping height, you sell twenty on the ground. But, what is the correct shopping height?

In "traditional" retailing, we talk about the "sight and take" position being the optimum position—this being between the chin and bellybutton of a typical consumer. This law still applies when selling plants, except the consumer prefers to look down at plants, but still doesn't want to bend down. This means you need to construct benches where the consumer can look down but pick the plant up without bending.

Benches

Bench heights will vary depending on the plant height to maximize sales. Benches are available in various materials and investments from a range of companies from around the world, plus many retailers get their own custom made.

When making a buying decision, consider the following factors:

Width. This is a retail unit, not a growing unit, and its aim is to maximize sales. If consumers are expected to walk both sides of it, then it can be twice as wide as a side unit. The width is based on an arm's length to allow all products to be shopped.

Mobility. A garden center retail outlet should be constantly changing. Benches should be constructed so they are easily moveable. Make them as light and flexible as possible.

Signage. Point-of-purchase signage is very important in selling plants. Ensure that your benches have the ability to carry a point of purchase signage system.

Durability. Remember, your benches will get wet, as you will be constantly watering. Ensure they are made so that you can water plants adequately and the benches will withstand water and allow it to drain away.

What style?

The key is not to spend large amounts of dollars on benching, but to maintain a consistent image for your business. This can be achieved cost effectively, and a bench system does not need to break the bank.

Although the overall image needs to be consistent, you will need different styles of benches to maximize sales. The styles to include are:

Photo 6-4. Linear benching.

Photo 6-5. This Stagecraft benching makes for sturdy and attractive benches.

Linear benches
Used for general sales of nursery stock in your "grid" layout plant categories.

Circular or hexagonal benches
These types of benches are ideal for your power spot display positions and lifestyle display arrangements.

Wedding cake benches
These maximize sales of plants in small containers such as ground covers, perennials, small shrubs, etc. Both levels of the bench must be at the "sight and take" position to maximize sales.

Tree rings
Trees are often difficult products to sell, but in my experience, I have found tree rings, or tree wheels, to be very effective. Trees are a browse product, and you need to create a browse shopping environment. A tree ring allows you to display by category: spring flowering trees, fall color trees, evergreen trees, etc. Plus, it allows you to position tree stakes at the ends of the ring spokes to maximize your add-on sales opportunities.

Sloping benches
These are ideal for products such as flats of bedding plants. By sloping

the bench toward the customer, the customer gains a more appealing view of the plants. This helps increase impulse sales.

Build Your Own Benches?

Retailers often look at how many benches they require, cost it out, and then realize that they cannot justify or afford the capital expense. In situations like these, you should consider constructing your own benches. You have a wide range of materials and designs to choose from, but keep in mind the overall look you wish to convey. What's cheap or easy to construct may not tell the customer that yours is a professional operation.

Photo 6-6. This hexagonal bench is easily shopped from all sides, and the suspended conifers really draw attention!

The cheapest option is to use pallets and PalletLegs. PalletLegs are available from registered suppliers and can provide you with the ideal cost-effective solution. PalletLegs are designed to clip onto standard pallets to create a rapid-assemble display bench, bringing the pallet and its products up to a shoppable height for customers. As pallets are unloaded by forklift from a truck, before the pallet

Photo 6-7. Portable small tables in the middle of plant benches improves the look of your merchandising.

is placed on the floor, the PalletLegs are clipped onto the pallet to create an instant display bench. The legs come in three sizes, which means

Photo 6-8. This tree wheel lets you attractively display several varieties of trees with easy access for your customers.

Photo 6-9. PalletLegs make functional, attractive displays from shipping pallets.

benches can be stepped, tiered, or sloping, just by changing the size of the legs being used.

PalletLegs have a range of accessories from wheels, rails, collars, cages, and canopies, which makes them ideal for power displays and gondolas, as well as general benching. They have a 1,102 lb. (500kg)/pallet load-bearing capacity, which makes them suitable for a variety of functions.

Innovation in Bench Design

Customized garden center merchandising units are becoming popular. The key is flexibility. Woodham Manufacturing (20 Parkhill Rd., RDI, Hastings, New Zealand, jwoodham@xtra. co.nz) is one company that specializes in outdoor garden center fixtures. They have developed modular units that are made from tough plastic and metal to ensure that the units are robust.

Photo 6-10. These modular units can be configured in many different ways and accommodate a variety of watering systems.

Purpose-Designed Benching

Designers of garden center benching often supply a design service to maximize the flow of your live goods area. You should work in partnership with these companies. Your involvement on customer flow, category placement, and profit per square foot for each category will help you achieve the optimum layout.

Keep focused on your objectives, whether for interior or exterior shop fittings. You should aim to amortize your shop fittings over three to five years, and the image you create should reflect the desires of your target market. The key is not to over or under invest on your retail furniture.

Supplier-Designed Fixtures

The objective of your fixtures is to increase sales of products. It should create a win-win situation for both yourself and your supplier. Because of their narrower focus, suppliers often are aware of the optimum way of selling their products and, therefore, invest in their own fixtures to sell their product.

Whether you use their fittings is always debatable, with camps for and against. My personal view is that in most cases they have a role where the supplier can provide fittings for the complete category, e.g., seeds, herbs, or garden care products. In this situation, their fixtures should save you money and enhance your image.

Photo 6-11. Herb Herbert's displays show a range of their product and attract customers with friendly signage.

My concern is where fixtures from suppliers are used to promote one product within a category. This often detracts from the consistency of your image and can be detrimental to the whole image you are trying to create. You will have to consider each fixture on its own merits. My word of warning is, do not spoil your image for the sake of saving a few dollars because a supplier will provide the display.

Many suppliers will contribute to the cost of your displays as long as you can guarantee that they will be allocated x linear feet of space for their product in prime location. Remember, if you do not ask, you will never know if a supplier is prepared to invest in fittings in your center.

Theatrical Props

Success is about daring to be different. Businesses that conform do not get talked about. You need to invest in theatrical props to create theater in your store. The list of props you could use depends on your imagination. They could include mannequins, furniture, drapes, costumes, wire animals, artwork, etc. (The next chapter is devoted to theatrical displays.)

6-12

Photo 6-12. Reeves Garden Center in Toronto used these old doors to make a theatrical display for Christmas, and they can adapt it for each season. This display allows them to sell a complete package rather than just one product.

Other retailers may have the props you need. Why not network? This month you may need a bath from a bathroom retailer for a promotion on indoor plants for the bathroom. Next month they may be looking for a group of plants for a promotion.

Many garden center retailers have started obtaining props, especially for Christmas, from specialist suppliers. If you do this, why not network with other garden centers so that you can provide a theatrical variety for your customers?

You will be surprised how many theatrical props are hidden in your team members' attics and garages. If they know what theme you are developing, they may be able to save the day.

As a final solution, you may make your own. It is surprising what your team can make with a few pieces of wire, papier-mâché, wood, and a little bit of imagination.

Provide Appropriate Carts

The garden center shopping cart evolved out of the supermarket shopping cart. When I was young, the supermarket carts were tall and narrow. Then researchers looked at the cart and found you and I would buy more products if the cart had a wider base. The psychology was that we needed to cover the base of the shopping cart to feel that we had had a good shopping experience. The supermarket shopping cart as we know it today, was born.

I have related this story for a purpose. You need a cart that is stable, easy to push (or pull), and has a large base to encourage shoppers to buy more.

Often the first exposure customers get to your business is your shopping carts. They expect them to be in the right location, readily available, and clean. And, of course, they must work properly—there is nothing that draws more frustrated criticism from a customer than a cart with a will of its own.

Selecting the Right Cart

Garden center carts come in a variety of forms. Most have been adapted from the supermarket or liquor industries. The real challenge for many retailers is to find a garden center cart that works in an outdoor plant retail environment.

Shopping carts need to be robust, strong, and stable, but also light and maneuverable. They also need to have a large capacity to allow customers to stack them with plants in an area that might have rough terrain. Carts also need to be low maintenance; tires need to be puncture-proof and durable with good traction.

My favorite garden center cart comes from New Zealand.

6-13

Photo 6-13. This cart is custom-made for garden centers and can carry a lot of plant material comfortably.

The Woodham cart (jwoodham@xtra.co.nz) is designed specifically for garden centers and meets the requirements of management, team members, and, customers.

Train Your Cart Assistants

Many companies employ young people to manage their carts. They are key personnel because, for most customers, these people are the first and the last ambassadors to represent your business during the shopping encounter. But often they are ill equipped to do the job. They should be recruited as cart assistants and greeters—and should be trained accordingly.

The role of a trolley assistant is to:
- Ensure carts are kept clean.
- Keep carts well maintained. This involves daily checking of the equipment and, for this, they should have a tool kit and oil available.
- Ensure carts are in a safe location and are retrieved regularly from parking lots.
- Collect carts in batches of ten, using special straps.
- Clean carts at the end of the day before storing them in a secure location overnight.
- Welcome and say good-bye to customers. In this regard, they should be recruited because they can make eye contact, smile, and have the confidence to verbally communicate with your customers.
- Look professional. Provide them with a staff uniform, even safety waistcoats, rain gear, hats, and sunscreen, when needed.
- Too often trolley assistants are not considered part of the team. If this is a practice in your business, you will find that, in time, the service they offer customers will decline. By involving them in team meetings and in sales training along with the rest of your staff, you could discover untapped potential and talent that can be applied elsewhere in the business.

Chapter 7

The Theater of Displays

Your objective is to inspire your customers to come back more often and purchase gardening products. If customers feel that every time they come back your center looks the same, the chances are they will visit you less often and seek alternative sources for their gardening needs. Theater displays are a practical means of making your center look different every time your customers visit. One of the most common questions asked is how often should you change displays. A display should have a maximum life of eight weeks, but in the spring you may be changing some displays weekly, or daily on that busy spring weekend.

Displays set the scene in the customers' eyes. The more upscale you wish your business to be perceived, then you need to introduce more lifestyle displays into your center. If you wish to be perceived as a price-led business, then more bulk displays with large price signs will be required.

Theatrical displays, I would define, as those that are not product- or price-led, but portray an added value perception that provides the customer with ideas, inspiration, and puts a smile on their face.

These major displays can be grouped in a number of ways.

Power Displays

Your most important display positions in the garden center are those where you can guarantee 100% of people will see products you put on display. These positions are called the power spots. You will only have a few power spots in your garden center. The key positions are indicated on the diagram of a garden center below:

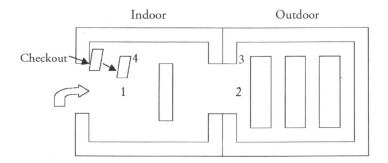

Figure 7-1. Map of power display locations.

7-1. Be creative with your power displays! Zanthomea in Western Australia spiced up a "boring" product with humor and style.

The key zones are (see above):

1. As the customer enters your store and has walked approximately eight feet into the store. This is the first product display she will focus on. If you place the display closer to the door, the customer may not focus on the display as she is taking in the new overall experience.

2. The first product display the eye focuses on in the plant area. Again give her space to take in the overall experience before trying to sell her a product.

3. The product display as she leaves the plant area.

4. The last display before she gets to the checkout.

These power display positions need to be used to maximum effect. Display positions 1 and 2 on the map should be used to inspire and excite people, whilst positions 3 and 4 should be used for add-on products after the customer has made a purchase.

A lot of research has been carried out on power positions, and it is critical that you plan the product displays well in advance and make someone responsible for managing these spots. Unfortunately, many businesses neglect these areas and do not maximize their return per square foot.

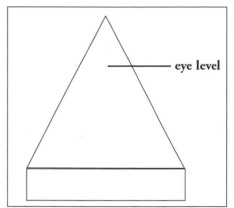

Figure 7-2. Optimal power spot display design.

The following are the golden rules when building a power spot:

Management Memo

Research carried out in the United States by the Russell R. Mueller Retail Hardware Research Foundation shows that sales of product increased by 229% when moved from a relay management position to an endcap position. For this reason, retailers should carefully plan such hot spots, as they can be one of the most profitable areas of a store.

1. To maximize sales, I recommend that you limit the display to one product.

2. Ensure the product you use is topical, in season, or fashionable.

3. Do not use this spot for price specials unless you are making an exceptionally good gross profit or you want the customer to receive you as a discounted retailer.

4. Build the power spot in a circle and pyramidal, if at all possible. This will create the most impact and sales.

5. Dummy up the base so that the middle of the cone is at the "sight and take" position.

6. Have a filling policy that means the display is managed on a full/half full/full/half full rotation. Once a display goes below half full, sales drop off dramatically.

7. The display must have a sign (see chapter 12 on signage).

8. Remember the "halo effect." Retail space surrounding the display is ideal for add-on lines.

Photo 7-1. Zanthomea in Western Australia uses Comex cutouts to celebrate autumn in this power spot.

Photo 7-2. This power spot is just before the doors to head back into the shop. Price is the key to this display.

Photo 7-3. This lettuce display features living labels, unusual container gardens that urge the customers to think differently about what a container can hold.

Living Label Displays

Living label displays are the best way of showing what a plant will look like when it matures. Most living labels are supplied by the wholesaler as part of the promotional package. Some retailers prefer not to sell the living label, whilst others would argue that everything is for sale, including the living label.

One of the most effective ways of displaying plants with a living label is to place the "label" in the center of the display and surround it with smaller salable product.

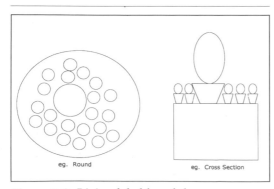

Figure 7-3. Living label bench layout.

Living label displays can be positioned as island displays, in the middle of merchandise "relays" (lines of plants on benches), or as endcaps. Some companies put a large price sign on the living label to emphasize the potential value of the smaller plants.

Creative Solution Displays

The majority of your customers are looking for ideas to solve what they perceive as problems in their garden. They often come to you, not for product, but for creative solutions to their problems. These problems can be solved through discussions, display concepts, or a combination of both.

You will create more loyalty and promotion via word of mouth if you construct displays that provide solutions for customers that relate to what you are verbally recommending.

Creative solution displays should be positioned in major positions in each major product department.

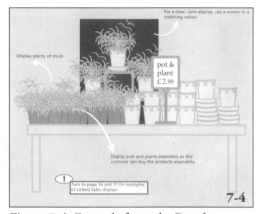

Figure 7-4. Example from the Dutch Promotion Council.

Creative solution displays need a number of ingredients if they are going to be effective.

- At least two products that will assist the customer with a perceived problem.
- Signage that explains the solution.
- Possible ancillary "props" to emphasize the message you want to get across.

Some examples of possible creative solution displays are patio plants with pots and growing media, trees with stakes and tree ties, hedging plants and pruners, and indoor plants and plant food.

Creative solutions can also be applied to your "relay" products, for example: bedding plants or roses displayed by flower color, shrubs displayed by height, perennials or indoor plants displayed based on light requirement.

Also look at how you can help your customer with creative solution services. These could include:

- Height marks up a tree so your customers can consider eventual plant height.
- A square yard frame positioned near your groundcover plants to enable customers to calculate how many plants they will need to carpet their garden.
- A yard mark along the path next to hedging plants can assist your customers when purchasing hedging material.

The key is to keep brainstorming creative solutions. Some solutions will be seasonal, i.e., winter protection; others will be fashion led; and others will be standard horticultural solutions.

Lifestyle Displays

As garden retailing has evolved, it's moved from being a plant/price-based industry to one that adds value to people's lives by providing lifestyle products. One reflection of this is the increase in landscape services and products such as "Gardens to Go" by Blooms of Bressingham in the United Kingdom.

> *Management Memo*
>
> The use of props that are not merchandise enhancing is a common error. There is a danger of selecting a favorite display prop and finding a use for it in almost every display. This creates monotony and leads people to believe that the display is never changing and they stop viewing.

Forward-thinking retailers are constructing lifestyle displays in their garden centers for two reasons: It shows the customers that they can relate to their needs and wants, and It increases the average sale per customer.

First, let me define a lifestyle display. Lifestyle displays reflect the lifestyle of a typical customer within your target population profile. The display then reflects how those customers would like to see their gardens. To gain an idea of a lifestyle display, the best examples can be seen in furniture stores such as IKEA, who build displays based on living rooms, kitchens, and bedrooms. To build these displays they introduce products from different departments into the display.

In the garden center industry, the "living rooms" are display gardens based on your perception of the customer's needs. Examples of living rooms could be: the rose garden, the patio, the native plant garden, the cottage garden, the woodland garden, etc.

To illustrate how to implement lifestyle displays I will use an example from the New Zealand industry. One wholesaler in that country provides a lifestyle display on a monthly basis and helps the retailer to set up the display using a merchandising team.

Photo 7-5. Permanent display gardens show your customers you understand gardens and fashion and can relate to their needs and dreams.

Theatrical Displays

One of the keys to success for small business is to be *consistently different*. These are two important words. First, you have got to dare to be different, which takes courage. Second, once you have introduced this culture into your business, you have to be consistent in your implementation. The worst thing you can do is let your customers down.

Theatrical displays are entertainment based and do not necessarily relate to the industry. A theatrical display could be contained in just one small area of your garden center or it can dominate the whole store.

To be successful at theatrical displays, there are a number of critical stages you need to go through.

Plan Well in Advance

Your first planning meeting should be at least three months ahead of the event. Some would argue with me that it should be twelve months ahead, and I would agree when it comes to events such as Christmas. This meeting should be open to all of your team members. Management's role should be to set the agenda, whilst the team should come up with the ideas. The key is to encourage an open brainstorming session. Do not criticize any suggestions because if you do, those crazy gems that could earn you a lot of money may not come to the surface.

Set the Budget

At the start of the meeting, management must set the budget for the promotion. You will soon destroy creativity if the team comes up with wonderful ideas and then you say, "We cannot afford that." Start the meeting with an investment target so that everyone can work toward it.

Collect Your Props

By planning your promotion so far ahead, it gives your team time to build, hire, borrow, or collect relevant props for the displays. Don't forget one valuable source is other retailers, many of whom would be happy to let you borrow mannequins, furniture, toys, or other materials. The time will come when you can do the same for them, and in the meantime they get their name out to your customers.

Build Your Display in the Dark

This is the theater industry; you are selling the magic, not the mechanics. The key is to unveil the final event, not show your customers how you build it. To build in the dark, you can get a crew together to transform your store once the store is closed. Or, you can do what one of my clients does in Australia. He puts a black drape around the area to hide it from the customer and puts a sign on the drape "All will be revealed in . . . 2 days [or 30 minutes, etc.]." This creates customer interest while the display is being built.

Take a Picture when It Is Finished

You may need to reconstruct or refer back to the display at a later date. It is therefore essential that you take a picture of the display and place it in a scrapbook with relevant notes. This should be your library of theatrical events, which can be referred to by any of your team.

Measure Your Success

Your reason for doing the promotion was to increase sales per square foot. You should measure the success of the promotion in dollar terms, because your aim is to beat this figure next time you do the same themed event.

What Events Should You Celebrate?

The list of events to celebrate is endless. There is no reason why you should not have a theatrical event in your garden center every day of the year.

The list of events can come from a number of sources: international events (the Olympics), national events (elections, Groundhog Day), annual celebrations (Valentine's Day, Independence Day), local events (county fair, neighborhood festivals), company events (your annual company birthday), industry-led events (new plant releases), media-led events (promo in a lifestyle magazine), or your crazy ideas (anything you can come up with!).

I recommend that you have an events calendar on display in your staff room. Team members can then add items as they think of them. The calendar could take the following format:

Month	Theme	Suggested Props	Suggested Products
January			
February			
March			
April			
May			
June			
July			
August			
September			
October			
November			
December			

Holiday Decorations and Promotions

Photo 7-4. Easter sales can see a boost with seasonal windsocks, baskets in pastels, and other items that lean toward Easter or spring.

Photo 7-5. Halloween has become a major American holiday, so celebrate it right. Pumpkins, gourds, hay bales, and home décor items will bring people in, and while there they will find your late-season bedding plants.

Photos 7-6 and 7-7. The same great idea on two continents. Using white fabric for a tent effect, the garden center in Belgium (left) and the one in Arizona both create a Christmas "room" in the greenhouse.

Photo 7-8. Of course nativity sets are popular at Christmastime, but don't forget about other religious statues. Saints are popular with Catholics, and angels appeal to a range of denominations and New Age thought.

Photo 7-9. Other than a Christmas tree, nothing says Christmas like poinsettias. Make sure you offer better quality and variety than your local mass merchant and supermarkets do. A range of colors and sizes will set you apart from the rest, and your customers will be proud to display these in their own homes or to give them as gifts.

Chapter 8

Financial Strategies

You may have entered this industry over another one because you enjoy plants, gardening, and the open-air lifestyle, but it does not take long to realize that you have to make a profit. To maximize that profit, you need a business plan as discussed in chapter 3. You also need effective bookkeeping so you know what is happening in your business. It is critical to success that you have accurate financial records. This allows you to monitor progress and make informed business decisions concerning the future investment and direction of your business.

The benefits of monitoring the financial aspects of your business are substantial. They reduce your yearly accounting costs, keep you aware of the financial condition of your business, allow you to make rational financial decisions, control your expenses, manage your prices, help with managing debtors, identify problems in your business, and monitor taxes and help outsiders such as accountants and consultants who advise you on how to improve the efficiency of your business.

Traditionally, bookkeeping was literally bookkeeping and to most of us it was a tedious operation. Now there are numerous computerized accounting systems to choose from, which make the task a lot less stressful and more accurate. The system you select will depend on the size of your business, your budget, computer power, personal understanding, training offered, and advice from local, qualified, business advisors.

This is a sound investment in your business, but you must select a package you can understand, operate and have confidence in. More important, you need to be assured that the benefits will reduce operational costs within your business. Analyze all the software options available and convince yourself it will give you the information you need to make decisions. Before buying, have a close look at the costs of purchasing and managing a system.

Benefits of Computer Use	Costs of Computer Use
Saving in management and staff time in performing tasks	Cost of training managers and staff in setting up the system
Improved record keeping	Capital cost and ongoing cost of upgrading systems
Quicker and better information	Ongoing training investment to make business decisions
Improved control over your business	System breakdowns
Stock control and quality improvements	Need for contingency plans
Improved speed at the pay point and improved customer service	Cost of training
Improved competitiveness	
Improved internal and external communications	

Based on a table prepared by Peter McSweeney and Nick Bailey for Nursery Computer Software Evaluation (NY99042) for the Horticultural Research and Development Corporation of Australia.

If you have a large garden center or are part of a chain or franchise, you may prefer an in-house customized software system for your business. Smaller garden centers will need to select an off-the-shelf option.

Prior to purchasing software, talk to existing users and get their opinion on the program. Find out how easy it is to use and if they have experienced any difficulties with it. Plus, talk to the suppliers—you will need to work with someone you trust. Ask them their views and what they provide in training, troubleshooting, problem solving, and so on.

You will need a computerized point-of-sale (POS) system to manage your stock control. To develop this, you will need a product numbering system, bar coding (or similar), and scanning equipment. Every product will need bar coding, since the system works as pictured in figure 8-1.

Figure 8-1

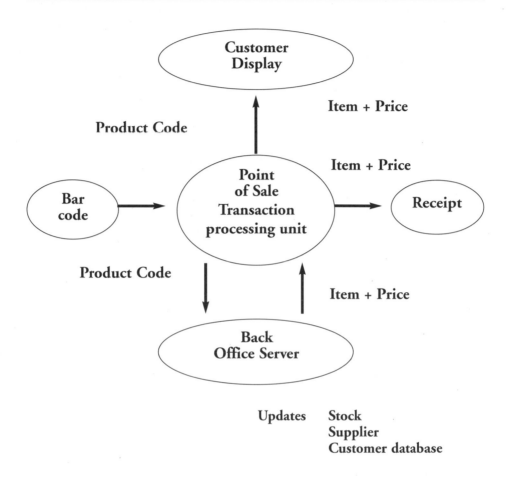

Ref: *McKeown P.G. 2000.* Information Technology and The Network Economy. *Harcourt: Fort Worth.*
*Based on Peter McSweeney and Nick Bailey for Nursery Computer Software Evaluation (NY99042) for the
Horticultural Research and Development Corporation of Australia.*

Cash Flow

The lifeblood of all business is cash flow. Without a healthy cash flow,
your business dies. You need to know you have enough cash to keep your
business afloat. With this in mind, you need to know in advance how
cash flows through your business, which you will learn with a cash flow
forecast.

A cash flow forecast is a summary of the money you expect to come
into the business and the money that is going out of the business each

A Selection of Software for Nursery/Horticultural Applications				
Product	**Company/Country**	**Grower**	**Wholesale**	**Retail**
ARC Products	ARC Growing Software Inc., U.S.A.	✔		✔
Bare Roots	Diverse Software Solutions Inc., U.S.A.	✔		✔
Customer Orders Software	Lowes Garden Information, Australia			
Dispatch & Accounting	Prophesy Transportation Solutions Inc., U.S.A.		✔	
FAMOUS	Famous, U.S.A.	✔	✔	
Fresh Solutions	Ibis Software, Australia	✔		
Garden Center Software	Garden Center Software, U.S.A.			✔
GartPlan	Denmark			✔
Greenlife Database	Botanical Nomenclature Services International Ltd., Australia	✔	✔	✔
Greenhouse/Nursery	Argos Software, U.S.A.	✔		✔
GrowIt Gold Works	Innovative Thinking Software, U.S.A.	✔		✔
GroSmart	Future Growth Solutions, Australia	✔	✔	✔
GroWare	SineQuaNon Inc., Canada	✔	✔	✔
Hortfarm	SMART Software Pty. Ltd., Australia	✔		
Hortlinks	Innovative Software, New Zealand	✔		
LogiVert	Paysage Software, the Netherlands	✔	✔	✔
Nursery Information System	Horticultural Computer Control, Australia	✔	✔	
Plantgro	Plantsoft Services, Australia	✔		
Plant, Order Entry and Control	Don Porritt, Australia	✔		
Plant Partner	Starcom Computer Corp., U.S.A.	✔		
PlantPic (and TagPic)	Norwood Industries, U.S.A.	✔	✔	✔
Production Plus+	Horticultural Cos. and Florists' Mutual Insurance, U.S.A.	✔		
UDS Applications	Industrial Software Inc., U.S.A.	✔		✔
Unique Horticulture	Botanical Nomenclature Services International, Australia	✔	✔	✔
WinPlant U.S.A.	WinPlant Software Corp.,	✔		

month. When the net difference between these two figures is added to the opening balance for the month, you can work out how much cash is in the business at the end of the month. With this figure, you can start managing your business. Remember, a business can look healthy, but its cash flow may mean it cannot pay its expenses each month as they occur.

The benefits of a cash flow forecast are that you can anticipate short-falls in cash and plan accordingly. It will also help you when you go to the bank and ask for extra finance. A cash flow forecast will help you plan the future and allows you to measure actual financial performance against projected financial performance. Finally, it protects your good credit rating.

The following table is an example of a cash flow forecast. It is purely a model and should not be used to compare your business against. It has been split up to help you design your cash flow forecast. The split is as follows:

Cash in or Recorded Receipts

    a) Cash Sales: This includes all transactions where payment was received at the point of sale

    b) Credit Sales: This is where you are providing extended credit, such as a garden design and build, paid for over a number of months.

    c) Sale of Miscellaneous Assets: This includes all cash injections to the business that do not fall into the above two groups.

Cash Flow Out or Recorded Expenses

    a) Operating Expenses: These are expenses that occur every month to run your business. They include electricity, cost of goods, telephone, wages, etc.

    b) Capital Expenditure: This can include your salary, motor vehicle purchase, and other equipment.

The aim is to use the cash flow forecast as a management tool in your business. You must monitor it on a monthly basis. Each month you may need to revise your business plan, arrange an overdraft, or inject more of your own funds if you find that the figures are on a negative side.

The following tips offer some ideas for improving your cash flow. They come from Peter Palmer's Bank of I.D.E.A.S.—Reducing Costs Workshop.

1. Payment in cash if at all possible.
2. Invoice people as soon as possible.
3. Reduce payment terms to the shortest term possible.
4. Clearly state your terms for payment and due dates on your invoices.
5. Consider charging a fee and/or interest for late payment.
6. Discounts for early payment.
7. Ensure that discounts are based on sound commercial judgment.
8. Promptly follow up on overdue accounts.
9. Make it easy for people to pay—e.g., direct credit to your bank account or by credit card.
10. Pay annual accounts by the month or semiannually.
11. Match timing of large expenses with months where you cash flow is the greatest.
12. Negotiate the longest possible payment terms.
13. Negotiate the best possible price.
14. Minimize the amount of stock you have on hand.
15. Increase net profit by increasing price or reducing costs.
16. Use credit, i.e., credit card (interest free period), overdraft, equity injection.
17. Be aware of your tax liabilities and provide for them.

Manage Your Gross Profit

Gross profit is your key financial guide for growing your business, and everyone working for you should have an understanding of gross profit and how it effects your business. Gross profit fits in the basic business formula as follows:

Sales Price - Cost of Goods Sold (COGS) = Gross Profit - Expenses = Net Profit

Understand Gross Profit

Garden centers generate a lot of money through the cash register. A large percentage of this money is used to pay for the goods sold, as well as the other expenses as a result of doing business. The aim of a garden center is to generate enough money from selling a product to cover the costs of purchasing that product, to cover all the related expenses, and to obtain a profit from entering into the venture. Gross profit is the dollars in

An Example of a Simple Cash Flow Forecast

Month	1	2	3	4	5	6	7	8	9	10	11	12	Total
Cash Flow In													
Cash sales	10,000	22,000	25,000	30,000	40,000	30,000	20,000	30,000	20,000	10,000	20,000	50,000	307,000
Credit sales	100	200	100	100	50	60	200	100	500	100	20	30	1,560
Sale of miscellaneous assets			4,000										4,000
Total Receipts	10,100	22,200	29,100	30,100	40,050	30,060	20,200	30,100	20,500	10,100	20,020	50,030	312,560
Cash Flow Out													
Cost of goods sold at 47%	4,747	10,434	13,677	14,147	18,823	14,128	9,494	14,147	9,635	4,747	9,409	23,514	146,902
Other Expenses													
Accounting					1,500								1,500
Advertising (2%)	202	444	582	602	801	601	404	602	410	202	400	1000	6,250
Bank charges and interest	45	45	45	45	45	45	45	45	45	45	45	45	540
Electricity		300		300		300		300		300		300	1,800
Insurance						825						825	1,650
Motor vehicle	300	500	600	1,320	200	300	500	160	200	300	400	500	5,280
Postage, printing & stationery	25	25	25	25	25	25	25	25	25	25	25	25	300
Rent	1,200	1,200	1,200	1,200	1,200	1,200	1,200	1,200	1,200	1,200	1,200	1,200	14,400
Telephone	137	137	137	137	137	137	137	137	137	137	137	137	1,644
Wages (17%)	4,428	4,428	4,428	4,428	4,428	4,428	4,428	4,428	4,428	4,428	4,428	4,428	53,136
Other	275	275	275	275	275	275	275	275	275	275	275	275	3,300
Loan repayment							320	320	320	320	320	320	1,920
Subtotal Expenses	11,359	17,788	20,969	22,479	27,434	22,264	16,828	21,639	16,675	11,979	16,639	32,569	238,622
Capital Expenditure													
Plant and equipment			3,500				8,000			1,500			13,000
Director's salary	3,000	3,000	3,000	3,000	3,000	3,000	3,000	3,000	3,000	3,000	3,000	3,000	36,000
Total Payments	14,359	20,788	27,469	25,479	30,434	25,264	27,828	24,639	19,675	16,479	19,639	35,569	287,622
Net Cash Flow	-4,259	1,412	1,631	4,621	9,616	4,796	-7,628	5,461	825	-6,379	381	14,461	24,938
Opening Balance													
Closing Balance													

Note: This does not take into account sales tax, which may need separate columns profit from buying and selling a product. Put another way:

Sell price — Cost price = Gross profit

Thus, a $5.00 sell price minus a $3.00 cost results in a $2.00 gross profit.

Although garden centers bank dollars, not percentages, they often talk about gross profit in percentage terms:

$$\frac{\text{Sell price} - \text{Cost price x 100}}{\text{Sell price}} = \text{Gross profit \%}$$

Thus, if you purchased a product for $3.00 and you sell it for $5.00, you will generate a 40% gross profit. It would be calculated as follows:

$$\frac{\$5.00 - \$3.00}{\$5.00} \times 100 = 40\%$$

Understand Markup

Markup is the profit obtained from the sale of a product when expressed as a percentage of the cost price.

$$\frac{\text{Sell Price} - \text{Cost Price}}{\text{Cost Price}} \times 100 = \text{Markup \%}$$

To continue with our example, the markup would be figured as such:

$$\frac{\$5.00 - \$3.00}{\$3.00} \times 100 = 66\%$$

This shows that a 40% gross profit is in fact a 66% markup. They are completely different percentages, and you do not want to confuse them when making your business plans or your cash flow forecast.

Avoid Costly Mistakes through Confusion

Confusion can cause major problems for a garden center. By looking at the calculations on the following page, it is readily understood that if team members confuse gross profit percentages and markup, the garden center can end up with some very misleading figures when analyzing sales.

Many people get confused in grappling with the terms markup and gross profit. By considering the chart on the next page, you can see why you must not.

Increasing Your Gross Profit

Theoretically, if you can increase your gross profit and maintain your volume of sales, you can improve your overall net profit.

Garden centers use a wide range of techniques to determine the sales price of products, but these should be based on:

- The gross margin that is expected on the product.
- The amount of competition in the catchment area.
- The demographics of your customers.
- Amount of product you have to sell within a given period.
- The garden center image you are creating.
- The perceived value of the product.

There are techniques you can use to increase your gross profit, including:

- Purchase your products at a lower price but maintain your retail price, hence increasing your gross profit.
- Change the product mix in your garden center.
- Reduce the number of markdowns you have in each department.
- Increase your retail price and hence gross profit.

Schedule of Comparisons between Markup Percentages and Gross Profit Percentages	
Mark Up %	Gross Profit %
10	9.90
15	13.04
20	16.67
25	20.00
30	23.08
35	25.93
40	28.57
45	31.03
50	33.33
55	35.48
60	37.50
65	39.39
70	41.18
75	42.86
80	44.44
85	45.96
90	47.36
95	48.73
100	50.00
105	51.22
110	52.38
115	53.49
120	54.56
125	55.56
130	56.52
135	57.45
140	58.33
145	59.18
150	60.00

- Stock more seasonal lines and turn them quicker.
- Provide fewer SKUs (stock keeping units) with a category. This is especially true in the garden care department. Many garden centers offer the customer too much choice, confusing the customer and resulting in no sale. I recently worked with a garden center that offered its customers fifteen ways to kill slugs and snails. A customer wants a maximum of three ways and for the garden center to recommend one of those.

Research in the U.S. by Arthur Andersen indicates the best method to increase gross profit is to change your product mix. The more non-known-value products included in your range that you can price-point effectively, the more opportunity you have to increase your gross profit. In addition, they recommend that the more added-value services you can include, the healthier your gross profit will be.

The reverse to increasing your gross profit is to be aware of and take steps to minimize a decrease in gross profit. Gross profit decreases are due to:

- Competition pressures, especially on like known-value products
- Too many garden centers within the same catchment area.
- A change in customer preferences and fashions.
- A change in the product mix that did not work for you.
- Having too much low gross profit product in stock.

Where's Breakeven?

The breakeven point in your business is the point where your income from sales is sufficient to cover all your costs of doing business. At this point, any extra sales at a profit will start generating a profit for you. Being aware of this point enables you to forecast the number of sales you need to make in order to cover costs.

If you take a single product, as an example, you would use the following formulas:

$$\frac{\text{Sales} - \text{Cost of goods sold}}{\text{Sales}} = \text{Gross profit}$$

$$\frac{\text{Overhead}}{\text{Gross profit}} = \text{Breakeven sales}$$

Let's use some prices to plug into the formulas. Your selling price is $5.00; your cost of goods is $2.00; and overhead for the department is $3,000.

$$\frac{\$5.00 - \$2.00}{\$5.00} = \text{Gross profit} = \$0.60$$

$$\frac{\$3,000}{0.60} = \text{Breakeven sales} = \$5,000 \text{ dollars of 1,000 unit sales}$$

The key is to monitor sales on a regular basis and take appropriate action when problems are indicated.

Net Profit-Your Real Goal

Everyone should be going into business to obtain a true profit, as this is the pool of money that allows you to develop your business and lifestyle. The way to figure net profit is as follows:

Sales − Cost of Goods = Gross Profit − Expenses = Net Profit

Remember, once you have made a net profit, you still have to pay your taxes, loans, living expenses, and future business expansion out of this pool of money. One of your aims should be to maximize your net profit, but not to the long-term detriment of your business. Every year when you have your financial results, you should take time to go through the following procedures.

First, look at the cost of doing business for the last twelve months. Where are your greatest expenses coming from, and are there any savings you can make in this area? In a garden center, your biggest expense will be your labor bill. Can you reduce this? Consider, are you using the right skilled people at the right times in your business? Are they fully trained in the skills they have to do? Is it more cost effective to go from full-time to part-time employees (or vice versa)? Are they working the best hours during the day? A review of wages can make a major impact. Be careful, though—you must not reduce the level of service and services the customers expect from your business.

Second, compare your actual business performance against your previous year's performance and your expected performance for the year. By doing this, you will identify if you have any problem areas where you need to take action. You may discover you need to change a supplier, eliminate unproductive services or unprofitable product categories, or reduce costs in some areas.

Third, I am a great believer that there is always a better way of doing things. Now is the time to reflect on the way you have been doing things over the last twelve months and to come up with a better way. Remember, we are creatures of habit and do not like change. But having always done it that way is no excuse in a changing world.

Management Memo

Is your stock making you a profit? One simple formula is to take gross profit and multiply by stock turn. If the resulting answer is higher than 120, then you are on the right road. If it is less, it is a time to take action and boost the numbers.

Fourth, be rational rather than emotional in your decision-making process. Yes, you are selling a product that is an emotional purchase by your customers, but do not become emotional in your business decisions. You often see bad business decisions because the owners have made decisions emotionally rather than rationally.

This means prior to making major financial decisions in your business you need to ask some pertinent questions of yourself. Such as, How will the decision affect your long-term goals for of the business? Can the business afford to support the extra financial burden? What are the alternatives—i.e., should it be leased, is there a cheaper version, can it be obtained secondhand or at an auction? Do not be afraid to ask consultants, peers, suppliers, other retailers, accountants, or friends if there is a better way. Often you are too close to your own business to make the right decision.

Book List

Andersen, Arthur, LLP. 1997. *Small Store Survival, Success Strategies for Retailers.* New York: John Wiley.

Davidson, William R., Daniel J. Sweeney, Ronald W. Stampfl. 1988. *Retailing Management.* New York: John Wiley.

Palmer, Peter. April 2001. *Reducing Costs Workshop.* Bank of I.D.E.A.S.

Stanley, John. 1999. *Just about Everything a Retail Manager Needs to Know.* Brisbane, Australia: Plum Press.

Chapter 9

Pricing Strategies to Increase Your Profits

Alas, it seems price is still the most important consideration in growers' and retailers' minds, even though all the research at consumer level gives it a lesser priority. Unfortunately, plant prices have not kept pace with inflation, leaving plants at a perceived lower value than a decade ago. As a result, many net profits have shrunk, and many businesses have been unable to invest in development for the future.

Many items in our industry are priced on the cost-plus basis. I would like to take issue with this approach because it does not take the customer's perception of value into account at all. In fact, the customer may perceive a plant or product as too expensive or too cheap. Either way, the result will be lost sales.

The pricing diagram here makes using the cost-plus approach look simple, but, in fact, it is far more complicated than I have illustrated and a more analytical approach is required.

The following discussion attempts to identify all the items of cost that should be considered by nurseries and garden centers when trying to set prices for their products. I would urge growers not to base their

PRODUCTION COST OF PLANT

OVERHEADS IN BUSINESS

PROFIT REQUIRED

GROWER
WHOLESALER
PRICING
STRUCTURE

SELLING PRICE TO RETAILER

COST TO PURCHASE

OVERHEADS IN BUSINESS

RETAILER
PRICING
STRUCTURE

PROFIT REQUIRED

SELLING PRICE TO CUSTOMER

pricing structure on a competitor's.

Obviously, you need to compare prices to see if you are competitive, but to base your price on theirs without doing your own price analysis is dangerous, as there are too many variables between yours and their businesses. Your competition could be paying different bank charges, land prices will be different, capital injection could be different, and so on.

The Cost of Plants

Wholesalers often look at retailers and complain about their "huge" markups. Retailers look at wholesalers and comment on how easy business is for them—all they have to do is grow the plants!

I do not wish to get involved in who has the best or worst part of the deal, but let us look at the cost of plants in a retail situation. It is not a license to print money. The equation is complex—if you get it wrong, you can lose a fortune; if you get it right, perhaps you will make a profitable living. As there are so many variables involved, I will have to make some assumptions. This means you will have to alter the figures to suit your own situation. All I can do is start you thinking in the right way.

Wholesale Value

For this exercise, let us consider a labeled plant comes into a retailer in a pot at $3.00 from a grower/wholesaler. This is the direct cost of the plant. We will assume a purchase of a hundred plants, for a total direct cost of $300.00

Management Memo

When researchers compare the effectiveness of these types of promotions, buy one get one free (BOGOF) always outstrips 50% off.

The natural reaction by many retailers is to take this product and add 100% (or 110% or 120%) and arrive at $6.00 (or $5.95 if we work to price points). This will provide a markup of 100% and a gross profit of 50%.

But this method gives us a completely false picture of our pricing structure. Like wholesalers, retailers also have two types of cost: direct and indirect. These costs have to be built into the equation, otherwise the bottom line may not be as healthy as it could be.

Indirect Costs

When determining your pricing, you cannot forget the indirect costs. If left out of the equation, your bottom line will suffer. The most common of these indirect costs are:

Shrinkage

This is a term used by general retailers for product that is purchased but never reaches the checkout in the form it should. It may have disappeared by being used in displays, been stolen, or deteriorated on the plant bench. Shrinkage is normally 2% of costs, but can go as high as 8% if not properly monitored. For this exercise, we will add $12, or 4%, to our costs.

Advertising

I am assuming you have an advertising budget, and the only way you can retrieve that expense is by selling product. Advertising budgets vary between 1% and 6% of turnover in garden centers. Take an average of 3% of turnover (which is closer to 6% on cost), which, as an indirect cost, has to be retrieved. This means another $18 has to be added, taking the cost of your plants to $330.

Labor

In the garden center industry, the biggest bill will be labor. A good rate would be 10% of turnover, while others find themselves in the high teens (hopefully not the low twenties!). The cost of labor will depend on your service policy, training policy, caliber of people, and management. For this exercise, let us assume your labor bill is 15% of turnover (which would be closer to 30% on cost). This means we need to add another hefty $90 to the cost of your plants, bringing the total to $420.

Return on capital

Car rental company charges are based on what it would cost to replace a car today, not what they bought it for. You have invested in a garden center and should expect a return on your capital. We need to add 15% as a hidden cost for a return on your investment capital. This adds another $45 to your plants. The one hundred you bought now stand at $465 before a customer selects one to place in their garden.

Overhead

These plants also have to help you pay for telephone bills, insurance, electricity, trips to conferences, heating, and other similar "invisibles." The figure for this will vary from garden center to garden center, but 12% of turnover (roughly 24% on cost) would be about right. So we need to add another $72 to the cost of our plants, giving us a total of $537 at this stage of our equation.

Cost of space

One equation that will vary from business to business is the actual cost of space. Let us take the following example to get the concept across.

A display bed is $21^{1}/_{2}$ square yards (20 square meters) in area and contains 300 shrubs when full. The bed is part of a 2,700-square yard (2,500-square meter) tree and shrub area for which the allocation of overheads is $21,600 per annum. Therefore, in theory the sales area has to be able to pay off or carry an annual overhead cost of $21,600/2,700 = $8.00 per square yard.

In practice, however, 40% of this sales area is not used for selling, but is taken up by paths, leaving only 1,620 square yards as selling area. Therefore, the true selling area cost per annum is $21,600/1,620 = $13.33 per square yard. That is, every square yard of bed carries an overhead charge of $13.33 per annum. The costing per square yard will need to be divided into plants sold. I know garden centers with a stock turn of five per year and others achieving twelve stock turns. This figure will need to be factored in based on stock turn and number of plant units per square meter.

Profitable Pricing

If you used a cost-plus system of pricing, the method we have just used, the pricing of your plants looks like the following (based on six stock turns a year):

Direct costs	Purchase of plants	$300.00
Indirect costs	Shrinkage	$12.00
	Advertising	$18.00
	Labor	$90.00
	Return on capital	$45.00
	Overheads	$72.00
	Cost of space	$13.33
Total cost of plants		$550.33

If you were to sell these plants at $6.00, they would actually cost you $5.50, leaving $0.50 for all those little incidentals you have forgotten to include, plus bank charges, paying the tax man, extracting some profit for yourself, and investing in the future of the business. Now a markup of 100% does not look very attractive!

Pricing from a Retail Perspective

The majority of retail pricing is completely different to cost-plus pricing. In this system, price is based on a customer's perception of the value of the product. It's up to wholesalers and retailers to work together to ensure the customers believe that they have value for their money.

Unfortunately, we find it difficult to determine what is value in a customer's eyes; the reason for this is we are too close to the product and know too much about the production cycle. Our most important "consultants" when dealing with price are the eventual customers—they should be involved in deciding on the price of the product.

Consumer Panels

Consumer panels, or focus groups, are essential when it comes to pricing products. A consumer panel should consist, for this exercise, of about twelve typical purchasers of the product.

The panel should be shown the product or products. I would suggest you keep numbers to no more than ten products and the session to no more than forty-five minutes. Each consumer then writes down how much they would be prepared to spend to obtain the plant in question. The totals are not discussed until each panel member has written down his or her value for the product.

Having obtained twelve prices, you can then obtain the perceived value as follows:

Sample Value Prices from Consumers	
1.00	2.55
2.00	2.75
2.15	2.75
2.25	2.75
2.25	3.95
2.50	4.00

Management Memo

Case Study

A grower held a consumer panel and found he could sell young hardy plants in trays for a retail price of $1.99. He then introduced the concept to retailers, and it proved to be a great success.

A competitor found he could introduce the same product for $0.99 and make a profit. He launched his product in a garden center alongside the $1.99 plants and waited for a quick stock turn.

The $1.99 plants sold three times quicker. Why? The consumers believed that $1.99 was value. They were suspicious of the $0.99 plants, thinking they might die since they were too cheap.

Of these results, you can disregard the $1.00 as too low; the consumer does not like the product. You can also disregard the $4.00, as this is not a typical price reaction. Of the ten prices that are left, average them out to find the price the typical customer would pay. In this case, it comes to $2.45. If you wish to sell the plant in relatively high volumes, you should enter the marketplace at just below that figure, say $2.35. At this price, the majority of people will believe this is excellent value and the plant will move in volume (as long as it is clearly priced!). If you sell it at $2.75

and upwards, it will move more slowly, as it will be perceived as expensive. But if it is priced at $1.99, it will be perceived as too cheap and, again, stock turn could be reduced.

The question the grower-retailer now needs to ask concerns margins. Is there enough margin in producing and then retailing the plant at $2.35? In some cases, the margin will be increased upon existing prices and in others reduced. It may mean some plants cannot be grown economically while others are found to be very profitable.

Consumer pricing groups are common in other retail sectors and are becoming more popular in this industry. If you aren't holding such groups, I would urge you to start and guarantee you will be in for some surprises.

Major Price Barrier	Minor Price Barrier	Your Price Should Be
$1.00		$0.95 or 1.25
	$1.50	1.35 or 1.45
	2.00	1.95 or 1.85
	3.00	2.95 or 2.90
5.00		4.95 or 4.85
	8.00	7.95 or 7.85
10.00		9.95 or 9.90
	13.00	12.95 or 12.85
15.00		14.95 or 14.90
	18.00	17.95 or 17.90
20.00		19.95 or 19.85
	23.00	22.95 or 22.90
25.00		24.95 or 24.90
30.00		29.95 or 29.85
40.00		39.95 or 39.85
50.00		49.95 or 49.85
75.00		74.95 or 74.90
100.00		99.95 or 99.00
150.00		149.95 or 149.90
200.00		199.95 or 199.80

Price Barriers

When deciding on perceived values many potential consumers base their values on a price barrier they would be prepared to pay up to. Therefore the product should be priced at a point below that barrier.

Price Barriers and How to Avoid Them

Everyone has a price barrier when they shop—a preconceived, perhaps subconscious, feeling of what is a "cheap" product and what is the point at which that same product becomes a "dear" product. This applies as much to green goods as to any other line. Pricing your products with these barriers in mind can dramatically improve your bottom line with no other effort on your behalf. Ron Marciel, of Western Nurseries, California, has studied customer reaction to price points over many years. The chart on the previous page shows some of his findings and recommendations.

Do Sales Work?

In difficult trading times, the temptation is to reduce prices and have sales to increase turnover. Continual sales may increase turnover, but can a business sustain the true cost?

The following table should be used as a guide when reducing prices. The figures may suggest reduced prices cannot generate sufficient new turnover to maintain profitability.

		Your Present Margin								
		20%	25%	30%	35%	40%	45%	50%	55%	60%
Price Reduction	2%	11%	9%	7%	6%	5%	5%	4%	4%	3%
	4%	25%	19%	15%	13%	11%	10%	9%	8%	7%
	6%	43%	32%	25%	21%	18%	15%	14%	12%	11%
	8%	67%	47%	36%	30%	25%	22%	19%	17%	15%
	10%	100%	67%	50%	40%	33%	29%	25%	22%	20%
	12%	150%	92%	67%	52%	43%	36%	32%	28%	25%
	14%	233%	127%	88%	67%	54%	45%	39%	34%	30%
	16%	400%	178%	114%	84%	67%	55%	47%	41%	36%
	18%	900%	257%	150%	106%	82%	67%	56%	49%	43%
	20%	-	400%	200%	133%	100%	80%	67%	57%	50%
	25%	-	-	500%	250%	167%	125%	100%	83%	71%
	30%	-	-	-	600%	300%	200%	150%	120%	
	100%									

This table shows how much volume sales must increase to compensate for price reductions. These percentages are the breakeven points with the prices before the promotion; you must go beyond them to increase profitability. (Chart is courtesy of Results Corp, Queensland.)

If Sales Do Not Work, What Does?

Price reduction campaigns can work in certain locations and economic climates, but they need to be planned and worked through carefully. I believe the garden trade should follow the lead of supermarkets with their specific price promotions. These promotions are positive, and I

believe they can be adapted for the ornamental horticultural industry.
Let us look at a few ideas.

Everyday Low Pricing (EDLP)

This is where a few specific products are selected as loss leaders and promoted heavily to encourage shoppers to shop at a specific store.

Variable Day Pricing

Prices vary depending on the day of the week or the time of the day. The
aim is to increase store traffic at quieter times. Gardeners' Day is a common way of creating such an event in a garden center. Shoppers are
offered a discount on the slowest day to encourage them to visit.

Some of my clients have "red pot" specials on specific days to generate sales during quieter periods. Kmart has a similar concept—their
BlueLight Specials, where various items are on sale for a short period of
time each day.

Image Pricing

The car industry especially knows how to develop image pricing. All cars
roughly do the same job—transport you from A to B. But the price tick-
et can vary enormously. The higher the perceived image, the more the
product is worth. The same principles can apply to topiary, extra large
plants, patio bowls, and rare plants.

Introductory Pricing

The magazine industry often uses this strategy to launch new titles.
Often the first edition comes with the second, and you get two for the
price of one. In my view, introductory pricing can have a role when
launching a garden care product, but if used when launching a plant, it
can devalue that plant.

Discount of Extra Purchases

An increasing trend is to offer a discount on a second product once the
customer has purchased one product at the full price. This is an excellent
way of adding value in the customers' mind whilst helping you move
slow-moving items.

Bulk Purchase Discounts

These are aimed at increasing the average sale per customer. One of the most successful in gardening has been the "four for three" promotion on plant materials. A client of mine, Dales Gardenworld in the U.K., used it during one month, October, to increase sales, whilst another company used it on weekdays during one specific month to increase sales.

Price Banding

Price banding is the band of prices in which a product will sell. For example, if the maximum perceived value is $30.00 and the minimum is $25.00, then this leaves a price band between $25.00 and $30.00 for flexible pricing. A retailer in a depressed area or in a lower economic demographic area may select a price nearer the $25.00 limit, which leaves flexibility to increase prices in the future. A retailer in a more affluent area or higher economic group area may price the product near the $30.00 limit and achieve the same volume of sales.

Increasing Your Price

The accompanying table shows what happens with a price increase. Compare this table with the one on price reductions. Don't be afraid to put your prices up. The key is to monitor sales. We are often afraid to raise prices because customers may perceive us as expensive. But the

		Your Present Margin								
		20%	**25%**	**30%**	**35%**	**40%**	**45%**	**50%**	**55%**	**60%**
	2%	9%	7%	6%	5%	5%	4%	4%	4%	3%
	4%	17%	14%	12%	10%	9%	8%	7%	7%	6%
	6%	23%	19%	17%	15%	13%	12%	11%	10%	9%
	8%	29%	24%	21%	19%	17%	15%	14%	13%	12%
Price Increase	10%	33%	29%	25%	22%	20%	18%	17%	15%	14%
	12%	38%	32%	29%	26%	23%	21%	19%	18%	17%
	14%	41%	36%	32%	29%	26%	24%	22%	20%	19%
	16%	44%	39%	35%	31%	29%	26%	24%	23%	21%
	18%	47%	42%	38%	34%	31%	29%	26%	25%	23%
	20%	50%	44%	40%	36%	33%	31%	29%	27%	25%
	25%	56%	50%	45%	42%	38%	36%	33%	31%	29%
	30%	60%	55%	50%	46%	43%	40%	38%	35%	33%

majority of customers doesn't know prices. With effective and creative merchandising and signage, you may find the consumer is happy to pay the price.

This table shows how much sales could decrease before you see a reduction in gross profit. (Chart is courtesy of Results Corp, Queensland.)

Book List

Stanley, John. 1999. *Just About Everything A Retail Manager Needs to Know.* Brisbane, Australia: Plum Press.

Stanley, John. 2000. *The Nursery & Garden Centre Marketing Manual,* 3rd edition. Sydney, Australia: Reference Publishing 2000.

Chapter 10

Managing Products

The aim of a retail business is to generate profit by "turning" products. This means that products need to be displayed and managed in a way that maximizes sales. All the team need to be skilled in product management, although the skills required may differ depending on the type of product.

The management of perishable products is more critical than the management of nonperishable products. If you neglect the management of dry goods, they get dusty, but you still have a saleable product. But if you neglect the management of live good such as plants, they die.

Living Product Management

In a typical garden center, living products could include indoor and outdoor plants, all with their own specific cultural requirements. The key objective is to ensure they maintain their "fresh" look until they are sold. Stale-looking plants will reflect on the whole business, as consumers judge the image of a business on its perishable plants.

As far as plant management is concerned in retailing, your priorities in product placement are illustrated in figure 10-1. The key is to place plants in the correct location. Plant placement is as critical as placing products in a supermarket. Some plants are planned purchases, whilst others are impulse sales. Planned purchases should be positioned in areas where customers are encouraged to pass impulse plants, such as bedding plants.

Figure 10-1. Product Placement.

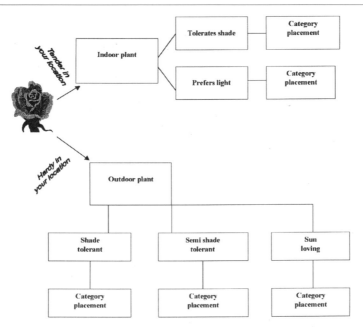

Covering the plant knowledge required to retail plants would take a book in its own right, so I will only give a brief overview of plant care here. I would recommend, however, that you consult other references for plant knowledge and specific cultural details.

Whatever the category of plant, there is basic cultural care that needs to be adhered to when managing plant material pre-delivery, receiving and holding, and management in store.

Pre-Delivery

The first key to success is to buy from the best. I have come across many retailers who buy solely on price without asking about what type of product they are buying. Prior to placing an order, you need to know that the grower can provide consistent quality. Plants should be grown in the correct growing media and ideally have been fed with long-lasting fertilizer that will feed them for at least their shelf life in a retail store.

Acceptable quality standards will vary somewhat by market sector. For example, the quality standard for a landscaper (planting in mass) will differ to that of a supermarket or a garden center. Quality is a perceived judgment covering a variety of considerations. Some of the key factors are:

Plant proportion in relation to pot
As a guide, the plant should be two thirds of the total height and the pot one third. Some species will not fall into this category, but it acts as a useful guide.

Number of branches on shrubby plants
Again, there will be species variation, but the general rule is that at least three branches on shrubby plants should emerge in the lower third of the plant.

Condition of foliage
People purchase freshness, so the plant should look fresh. The foliage should be true to type.

Pest and disease free
This should go without saying, but it does occasionally occur. Plants should be pest and disease free when sold.

Weed free
The container should be weed free. This is not always the case—liverwort and other annual and perennial weeds are occasionally found in pots.

Clean pot
Many nurserymen will argue you are buying the plant, not the pot. But customers look at the whole product and the condition of the pot is critical. As a result pot washing machines are now becoming a common feature in some nurseries. Plants are also being grown in colorful and branded pots to further enhance the plants' appearance to customers.

Growing media level in pot
The growing media should come to about a fingernail's depth from the top of the pot. If the media has settled any further down the pot, it should be topped off.

Root growth
Roots should not be protruding from the base of the pot. With woody species, secondary root curl should be avoided, as this will result in an unstable plant. The practice of potting up only a few weeks before a plant is sold should also be discouraged, as the plant will not have fully established in its new medium.

Taking cuttings from sold material
This rarely happens, but it does occasionally. If customers have purchased an "as seen" product, that is what they should receive. Taking propagation material from the plant after a sale should be frowned upon unless, as in the case of some coniferous plants, it improves the quality.

Labeling
I have written a chapter on signage and labeling that discusses the various factors involved. Plants must be labeled. For the landscape trade, batch labels may be appropriate, but for the retail trade, every plant must be labeled. Most retailers will also prefer a colored pictorial label.

Feeding
A drip liquid feed system may product excellent plants in a wholesale nursery, but once the drip is switched off, the plant will soon start to show signs of neglect. A slow-release fertilizer will keep the plant well fed through its time on the shelf.

Various nurseries and associations have a minimum quality standard that is adhered to by the industry; the following is one example to act as a guide when you are developing your own standards.

Holding Procedures
Once the plants have arrived at your retail establishment, it's essential that they are inspected. You should sign the delivery note to accept the plants only if:
- The plants are true to type.
- They are to the quality standard you require.
- They have been counted and tally with the order.
- They are pest and disease free.
- They are labeled correctly.
- The plants have not become stressed or otherwise damaged in transport.

Quality and Plants					
Amenity and groundcover grade	Volume in liters/ minimum height in centimeters	Plant habit	Number of breaks in lower third	Caning	Example
1	2	3	4	5	6
Berberis, vigorous	2/45	Bushy	3	-	*B. × stenophylla*
Berberis, medium	2/30	Branched	2	-	*B. thunbergii*
Berberis, dwarf	1/10D	Bushy	3	-	*B. buxifolia* 'Nana'
Bergenia	1/15D	Crown	-	-	*B. cordifolia*
Betula	1/30	Leader and laterals	-	-	*B. pendula*
Brunnera	1/10D	Crown	-	-	*B. macrophylla*
Calluna	0.3/7D	Bushy	3	-	*C. vulgaris*
Campanula	0.3/7D	Crown	-	-	*C. poscharskyana*
Carpinus	1/30	Leader and laterals	-	-	*C. betulus*
Carex	0.3/7D	Crown	-	-	*C. morrowii* 'Variegata'
Castenea	1/30	Leader and laterals	-	-	*C. sativa*
Chaenomeles	2/40	Branched	3	-	*C. japonica*
Chamaecyparis	1/30	Single leader furnished to base	-	-	*C. lawsoniana*
Cistus	15/20D	Bushy	3	-	*C. corbariensis*
Clematis	1.5/60	Single or several shoots	-	-	*C. vitalba*
Cornus, vigorous	2/45	Branched	3	-	*C. alba*
Cornus, dwarf	0.5/7D	Several shoots	2	-	*C. canadensis*
Corylus	2/45	Branched	2	-	*C. avellana*
Cotoneaster, medium	2/45	Branched	3	-	*C. simonsii*
Cotoneaster, prostrate, vigorous, medium	1/30D	Branched	2	-	*C. horizontalis*
Cotoneaster, prostrate, slow	1/30D	Branched	2	-	*C. dammeri*
Crataegus	1/30	Leader and laterals	-	-	*C. oxyacantha*
Cupressocyparis	2/45	Single leader furnished to base	-	-	*C. leylandii*
Cytisus	1/30	Bushy	3	-	*C. scoparius*
Daboecia	0.3/7D	Bushy	3	-	*B. cantabrica*
Elaeagnus		Branched	3	-	*E. angustifolia*
Epimedium	0.5/7D	Crown	-	-	*E. rubrum*
Erica	0.3/7D	Bushy	3	-	*E. carnea*
Euonymus, vigorous	2/45	Several shoots	-	-	*E. europaeus*
Euonymus, dwarf	1/15D	Several shoots	3	-	*E. fortunei cvs*
Fagus	1/30	Leader and laterals	-	-	*F. sylvatica*
Festuca	0.3/7D	Crown	-	-	*F. glauca*
Fraxinus	1/30	Single leader	-	-	*F. excelsior*
Gaultheria, vigorous	1/15D	Several shoots	2	-	*G. shallon*
Gaultheria, slow	1/10D	Several shoots	3	-	*G. procumbens*

From the British Container Growers Standard.

In some situations, plants may have traveled great distances from a different climatic zone. If this is the case they may need acclimatizing prior to being placed on sale. The acclimatization process will vary depending on the origin of the plant and the climate at the destination; e.g., plants originating in a warm sunny climate and being sold in a cold glasshouse.

Plant grown outdoors in a tropical climate for sale indoors in a cold climate will need acclimatizing to adjust to both the temperature variation and the daylength and light intensity variation. In this situation, it may be advisable to put plants under shade protection.

Once in the retail plant area plants need to be watered, checked for pest and disease damage and maintained to maximize eye appeal.

New plants should be placed at the rear of the display and plants already in the sales area of the same type should be moved to the front of the display.

Management in Store

Watering
The real key to success is maintaining the correct water-to-air regime in the growing medium and keeping the foliage looking healthy. The application technique for watering is therefore critical.

Water can be applied from the base of the container or from overhead. As with any situation there are advantages and disadvantages to consider.

Basal watering
Advantages
- More water conservation, water goes where it is actually needed.
- Water is recycled, an increasingly important environmental issue.
- Equal distribution of water to each plant is achieved.
- Eliminates water damage on the plant foliage.
- Water is available to the plant on hot days when it would normally be stressed.
- You can water when consumers are in the garden center without them getting wet.
- You can use more aesthetic displays in the store without the decorations being damaged by water.

Disadvantages
- If plants do not turn quickly, salt could build up in the growing media, effecting plant growth.
- *Phytophthora* and other water-borne diseases can be spread more easily around the plant center.
- Regular cleaning of the benches is required to prevent the build-up of liverwort on benches.
- The capital installation cost is high.

Overhead watering

Many garden centers prefer to water from overhead, but you still need to consider the pros and cons.

Advantages
- The system can be used to water the plants and to mist the plants to keep them turgid in low humidity and hot conditions.
- Reasonably inexpensive to install and flexible to change around.
- Warm water can be used to protect plants from frost damage in frost-prone areas.

Disadvantages
- The "umbrella" effect of the foliage means that all plants do not get an equal amount of water.
- Staining of foliage if excessive nutrients are freely available in the water.
- Water is wasted, as it is difficult to control water placement.
- Some flowers bruise with water spray on the petals.
- It restricts watering times to times when customer are not shopping, which may not be the optimum times for the plant.
- It limits your opportunities to create adventurous displays.

Whichever system you select, you must still check your plants daily and be prepared to hand water. Even with the most sophisticated watering systems, you still need to check dry pockets in the garden center and provide additional water for those plants that naturally need more water.

Protecting plants

Wind can be one of the biggest causes of damage to plants in a garden center. Ideally, you have selected a sheltered site, but the majority of sites still have some areas where wind can be a problem. Wind will accelerate dehydration and in severe situations cause foliage damage.

Wind protection can take the form of artificial or natural shelter.

The key is to filter the wind rather than put up a solid barrier, which can actually increase your problem by creating wind eddies.

The other natural phenomena that can cause problems is frost. The most damaging frosts are the unexpected ones, especially those in late spring that catch the retailer and consumer unaware. Frost protection varies depending on the degrees of frost you are exposed to in your region. The key is to be prepared. A constant monitoring of forthcoming weather conditions can save you a lot of dollars and heartache.

Remember, problems occur if you put plants under stress. If you maintain a healthy environment for plants, you shouldn't have any major problems.

Protecting customers

Plant management is one area where you need to know your plants to ensure you provide the correct conditions for the plant. But, remember, you also have a duty of care to the public. You should especially be aware of:

- Placing eye protectors on canes used to support vines or other plants.
- Poisonous plants, advising customers accordingly.
- Plants that commonly cause rashes with some people (e.g. some plants in the Primulaceae family).
- Plants that have pollen that can stain people's clothes (e.g., lilies).
- Heavy plants where customers could strain their backs handling the products without assistance.

Stoneware and Statuary Management

One product category that needs looking at on its own is the statuary and stoneware category. Stone ornaments are becoming more popular in gardens and garden centers, but they do have some unique attributes.

Stoneware works well when it is used amongst plants to create lifestyle displays rather than being used as a category on its own, but do ensure it is safe. They are heavy items that in a garden center are not secured into the garden. You must ensure they are safe. Garden centers will attract families with young children, and these children will wander off to look at features. Deaths have already been recorded in garden centers where statues have tumbled onto children trying to climb them. You will need to secure large stone features and to keep an eye on children around those products.

Consumers like to buy clean products. How often do you venture into a garden center and see dirty water and leaves in birdbaths. These baths should be kept clean, with fresh water placed in baths at a regular interval. Clean birdbaths sell, dirty ones do not—it's that simple!

Finally, be careful with loading large stoneware into customers' vehicles. Remember, they have to take them out at the other end. Often, you see statues placed in vehicles and wonder how a frail customer is going to unload it at the other end. Perhaps this is where a delivery service could be a major attribute.

Dry Goods Management

The skills required to manage dry goods in the shop are very similar to those in other retail environments. For this reason, many employers will employ a retailer rather than a horticulturist to manage this department. The dry goods department will cover product categories such as garden care, lawn care, garden machinery, bird and pet products, growing media, ornaments, and watering equipment. Whichever category you are responsible for, there are some basic management rules common to all.

The first rule, which also applies outdoors, is cleanliness. Consumers prefer to shop in a clean environment and, therefore, your daily cleanliness program is critical. Plus, you and I notice the little things rather than the large things. A dirty shelf, fingerprints on glass doors, and unemptied garbage cans are an indicator of how the business is run. Every business should have a cleanliness checklist that they adhere to in their store.

Remember, retail is detail. Customers admire detailed retail stores. Always check:

- Fingerprints on the front door (especially if it is glass).
- The condition of the floor.
- Toilet paper in the restrooms.
- The cleanliness of worktops and the checkout.
- Posters that are out of date or ripped.
- Cobwebs.
- Dead flies in the store window.

Apart from hygiene, you also need to ensure that stock turns quickly.

It is very rare we have products supplied by a manufacturer with a sell-by date, but you should run your business as if all your products have a sell-by date. In other words, "first in first out" should be a company policy. In practice. this means that when refilling shelves, your team should take the product off the shelf, put the new product at the back of the shelf, and then face the front of the shelf with the old product.

We work in a seasonal industry; the variation in seasonal trade will vary greatly depending on your geographic location. For example, if you have a garden center located in Edmonton, Canada, your trading pattern will be completely different to one located in Tampa, Florida. Even so, you will have seasonal trading cycles, and you will need to manage your dry goods to maximize sales each season.

In the garden care department, there are products that will only be sold in volume in either spring, summer, fall, or winter, and you have to place these products in the optimum position at the optimum time.

Many businesses now produce a planogram of their shelving system to maximize sales each season. A planogram is a diagram produced manually or via computer that shows the optimum position of products at any one time on a merchandising layout. In some retail sectors the planogram is supplied by the manufacturers, whilst chains or franchise retail organizations will produce them for their own retail group.

The advantage of a planogram is that management can analyze the

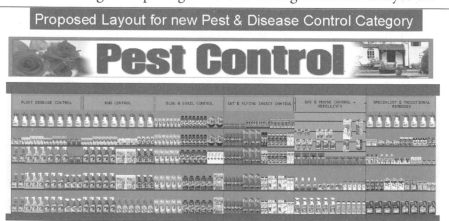

Proposed Layout for new Pest & Disease Control Category

Proposed Strategy: - REDUCE DUPLICATION – SIMPLIFY FOR CONSUMER – EXPLOIT UMBRELLA POTENTIAL

Help the consumer shop across the Category and build staff confidence to give better advice. Exploit growth in Care & Control products and increase Link Sales potential with Plants. Reduce number of Brands. Take distress away from consumers shopping experience. Manage Margin Mix to use category as Cash Cow. Push RTU as a mechanism to bring NEW users into the Category. Look for opportunities to highlight Environmental benefits of Integrated Pest Control.

retail data and produce a scientifically based plan for a product category. This plan can then be implemented in the store very simply by following the layout provided on the diagram.

In planning your planogram, you need to consider:

- Top-selling seasonal lines should be placed in the "sight and take" position (chin to bellybutton on an average height person).
- Out-of-season lines that you feel should be kept on the shelf should be placed in the bend position, as this is the least popular sales position
- If you have a number of products that perform the same task— e.g., slug and snail control—I would advise that you should stock only three options. The key is to put the one you recommend in the sight line and the others outside of the sight line. Research also indicates that the product you recommend should have a facing of between three and ten products at the front of the shelf.
- Heavy items such as large bags of growing media should be

Percentage of Units Sold in Each Shelf Position	
75%	Stretch position
100%	Sight and take position (chin to bellybutton on targeted customer)
55%	Stoop position
20%	Placing products on the floor

placed near the ground. If you place them higher, you may cause back strain when people lift products. Make sure all your team are trained in safe lifting practices.

- You will have products that state "Warning: Keep out of the reach of children." You have a duty to your customer to ensure that these products are kept at least three feet above ground level.

The management of this department also includes keeping the department safe, but accidents do happen. If garden chemicals are spilt, you should cover the spillage with sawdust to absorb the chemical and then clear the area up. A bucket of sawdust should be positioned near this department, and everyone should be trained in the cleaning up process.

Stock Control—The Key to Your Success

As I have already mentioned, stock control management is the key to success. Today we have elaborate systems available to control stock, especially as bar coding is now being used successfully by many horticultural businesses.

The challenge is that the "stock life" of products we deal with varies enormously. For example, we would expect to sell all our bedding plants in days, but shrubs may take weeks, and trees up to six months. This should not deter a retailer from introducing a stock control system; it is the lifeblood to the success of the business.

The key to stock control is managing the life of the product whilst it is in the retail environment. Every product should have a sell-by date, and the product should be managed accordingly. As every plant and product has a different life cycle, it is best if I use an example to illustrate the management procedure.

Week No.	Expected Cumulative Sales	Actual Cumulative Sales	Action Plan
1	10	3	Change one thing in your merchandise strategy—e.g., change position in garden center, change sign, change shape of display, or change information given to customers
2	20	6	Change one more thing in merchandise strategy
3	30	9	Change one more thing in merchandise strategy
4	40	12	Change one more thing in merchandise strategy
5	50	15	Change one more thing in merchandise strategy
6	60	20	Move from merchandise strategy to financial strategy. With some products you may want to put the price up for one week. Your perceived price may be too low.
7	70	24	Try selling three for the price of two. Multi-selling may work for you
8	80	35	Start reducing the gross profit of individual plant units.
9	90	40	Reduce price below cost price. You need to clear the product in a week.
10	100	70	Use the remaining stock for demonstrations, adding value or promotions. It must be cleared by the end of this week.

The plant buyer purchases plant Y. The role of the plant buyer in this situation is critical, he has to make the following decisions:

- What shall I buy? Plant Y
- How many shall I buy? One hundred plants
- What should the retail price be? $10.00
- What is its shelf life? Ten weeks

In this scenario, the plant manager now knows that they are expected to sell ten plants a week over a ten-week period to clear this batch of plants. The only exception to this rule would be unexpected weather conditions, which could slow down the plants' retail cycle.

In most situations, the plant will perform as expected and sell at the rate of ten a week. But the retail world does not always run that smoothly, and there are times when you have to manage the plant differently to ensure you obtain the desired stock turn.

If the plant is not performing, then you must make managerial decisions to move the product. My approach would be as follows:

I realize that not all products are going to perform as I have indicated, but the key is you always monitor product cycle from week one and manage it accordingly. Do not start taking action when it is too late; this will result in sales per square foot will being lower than you should expect.

You should also use your historical records as a tool to develop future buying patterns. If you had a surplus of one plant variety last season, buy less of this variety this season so your order more closely matches units sold.

Managing Consistency

McDonald's is a worldwide retailer. Their success story is one that has been written about many times. The part of their success that applies to a garden center is their commitment to consistency. A McDonald's in Paris or Beijing applies the same standards of consistency as a McDonald's in Chicago. McDonald's knows that to be successful they have to provide a consistent package to the customer, and the same applies in your business.

To achieve this, ideally you need a checklist and you should use that on a daily, weekly and monthly basis. You can create a checklist from scratch for your business, or you can use a ready-made one and adapt it to your business. The following is an example of an ideal checklist for garden center owners. It was produced by David C. Seavey at the University of New Hampshire. The full critique is available from the university.

Garden Center Checklist
Exterior Signage

	Yes	No	Needs Improvement
1. Are business road signs simple, easily read, attractive, landscaped, innovative, and eye-catching?			
2. Are directional signs used effectively?			
3. Do department signs help customers find plants and hard goods quickly? (e.g., perennials, shade trees, fruits, statuary, mulches)			
4. Do informational signs or literature provide instructions for placement, planting, and maintenance of plants?			
5. Are picture signs accurate, readily visible, and attractive?			
6. Are price signs accurate, readily visible and attractive?			
7. Are there signs that use negative words such as *no* or *don't*?			
8. Does a sign explain policies regarding quality and guarantees?			

Quality

	Yes	No	Needs Improvement
1. Are green and hard goods of high quality?			
2. Are plant selections appropriate for the various hardiness zones in your region?			
3. Are bare-root and root-packaged items, bedding plants, roses, and plants with new growth protected from freezing?			
4. Do employees handle stock carefully? (Are plants picked up by their tops without support to the soil ball and/or dropped hard on the ground?)			
5. Is B&B (balled and burlaped) stock protected against drying by frequent watering and/or mulching?			
6. Have container-grown plants been fertilized with slow-release fertilizers that will be effective in either a maintenance or growth program?			
7. Is overhead or drip irrigation installed in display beds?			
8. Is recently potted stock maintained in a high-humidity location and protected from wind and bright sun?			
9. Are plants shaded under lath when they should be in full sun?			
10. Are containerized plants and balled stock displayed on a base that allows good drainage?			
11. Does container-grown nursery stock have a well-established root system, without being pot bound?			

Book List

Seavey, David C. 1999. *The Garden Center Critique and Merchandising Guide.* University of New Hampshire Cooperative Extension.

Chapter 11

Retailing Plants Successfully

We have seen a rapid evolution in the retailing of plant material. In the late 1950s and 1960s, the traditional way of retailing plants was via the nursery gate. The grower was also the seller to the eventual user. Over the intervening years we have seen the industry become more sophisticated in its production, distribution, and retailing. Many factors have led to the changes in retailing, but the primary developments that have led to those changes are:

The Container Revolution. In the late 1960s and early 1970s, a great deal of research was carried out into growing plants successfully in containers. To master container growing, research was carried out on containers, watering systems, fertilizers, and growing media, with the result that we can now consistently grow a quality plant in a container with a prolonged shelf life in that container. The result is a container-based industry rather than the traditional field-based industry, and the quality of the ground soil is no longer a critical issue in the location of the business.

The Consumer Revolution. During the same period, we have seen consumers change their lifestyle and wants. Consumers have steadily accumulated wealth and have moved beyond buying staple items to purchasing goods to make lifestyle statements. As a result, a number of industries have grown rapidly. We have seen rapid growth in the travel, sports, restaurant, and gardening retail sectors as a result of a changing consumer who has increasing leisure dollars to spend.

Gardening has benefited more than most due to consumers who are becoming more affluent, looking for products that enhance and reflect their lifestyle, and that are often considered as a status statement outside their home.

The Profit Revolution. Although many people may feel they should receive more profit for their investment, plants at a retail level have a higher gross profit than many other products on the marketplace. The result is that retailers who look at the sales and profit per square foot find the results attractive when compared with many other products on the marketplace. What they do not consider is that wastage is higher, plus the amount of skill, time, and money required to manage a perishable product is far higher than most retailers initially expect, which does balance out the equation slightly.

The Distribution Revolution. Moving perishable products around the country or globe was a real challenge. With more sophisticated and rapid distribution channels this barrier has now been removed. Today, it is not unusual for a supermarket to have fruit and vegetables on the shelf from fifty countries. Having plant material available from the nursery industry is no longer a challenge in their minds.

The Evolution of Distribution. From nursery gate sales we saw the development of plant centers operated by horticulturists who were trained in plant production. As these centers matured, many evolved into garden centers and the operation of these businesses was taken over by business people who were trained in retailing. Garden centers provide for the gardeners' needs and sell plants, garden care products, and ancillary garden accessories. The garden center has now evolved into the lifestyle center, oftentimes complete with restaurant, pet department, outdoor furniture, and craft center. The plant division, although still a core category, now takes a less prominent role in the overall retail picture.

In the 1990s, the hardware store revolution also took place with the corner hardware store evolving into a box store to supply all the needs for the handyman. This retail sector then saw an opportunity to grow its hardware division if it could attract more women. The result is that the garden center is now an integral part of the hardware store. Companies such as The Home Depot (U.S.), Lowes (U.S.), Bunnings (Australia), Ogi (Germany), and B&Q (U.K.) are now recognized globally as leaders in the retail industry.

Supermarkets have also entered the plant industry as they realize that female shoppers will impulse spend on perishable products, and this sector of the market is now seeing a growth phase. Historically, the wholesale nursery people believed that they "owned" the plant market. At a recent conference I attended, a garden center owner took the same stance. Plant retailing is now a multifaceted industry with nobody having the high ground. It will continue to diversify with other retail opportunities occurring. Already we are seeing growth in finished garden retailing, Internet plant retailing, and global retailers. The evolution of the last forty years is going to continue at a greater speed.

The key to success is knowing where your retail business fits into the retail plant web. In other words, you need a successful retail strategy.

Strategies for Garden Centers

In an industry with so many different outlet options, you need to offer the customer a clear and precise reason to visit your company. This is often called your USP, or unique selling proposition. In other words, you need to identify what makes your business unique in your market and to promote and develop it accordingly.

Garden centers should be recognized as unique destinations that have a core strategy of providing for all of the consumers' needs. Consumers expect to find a wide range of plants, expert advice, and a full range of garden center products.

The strategies for a garden center should be different to other outlets of plant material. In developing a garden center strategy, the key points are:

1. You provide a wide and deep range of plants that are suitable for your local conditions.
2. You have a clear and precise promotional plant strategy that provides you with a clear point of difference.
3. Your signage system provides customers with ideas as well as price. You need to show the customer you know the product.
4. Your team is made up of trained horticulturists who have retail skills and personality.

5. You have an ongoing training program that ensures your team is up to date with new plants, product knowledge, and garden trends.
6. The displays must reflect lifestyle, as the impulse sale is exceptionally high. People come to garden centers for ideas, not products.

Your objective should be to be recognized as the regional center for gardening advice. You must become the destination. Failure to be recognized as such is a recipe for disaster. Over the last few years, we have seen independent garden centers fail and close down. Often, they have used the excuse that it has been the competition. In the majority of cases, it has been due to the lack of focus in their own strategies. In this market sector you cannot afford to be perceived by your customers as an also ran. The competition today is too fierce, and the result is a declining market share.

Strategies for Hardware Stores

A decade ago I was told hardware stores would never make it in the gardening sector. Today, they have some of the most sophisticated and successful garden centers on the globe.

They did make mistakes in the early days—they did not understand the complexities of retailing perishable products, something that was quite new to them. But that is now behind them, and the start of the twenty-first century has seen a rapid proliferation in hardware stores, and I feel we will shortly see saturation in this sector and a thinning out will then be inevitable.

Hardware retailers, to be successful, need to consider the following strategies:

1. Hardware stores came into the industry understanding retailing but lacking expertise in the gardening sector. These skills were rapidly brought in via the use of consultants and full-time horticulturists. Successful hardware retailers need access to an experienced retail horticulturist who is part of the team.
2. The range of plants will often be shallower and narrower than in a garden center. Hardware stores tend to deal with less-educated gardeners than a garden center and therefore do not need to supply the more unusual plant material. The key to success is

stock turn, and to maintain a high stock turn a hardware store needs to stock proven winners.

3. The merchandising technique is completely different to a garden center. Customers are looking for product. They are in a do-it-yourself store, not a do-it-for-me store (e.g., garden center). They are not looking to purchase finished lifestyle statements; they are looking for the different plant units and accessories so they can make their own. This means that the majority of plants are displayed on a grid layout to maximize sales.

4. The wages-to-sales percentage is about 4% lower in a hardware store than in a garden center. This does not necessarily mean that team members are less skilled; it means that the time to provide advice is less available. As a result, hardware stores tend to invest more in technology to keep the labor bill down. They rely on automated watering and more sophisticated stock control systems to maintain efficiency.

Strategies for Supermarkets

The retailers with the highest traffic flow are the supermarkets, but there are differences between these retailers and the others. The garden center generally attracts the family, and their marketing strategies tend to be family based. Traditionally, the hardware store has been a male domain, and garden departments have been introduced with the aim of attracting more women. The supermarket has always been a female domain, and research shows that impulse sales increase when women shop alone or with other women. The supermarket already had a high traffic flow of potential high-impulse spenders.

The supermarkets know that grocery products have generally been low gross profit products. There is not a lot of profit, if any, on a can of dog food! This industry has found that it can only maintain an acceptable gross profit on perishable products such as bread, cheese, meat, fruit, vegetables, fish, and flowers. As a result, we have seen investment in the perishable categories to enhance profits. Fully developed delis, butchers, bakeries, florists, and liquor departments are now commonplace and being positioned in prime retail locations within the supermarket. The key to success is to locate perishable products in prime spots to increase impulse spending on high gross profit items.

It is within the above scenario that garden products are looked on as an attractive category within the supermarket industry. Supermarkets have traditionally had a garden department for "dry" products for a number of years, but it is only recently that, as an industry, they have started to develop the "live" or "green" categories within the store.

As a supermarket owner, the following strategies are important:

1. This industry stocks a very narrow and shallow product range, as it is a purely impulse market. The consumer must know what the plant is, and it must be an impulse plant. It must be in flower or have attractive foliage, and the whole batch purchased must look consistent. I know a supermarket that specifies that, for example, cyclamen must have five flowers on them—no more or no less. If they find some have three, four, or six flowers on them, then they will reject the whole order.

2. The team employed by the supermarket will not be horticulturists and will most likely not know the plant and how to care for it. Any plants that are difficult to care for in an indoor environment should be rejected. Team members should only need to price it and restock it.

3. Stock turn is the lifeblood of this sector. If the plant does not turn, it will be rejected. Plants are often needed to turn in two or three days (compared to one or two months in garden centers for some products).

4. Plants will be placed in prime selling zones in the supermarket and are there to attract customers and increase impulse sales. The store therefore wants to make a good gross profit. Plants are competing with a whole range of other products for this space. The winning product is the one with the expected highest gross profit return per square foot.

5. This is a season- and events-led retail sector. Plants need to be decorated to celebrate: Chinese New Year, Christmas, Valentine's Day, Halloween, Easter, Thanksgiving, Independence Day, and any other events or holidays important in your area.

6. The product mix may change weekly within the category to maximize sales.

Strategies for a Market

The oldest retail environment was the bazaar or village market. They started in Mesopotamia in Asia Minor and are as strong today as they have ever been. Today, farmers markets, flea markets, car trunk sales, garage sales, and stalls in shopping malls are the modern day village markets. Their role today is the same as they have always been—a point of social contact.

Retailing Plants in Different Retail Sectors			
	Supermarket	Garden Center	Hardware
Layout	Grid	Boutique	Grid
Range (SKUs)	Low (often less than 500)	High (often up to 6,000)	Medium (often 1,000–2,000)
Price perception	Low	High	Medium
Team's horticultural knowledge perception	Low	High	Medium
Plant category within total product categories sold	Impulse lines	Core category	Additional category to attract wider market
Promotional strategy	Price-led on flowering products	Promotion-led on lifestyle	Price-led on top-selling lines
Consumer target	Impulse female buyer	Lifestyle gardener	Do-it-yourself gardener
Location	Urban	Urban/Rural	Urban
Add on selling	None provided	Essential	Desirable
Shelf life	Very short (days)	Can be months	Normally weeks

Although many in the industry despise this type of outlet as a means of selling plants, this is an integral part of plant retailing and will continue to be. This style of retailing is seven thousand years old and is not about to disappear. If anything, we are seeing a resurgence in this type of retailing, as consumers shop these outlets looking for entertainment and a bargain. Whereas the supermarket is looking for consistency, this is the last thing you want in a market scenario.

To be successful in a market situation, the following points need to be considered.

1. This is personality retailing. The more personality you have, the more you sell. The consumer is looking for old-fashioned banter with the seller to remind them of the old greengrocer. The type of person who sells in the market would never "cut it" in a supermarket or hardware store.
2. Repetition is death. Customers are looking for unique one-off items. The key is to display just one of everything. Different styles of pots, quality of plants, labels, and product mixed together is acceptable—it adds to the theater.
3. Plants need to be clearly priced, as they are purchased on price. This does not mean to say they have to be cheap—often they are more expensive than in a more formal retail environment. Price bartering is part of the fun of market retailing.
4. This style of retailing cuts out the middleman. The grower is often the seller to the consumer. The result is that the grower gets to know eventual customers and can carry out his own consumer research.

Strategies for Cyberspace

The opposite end of the retail spectrum from the market must be selling in cyberspace. This opportunity to sell plants via a computer only became possible due to Internet communications developed in the early 1990s. But, in an exceptionally short time we have come from invention to a situation where about 70% of first-world homes have access to cyberspace.

The late 1990s saw an Internet boom, with fortunes being made as new Internet companies hit the market. The turn of the century saw the inevitable "Internet recession," where many such companies went under. This was inevitable. It has always been the case that 80% of companies fail in the first two years of their life. Internet companies were not immune to this sad reality. Those that survive will become the Internet companies of the future. There will be cyberspace retailing of plants in the future.

I have a whole chapter on Internet at the end of this book, where we will go into the subject in depth.

Mail Order Strategies

Over the last few decades, mail order plant retailing has grown steadily. The advantage of mail order is that it stretches the geographic distribution zones for your products. Plus, companies such as FedEx have improved the distribution of parcels around the country and the globe. Bulb, perennial plant, young plant, and rare plant suppliers have used this format for retailing for a number of years.

The key to success is in the marketing. In the majority of situations you will need a glossy catalog. This is the ultimate example of selling dreams. The customer does not see the product until the parcel arrives, often many weeks or months later. Many mail order companies have failed by overselling the dream in their catalog and sending the customer a product that does not live up to the perceived dream. If you are in the mail order business, your customers need to put a lot of trust in what you are and what you are going to deliver. Do not oversell the dream at the beginning, as you need repeat business.

The other key to success is communication. With modern distribution and handling procedures, the customer expects you to be able to communicate with them and to be able to update them with the delivery process.

Chapter 12

Signs: The Silent Communicators

The average urban American is exposed to over 30,000 visual messages a day. Retailers tell you that people do not read signs. It's true—there are far too many for anyone to read, digest, and understand. This does not mean that you should ignore or minimize your signage. Signs are a crucial part of your business, and a well-thought signage strategy can give you the equivalent of at least one extra full-time employee serving customers.

Due to consumer signage overload, you need to think through your signage plan very carefully. You need a system that is simple, uncluttered, and helps rather than bamboozles your customers.

A good example of signage strategy can be found in most major airports around the globe. Next time you are in an airport, take a look at their signage. It probably got you from the parking lot to your airline seat with little confusion. Yet some companies cannot get the customer from the parking lot to the climbing roses, which is a far simpler operation.

A sign should achieve two objectives: It should be easily understood (function), and it should be pleasant and good looking (aesthetics).

Develop a Signage Strategy

Signs should be used to establish a brand image in the consumers' mind, direct them to specific product categories, and increase the sale of selected products. You will need to plan your signage strategy; otherwise, you may well end up with a selection of signs that confuses both your customers and your sales team.

Photo 12-1. Promotional signage provided by the supplier.

Photo 12-2. Herb Herbert's signs leave no doubt about what this product is for.

Before discussing signage in depth, let us look at the types of signs you will require in your business:

- Corporate signs: These inform the consumer what business they are actually in. These are your branding signs. For example, your company name is your corporate sign: "John's Garden Center."
- Product category signs: These direct the consumer to specific product categories. One of many possibilities is "Cottage Garden Plants."
- Promotional signage: These highlight specific promotions and have a short life span, based on the stock turn of the promotion.
- Information signage: These identify service and service policies within your business and are information signs: "We Guarantee Our Plants."
- Product signs: These educate consumers about the specific products you sell.

The key to success is that you need a signage strategy. Prior to looking at your own business, I would encourage you to look at a McDonald's, BP, Wal-Mart, or Home Depot store. All these retailers have very specific signage strategies. You rarely see faded or outdated signs or promotional signage randomly scattered around the store without any logic in a belief they will eventually sell products that are not situated near the signage.

You need to have the same discipline in your store. Signs should help the customers shop your store and make buying decisions, not confuse them and take the attention away from the product you are trying to sell.

Let us now look at each signage category in a lot more detail.

Corporate Signs

The aim of a corporate sign is to set an image standard and to inform the consumer where they are. Corporate signage is part of your branding image and should marry in with your image objectives and corporate message.

For example, when I mention the name McDonald's you probably think of the big yellow M, Ronald McDonald, and hamburgers. The consumer needs to build a similar picture in their mind concerning your business.

The key to corporate signage is consistency—once you are satisfied with it, you keep it, as it takes a long time to get a corporate message across to a consumer.

I recently worked with a client who every twelve months changed the color of the corporate sign. Why? Because the team had become bored with the colors. The result was confused customers. Color is part of your brand!

Corporate signage needs to be seen by passing traffic; therefore, you will need to take the following into account:

- The speed at which viewers are passing (on foot or in vehicles)
- The height and width of the letters
- The style of printing
- Color combinations
- The amount of words used
- The message you need to get across.

The crucial need of an entrance sign is that it can be seen and still allow ample time for the passer by to enter your establishment. Ideally, the sign needs to be sited in advance of your site entrance. The following table, produced by the United Kingdom Ministry of Transport, should act as a guide:

Speed Limit	Sign Distance from Turning
30 mph (50 kmph)	550 yards (500 m)
40 mph (65 kmph)	740 yards (675 m)
50 mph (80 kmph)	820 yards (750 m)

Note that depending on you location, you may not be able to place signs half a mile from your garden center. These are suggestions for ideal placement; try to get as close as local ordinances or your situation will allow.

Readability of Outdoor Signs		
Height of Letter	Maximum Distance for Easy Visibility	Approximate Time Visible at 35 mph
1 in.	25 ft.	$1/2$ sec.
2 in.	50 ft.	1 sec.
3 in.	80 ft.	$1 1/2$ sec.
4 in.	100 ft.	2 sec.
5 in.	140 ft.	$2 3/4$ sec.
6 in.	170 ft.	$3 1/3$ sec.

From James Milmire, Roadside Marketing *(University of Delaware Food Business Information, 1965).*

Surface Color in Various Lighting Conditions				
Daylight	Sodium Streetlights	Mercury Streetlights	Tungsten Indoor Lights	Fluorescent Indoor Lights
Red	Brown	Brown/black	Bright red	Dull red
Blue	Brown/blue	Deep violet	Dull green/blue	Bright blue
Green	Brown/yellow	Dark green	Yellow green	Cool blue green
Yellow	Yellow	Green/yellow	Intense yellow	Green yellow
White	Light yellow	Blue/white	Cream/off white	White

From Bill Stewart, Signwork: A Craftsman's Manual *(Collins, 1984).*

Corporate signs should look attractive in daylight and in artificial light. It is therefore worth considering the effects of artificial light on color.

Product Category Signage

Once in the store, the potential customer wants to find specific departments and categories of products. The most common way of directing customers is by signage. When considering departmental signage, take the following into account:

- The bigger the garden center, the greater the need for department signage.
- The customer should be able to enter your store and clearly see where the major departments are situated.
- Keep the sign simple so it can be easily read.
- Be consistent in the style used on all departmental signage.

The words used on departmental signs depend on your position in the marketplace. A product-led store may use words like *roses, native plants, perennials, furniture, garden chemicals*, and *trees*. A lifestyle-led store may use words such as: *the rose garden, the natural garden, the cottage garden, outdoor living, garden care*, and *living shade*.

Use capital letters sparingly. Resist the temptation to write messages in capital letters, although a simple word in capitals is acceptable. Your reader will find a lowercase message, in serif type style, easier to read than one in capitals.

Promotional Signs

The objectives of a promotional sign can be varied, and this type of signage is often misused. The aims could be:

- To promote one specific product (*Scabiosa* 'Blue Butterfly')
- To promote a category (Herb Herbert Herbs)
- To promote a theme (the perfumed garden)
- To promote an event (company birthday)
- To identify a season (spring)
- To identify a specific time (Valentine's Day)

Promotional signage can either be produced in house or by a supplier. Whichever the case, abide by the following rules:

- Only use the signs in the key, relevant areas (do not promote roses in the conifer department).

- Give the promotion a life span and keep to it (customers do not want to see dated, faded, and ripped signs).
- Use promotional material in an exciting way. Rather than just hang up posters around your garden center, group them to catch the customer's eye.

Figure 12-1. Group posters to generate interest.

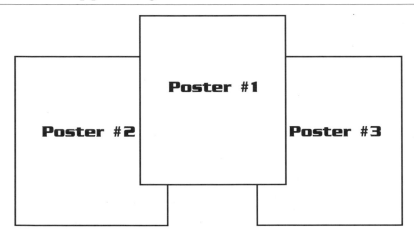

Information Signage

These signs identify your service, services, and policies. Their aim is to inform the customer. These signs should also be written in positive language; negative signs do not build consumer loyalty.

Having said that, how often have you seen signs such as: "Do not touch," "Breakages will be paid for," "Do not eat on these premises," and so on. You should be encouraging your customers to want to spend their dollars with you. Always write your signs in positive English, such as: "Do handle us with care," "We love your company, but we would appreciate you not eating while you shop. Thank you." You can also use humor to get your point across, as evidenced in photo 12-3.

Photo 12-3. Make people smile, even when you're giving them a warning.

Product Signs

The aim of these signs is to focus the customer's eye on a specific product.

What do you write on a sign?

The objective of a sign is to motivate customers to purchase. This means, in most situations, that you need to make them aware of the benefits to them, rather than the features of the product.

Benefits are reasons they should buy, whilst features are what the product is. Take a look at many plant signs, and you can see how many non-horticulturists are often confused by the language used and the amount of information provided.

The key to using signs is the K.I.S.S. principle (Keep It Simple Sells). There are rules that if adhered to can increase your sales.

1. Highlight the benefits to the customer rather than the features of the plant.

For example:

Feature	Benefit
Grows in full sun	Ideal for sunny positions
Perennial	Plant once and it will regrow each year
Disease resistant	No need to use harmful chemicals
Grows in pH of 4.5	Ideal for peaty soils
Groundcover plant	Ideal for covering the ground quickly

2. The majority of plants are purchased on impulse, and your consumers do not want to read long messages to stimulate them to buy. Identify the three major benefits for the majority of your consumers and highlight these in a bullet point format. This is easier to read and will stimulate more interest.

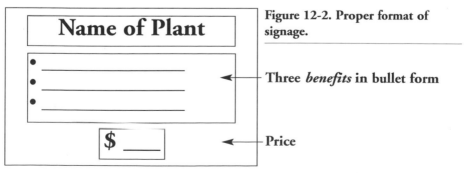

Figure 12-2. Proper format of signage.

Three *benefits* in bullet form

Price

3. Do not use jargon. Jargon is the language of the industry, which is not in common usage by the general public. Examples of commonly used jargon in our industry include systemic, pH, perennial, F_1, acidic, H.T. These are words rarely used in general conversation and should be avoided on signs promoting products.

4. Latin name or common name—which comes first? The industry has debated this many times over the years and has still not come to a mutual industry decision. It is my view that the scientific name is essential for wholesale purchase of product, but when it comes to selling, the common name is more important.

Photo 12-4. Ferndale Garden Center in the U.K. has creatively solved the problem of older customers not being able to read labels, and it shows the customers that they care about them.

I know many purists will disagree and will argue that we should educate our consumers to use scientific names. I do not disagree with that sentiment, but I believe our objective should be to encourage as many people as possible to enjoy plants. Latin names put people off, as many people get embarrassed because they do not know or cannot pronounce the Latin name. Over the last few years, products such as Flower Carpet Rose, Herb Herbert herbs and Blue Butterfly have proved that a name that catches the consumer's imagination sells more product.

5. Write signs in lowercase letters. Consumers find it easier to read lowercase serif-style letters, and our job should be to make it easy for people to read signs.

6. The majority of plant buyers are in their forties, fifties, and sixties and are experiencing failing eyesight. For this reason, companies such as *Time* magazine and *Readers Digest* have identified the need to produce publications in larger print. Many people will visit your garden center

and accidentally leave their reading glasses at home. Do make sure your signage has lettering large enough for your target market to read it.

I have one client who has positioned a magnifying glass next to the garden care department. He has found that many customers forget to bring their reading glasses into the center; they arrive at the garden care department and cannot read the information on the labels. His magnifying glass has definitely increased sales.

> **Management Memo**
>
> Use Words That Sell
> Certain words have positive suggestive meanings on signage and should be used whenever possible. Words that sell include: at last, attention, back by popular demand, check out these, exclusive, finally, for the first time, for those who insist on the best, good news, huge savings, hurry, in a class by itself, it's here, new, new low price, only, gives you . . . , quality doesn't have to cost you, reasons why you should, save big, state of the art, switch to, take a look at these features, take the _____ challenge, the _____ advantage, the smart choice, urgent.

The power word alphabet

Donald Caudhill of the University of North Alabama developed the power word alphabet. These are some words that help promote products:

A: Action, accomplish, ahead, anybody, achieve, answer, announcing, amazing, at last

B: Benefit, best, bible, big, bargain

C: Can, calm, care, career, clean, comfort, challenge, compare, cash, control

D: Discover, deliver, destiny, definite, dynamite, decide

E: Easy, earn, effective, efficient, entertain, extra, exciting

F: Free, famous, full, fancy, fun, future, facts, friends, fast, found

G: Guarantee, get, glamour, great, gold, give

H: Health, happy, heart, heaven, help, home "how to," hurry, honor, hot, hope, honest

I: Introducing, intelligent, invention, invite, innovate, incredible, interest, improve, immediate, important, instant

J: Join, jewel, jumbo, joy, just arrived, juicy

K: Know, key, king, keep, knowledge, kind

L: Love, land, liberty, luxury, look, last chance, life, lasting, listen, learn

M: Money, magic, more, maximum, minute, modern, miracle, most, mind, mine, many

N: New, now, need, nude, nice, neat, never before

O: Opportunity, occult, open, on, original, occasion, own

P: Proven, power, positive, promote, protect, payoff, pro, pleasure, profit, performance

Q: Quality, quick, quiet

R: Results, respect, revive, right, rich, revolutionary, remarkable, record

S: Save, safe, sale, satisfaction, self, service, sensational, special, smile, super, startling, secret, suddenly

T: Today, take, taste, thanks, time, true, try, total, tempting, think, trust

U: Urgent, unique, understand, ultimate, useful

V: Victory, vitamin, vacation, VIP, value, valor, volume

W: Win, wise, wanted, worth, willing, wow, which, when, why, who else, wonderful

X: Xanadu, Xavier, x-ray, X

Y: You, your, yes, young, youth

Z: Zest, zodiac, zip, zenith, zeal, zero

Use the right sign at the right time

Signage should be used at key times in a product's life cycle. The following diagram illustrates the life cycle of a typical product and shows the key times when you should use signs to promote the product to achieve maximum sales.

The product will remain the same, but the message will be different at various stages in its life cycle:

Figure 12-3. Signage in life of product.

Point in life cycle	Words to use
Testing	NEW!
Rapid sales growth	IT'S HERE!
Pre peak period	ATTENTION
Peak period	Look at these key features
Early decline	Check out these
High promotion period	Attention
Clearance	Huge savings

Figure 12-4. Signage checklist.

Weekly Signage Review Checklist		
Activity	Good Ideas	Problems
Review this week's sale signing Are all advertised items signed? (list) ☐ Do any advertised items have traditional problems such as always needing two sides for back-to-back signing etc? ☐ Are all advertised items easy to locate? ☐ Are there problems with customers confusing sale merchandise with adjacent non-sale merchandise? *Review general signing policies* ☐ Are there any out-of-date signs still up? ☐ Are there enough signs, per agreement, per fixture, gondola, etc? ☐ Are there too many signs in any area? Too few? *Review general sign quality issues* ☐ Are signs consistent, legible, and neat? ☐ Are the benefits well presented? ☐ Do the signs, in general, enhance the appearance of the store? *Review trend signing* ☐ Is what's new proudly out in front for the customers to see and is it properly signed? ☐ Are there any trends without signs? ☐ Does the customer understand the trend? ☐ Review any problems identified by store managers and associates ☐ Communicate this checklist to buyers and sign personnel ☐ Check sign department and store to make sure proper signing has been prepared and sent		

Use the correct material for your signs

The challenge is finding suitable materials for outdoor signage systems. Over the years, various materials have been available, but do make sure they are weatherproof. Many retailers still prefer to use corflute (Correx or printflute) or the newer weatherproof vinyls. Make sure you use nonfading inks, especially if using colors, as you will find red will fade out-doors rapidly if the wrong ink is used.

Manage the signs in your garden center

Signage needs to look fresh and professional. Indeed, a well-presented sign could be considered as an extra salesperson in your garden center. Unfortunately, many garden centers do not realize the sales opportunities that signs can offer, with the result that signs are often managed quite inappropriately.

The Rules of Product Signage

Although writing signs is an art, anyone can write one—provided they abide by a dozen simple rules:

1. Be specific in what you want to say to your customer
2. Make the price easy to understand
3. Sell the romance and sizzle
4. Write facts, not fiction
5. Don't state the obvious
6. Explain what is not obvious
7. Help the customer buy the best product
8. Help the customer comparison shop
9. Remind customers of logical needs
10. Always state what they will save
11. Stay positive and sign-friendly
12. Break the above rules—if it fits your strategy

It's not the sign, it's the stand!

It is relatively easy to come up with a sign, but getting the right support system for your signs has always been a challenge.

Over the years, many systems have been developed and discarded, but I still believe that for outdoor plants, there are only two real alternatives.

- Labeledge was developed in the United Kingdom in the early 1980s, and this system still has merit where plants are arranged along a horizontal merchandise layout.
- With the trend towards more promotional displays, the best sig-nage support system I have come across is a metal stand where the sign slides in. The key is that the base of the stand has to be large enough to ensure it remains stable in windy conditions.

The Plant Label

Long gone are the days when the sole purpose of a plant label was to provide the botanical name of the plant. Labels are now crucial selling tools and are an essential item in the sale of the plant.

It's the wholesaler's role to label the plant with the objectives of making sure the label stays on the plant, providing essential information for the customer, creating a desire to purchase the plant, and assisting the retailer with stock control.

Make Sure the Label Stays on the Plant

Labels can either be tied on to the plant, stuck in the pot, or wrapped around the pot. Tie-on labels are normally placed at least two thirds of the way up the plant to ensure they are clearly visible and easily read. Such labels are designed to be self-locking or are produced with a tie, which is twisted around the plant stem.

Stick-in labels are preferable for small outdoor plants, bedding plants, and most of the smaller indoor plants. The Harrison Tagging Machine inserts labels mechanically. Labels come in a variety of sizes and shapes, but most have a pointed base for easy insertion into growing media.

The main disadvantage of stick-in labels is that customers can swap them around in the garden center. This has been a problem, particularly in the bedding plant industry, where confusion can easily occur. To overcome this, label manufacturers have developed self-locking labels that are firmly secured to the container.

Some bedding plant nurseries have altered the shape of their labels depending on the perceived value of the plants. Their "base" range of plants has a standard label; the more prestigious and expensive plants have a different shape; and new plant introductions have a third shape. This differentiation has helped retailers and customers to select from three product groupings.

Self-adhesive pot labels are relatively uncommon and tend to be used on indoor plants. It can look very attractive in the garden center, but remember that if the plant is repotted, the label will be left on the old container. If using this technique, you must use a strong adhesive and colorfast inks on the label.

Provide Essential Information for the Customer

Having decided on how you wish to attach the label to the plant and pot, you then need to consider what essential information is required on the label. Customers need to know:

- What is it?
- When does it flower (if relevant) and what do the flowers look like?
- How do I plant it?
- Where should I plant it?
- How do I care for it?
- How tall will it grow?
- How much does it cost?

You have to decide what is the most appropriate way of getting these messages across without confusing the customer.

What is it?

Traditionally, botanical names were placed on labels. But the public doesn't understand botanical names and often cannot pronounce them. Common names are preferable to botanical names from a marketing perspective. I am not proposing that botanical names be dropped completely, but I do believe that the common name should catch the customer's eye and that the botanical name should be in smaller print.

If the plant at present does not have a common name, then invent one. That will increase its sales appeal (as long as you keep within the law and business etiquette). There are several good plant dictionaries that list both common and scientific names. It's a good idea to keep it around the information or checkout area in case a customer comes up with a common name you aren't familiar with.

When does it flower/what does it look like?

A picture is worth a thousand words. This could not be truer than when it comes to plant labels. A colored picture is almost essential. There are multinational label companies who have large libraries of plant photographs, which can be used for this purpose. The only guidelines are to make sure the photograph is true to type and of excellent quality. The key is in the skills of the photographer.

How do I plant it?

Don't assume customers know how to plant. If they are not devoted gardeners, it may be a new skill which they will require learning. Don't assume they read gardening books and magazines—the majority of plants are purchased by impulse buyers who may not be dedicated to their gardens. The customer expects the retailer to provide basic information on planting. This may be on a complimentary leaflet given to customers or by the wholesaler providing that information on plant labels. If you do provide planting guidelines on the label, you would be advised to use diagrams with a step-by-step approach.

How do I care for it?
Having provided planting information, the customer also needs to know how to care for the plant. That information needs to cover subjects such as: When to water? When to feed? When to prune? Where to plant it? Again, this information can be provided with symbols, diagrams, or words.

The main point is: Do not be vague. Words such as *water frequently* and *feed occasionally* are up for dispute, as we will all argue on what frequent and occasional really mean. Use phrases such as "water every four days" or "feed once a month." We need to be specific when providing technical information.

How tall will it grow?
The average person moves to a new house every three to five years, and we need to relate to the customer's needs when providing size information. Informing a customer that a specific conifer will reach x height in thirty years is not going to help you make a sale. Information such as "In five years this plant will reach x height" puts it into a perspective customers can relate to in their own garden.

How much does it cost?
Price is an important consideration when buying a product, but not the first consideration. First, you must inspire customers to buy, then provide basic information to meet their needs, then the details of how much they must invest to meet those needs.

The price should be on the label or on the pot. (I have even seen it in some cases on leaves!) It should always be in a set position to help the customer and should be printed in nonfading ink. With stock management now so critical, there should also be a bar code—essential if you are marketing to supermarkets and hardware stores.

Create a Desire to Purchase the Plant

The first and most important job for the label is to create a buying desire. This can be achieved in a multitude of ways, and all we can do in this chapter is start your imagination on what is possible.

Labels cost money, which has to be carried by the plant. It's easy to come up with elaborate ideas, but they must be cost effective. A label perceived to be too elaborate and expensive could cause customer resistance.

Artwork

When producing artwork, always keep you targeted customer in mind. Artwork aimed specifically at children can be very effective, and so can artwork aimed at encouraging impulse buying.

Substitute labels

Plants do not flower all year around, yet they are displayed in garden centers for long periods, often at times when they are not at their peak. The ideal situation would be to have the plant in flower or fruit for longer periods in the retail environment, and this is where substitute labels come into their own. Substitute labels originated over twenty years ago but are still relatively uncommon. The label is cut out to the shape of the flower or fruit so that it gives the impression from a distance that the plant is in flower or fruit. Substitute labels have been used around the world on orange, apple, lemon, and avocado trees, clematis, lilies, and violas.

"I'm" labels

Research shows that the people often talk to their plants as if they were pets. Therefore, it is worth considering personalizing your labels to enable them to talk back. This is where "I'm" labels come into their own. They may sound corny, but they work. Such labels could say "I'm ideal for a sunny location" or "I'm an ideal patio plant."

Guarantee labels

Customers need assurance when buying products. They want to know that they're purchasing a healthy product that, assuming they follow the instructions on the label, will survive. This is where the guarantee label comes into its own. It, in fact, serves a number of purposes.

First, it assures the customer that in the retailer's eyes they are getting a first-class plant. Second, if the plant dies, the customer is most likely to return the plant to where they purchased it rather than go to another retail outlet for future products. It therefore builds customer loyalty. Finally, when customers return with a dead plant and are serviced by staff professionally, they tend to buy more plants. It also can increase the average sale per customer.

Brand labeling

The objective of brand labeling is to encourage the customer to purchase plants from a specific supplier. Growers obviously consider this to be a desirable situation, but realize that brand loyalty can take a very long time to build and the process can be expensive. Having said that, it is achievable. Companies such as Monrovia (U.S.A.), Hilliers (U.K.), and Herb Herbert International (Australia) have established themselves in the public's mind. If you do proceed down this route, it is important that the label clearly identified that this is a branded product. Pots imprinted with brand names are also being used to establish supplier identity and have the advantage that their message can be seen from further away than with labels.

Labels used for add-on sales

Our industry is one of the few where every product sold has an add-on sales opportunity. This may come in the form of growing media, plant food, stakes, climber supports, garden care products, or an associated plant.

Add-on selling can be promoted through plant labels. "Don't forget" labels were developed in the U.K. and proved to be successful. Allied traders have also sponsored labels to ensure their product is mentioned. With the advancing technology of printing, labels are bound to become more appealing to customers and will help sell more plants.

A word of warning: Do not overdo labeling. The maximum number of labels on a plant should be two. Excessive labeling can be a negative to the customer. Also, remember the plant should look good enough to sell. The label cannot act as a substitute for a bad plant; its objective is to enhance what is already a desirable product.

Living labels

Living labels are large display plants supplied by the wholesaler to help sell smaller grades of the same plant. Living labels should also be available for sale in your center. An example is a fully grown camellia specimen (your living label) surrounded by small pots of the same variety or cultivar.

Brands and Branding

For many suppliers of living products, branding is an expensive operation that would cost too much to consider. Yet products such as Flower Carpet rose, Herb Herbert herbs, and David Austin roses have achieved international brand recognition.

What Is a Brand?

The basic definition is a name, symbol, or design or combination that identifies the product of a particular organization that places it apart from the competition. To the customer, a brand is reliable, familiar, and predictable.

Prior to branding, companies go through a process called brand mapping to identify where they are positioned in the marketplace. Brand mapping is an exercise where the supplier reviews all the consumer options available and then where they should position their product. The chances are if you are launching a new product, it will fail—90% do—and, therefore, the cost of branding needs to be taken into consideration.

Do Labels Really Work?

Many growers ask if the cost of labels is worth the effort as plants sell themselves. The important answer to this question is to ask the customer, and in 1992 Mary D. Zehner of Michigan State University did just that for the Professional Plant Growers Association of America. The Master-Tag and John Henry companies funded her research.

She asked regular buyers of plants for their opinion and her results are shown here. In descending order the public wanted the following information on labels:
- Where to plant it (sun/shade)
- Annual or perennial
- General care information
- Plant height at maturity
- Common name of plant

The Future of Signage and Ticketing

As mentioned at the start of this chapter, the consumer is exposed to over 30,000 messages a day, and this is increasing. Therefore, we will see developments in signage and ticketing over the next few years for two reasons: to grab the consumer's attention and to reduce costs and shrinkage. Posters and signage will have to become more attention grabbing. This means signs will have less words and more lifestyle pictures. The sign with a picture of a flower and the benefits written on it will be replaced with lifestyle photographs showing consumers enjoying the product.

The pharmacy industry has already done this. They used to show pictures of product. They now show people enjoying a healthy lifestyle. Why? Because people can more easily relate to this. The same thing will happen in the gardening industry.

Book List

Hughes, Vera, and David Weller. 1989. *Profitable Retailing.* New York: Macmillan.

Larsen, Sonja. 1991. *The Handbook of Successful Merchandise Signing.* Insignia Systems Inc.

Stanley, John. 1999. *Just about Everything a Retail Manager Needs to Know.* Brisbane, Australia: Plum Press.

Chapter 13

Managing Your Business

Retailing is a business that is constantly changing, and to manage a retail business you need to be an astute businessperson. To make matters worse, in the garden center sector we are dealing with a perishable product, and if you get your management procedures wrong, the product literally dies on you.

For those reading this book who are thinking of starting a garden center, you need to be entrepreneurial. For those who have established businesses, you need a team of entrepreneurs to make the business work effectively.

The key to managing your business is to start with the end picture of what your business will look like in your mind and then work backwards. You will need a team that can take your business into an exciting millennium that has already shown us that times are rapidly changing. The team will need to consist of a number of people with different skills. A typical garden center could be structured as shown in figure 13-1.

Figure 13-1. Structure of garden center team.

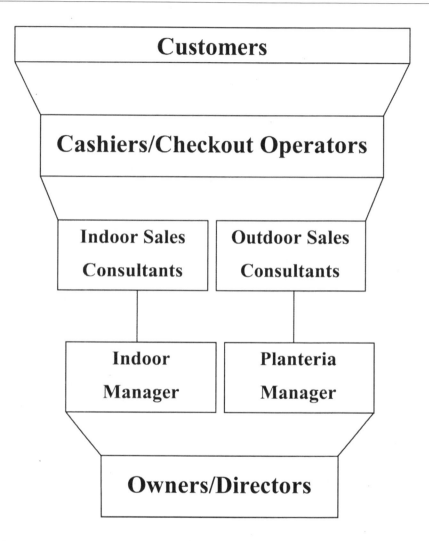

To maximize output, direction, and motivation, each team member should have a job description. This should clearly explain what their role is and how it will be measured. Job descriptions must be in writing and the person responsible for the job should sign the document to confirm they agree with their responsibility zones. You should review the job description with the team member every year. This should be a positive experience for all concerned. The aim should be to build confidence, not find fault.

Job Description: Garden Center Sales Consultant	
Tasks	**Measurement**
1. To assist customers with product information.	A working knowledge of plants that will successfully grow in your area.
2. To sell products to customers.	Average sale will be $x per customer.
3. Maintain all plants in the shrub department.	Shrinkage due to lack of care in the planteria will be less than 2%.

Two key people in your team will be the shop manager and the plant manager. The people recruited to these positions could make or break your business. We should therefore analyze the needs of these positions.

The Planteria Manager

Historically, planteria managers were employed to water and care for plants until they were sold. In today's high-pressure world of retailing, that has changed. A modern garden center needs to be big enough to allow the manager creative opportunities whilst building a team of people who can inspire customers into making their dream gardens become a reality. Recruiting the right planteria manager is not easy. There are not a lot of good managers around; those that are are worth their weight in gold!

Policy Plan

According to Will Tooby, director of Bransford Plants, U.K., his policy plan would be divided into three sections. The first is a mission statement, such as "To inspire people into making their gardens wonderful healing and pleasurable spaces using our plants." Next is a values statement, which would cover the company values concerning ethics, responsiveness, sustainability, and profitability. Finally is a "raving fans" policy, which is a customer care policy where everybody listens, is responsive, and is beating customer expectations. The above is really a global perspective of the business and should be shared by all team members in the business.

Detailed Policies

A category manager, such as a planteria manager, needs also to get into more detailed policies and planning. This manager would have:

A people policy

This would have training procedures and objectives for all team members, to ensure they are maximizing their own potential within the business. A training manual and/or video is an excellent tool. Reviewing these materials at specific times during the year or when your or the employee feels it is helpful will keep the commitment to excellence paramount in your team's focus.

> ### Management Memo
> "If someone fails in your business, they did no fail as a person. You failed as a leader because you did not establish a standard and enforce it."
> —Norman Schwarzkopf

A marketing strategy

This would be split into several areas. First, you would need to identify your target market. A typical garden center planteria manager may decide that their target market is one of the following:

- Keen knowledgeable gardeners—which would be a small select group.
- Keen decorator gardeners—which would be the majority of gardeners.
- Less-keen decorators—those looking for an instant fix in the garden.

Having identified the target, the planteria manager can then decide on the variables within the market mix to suit the target client. These variables would include product mix, price brackets, promotions, and placement of products. These factors will help define the plant purchasing policy, financial planning, merchandise, and display policies.

I must stress at this point that all of the above have objectives, and an astute planteria manager will have specific, measurable, achievable, realistic targets within a predetermined time frame. For example:

- By the year 2005, our average sale per square foot will be $500 per year.
- The average sale per customer will be $45 by the end of 2004.
- We will have implemented the best customer service policy in the industry by 2004 and have it measured by independent mystery shoppers.

Product strategy

One of the biggest challenges for a plant manager is getting their product strategy right. The strategy could well be:

- Seventy-five percent of product sold will be seasonal and stocked in minimum quantities of twenty-five. These products will be high impulse and zone merchandised, based on solutions or lifestyle.
- Ten percent of plants will be in an A-to-Z library area on triple shelves with two plants on each shelf. They will be in small quantities and delivered by a specific wholesaler weekly.
- Fifteen percent of sales will be generated by living labels (large specimen plants giving instant impact and aimed at selling smaller product of the same species).

Quality audit

A daily audit of the planteria must be carried out. This should be documented and signed. An audit should check weed control, watering, pruning, pest and disease control, spacing, facing, display, signage, and so on.

Neville Passmore's Garden Center Assessment and Management Tool (www.jstanley.com.au) is an excellent product for quality auditing. This pictorial guide will assist you to measure and manage your garden center performance. It enables you to numerically assess the performance of your garden center on over sixty descriptors in nine categories.

Price strategy

Pricing is always debatable in a garden center, and we have a whole chapter on it in this book (see chapter 9). As a manager, you need to base your pricing on perceived value, stock turn ratio over gross profit, discount on multibuys, contract-grown sensitive-price lines, and branded products.

Promotion strategy

Ten percent of every plant category needs to be promoted at any one time on a monthly changeover. The promotions must be topical, and one person needs to be made responsible for supervising promotions. If you don't do this, you could find yourself losing a lot of dollars.

The Shop Manager

Historically, garden centers were plant led, and the shop was the adjunct to the core business. All that is now changing, and we are seeing a complete turnaround. Statistics are starting to show that plants make up one third of the garden retail industry and non-living products are two thirds of the industry.

A lot of the skills you are seeking in a planteria manager also apply to a shop manager, and the shop manager often now carries the greater responsibility when it comes to dollar return per square foot of retail selling space.

The key product ranges in the shop can be split into two major categories: garden care and garden enhancement.

Garden care products are those closely related to the plants that help the customer care for their garden. This department will cover categories such as garden chemicals, fertilizers, growing media, garden tools, seeds, and lawn care. This department in many garden centers has remained static, except for garden chemicals, where many retailers have actually seen a slight reduction in total sales as consumers become more environmentally aware.

Garden enhancement has seen major growth in recent years. This department covers categories such as outdoor lighting, outdoor furniture, water gardens, statues, and large outdoor containers. Some of these products can take up a large amount of floor space and can be big-ticket items.

The shop manager may also be responsible for other categories, such as outdoor clothing, floristry, indoor ornaments, pets, and catering.

In searching for an indoor manager, you may find the person you are looking for in other leisure retail industries. You will need someone who is a good buyer, aware of trends, and understands how to sell, merchandise, and display such products.

Entering "Retail Heaven"

Those of you old enough will remember the Genesis hit "Seven Steps to Heaven." For you to find retail heaven, there are seven steps we need to consider. Some of these subjects have been covered in other chapters, but it is worth emphasizing them again at this stage.

As your business grows, you will employ managers to manage your business. This gives you more opportunity to work on your business and to lead your team and develop future growth.

To be an effective leader, you need to develop the key seven steps in your business.

Step One: Determine What Your Real Market Position Is

When we start in business, we often try and get any customers we can. In reality, only certain types of customers are attracted to our business. It is these people we should concentrate our efforts on.

The majority of garden center customers are between the ages of twenty-five and seventy-five and own a property with a garden. In gardening, the real target is a woman aged between thirty and fifty-five and in socioeconomic groups 2 to 4 (commonly called the middle class).

It is essential that you evaluate the competition in your marketplace for these customers. I will guarantee you will be able to divide your competition into three groups.

Group one: Market leader. This will be one company who at this point in time leads the industry in your area.

Group two: Market movers. These are companies who have yet to become leaders, but are moving their businesses forward.

Group three: The lost tribe. These retailers have lost the plot and have no idea what is happening in the garden retail industry.

You should aim to be a market mover or a market leader. Your objective should be to be an aggressive marketer who is providing the complete garden solution and ideas package for your customers. You need to invest in new retail models and in marketing to your target group with an added value proposition.

Step Two: Obtain the Right Location

Chapter 2 covers location in depth. I cannot stress enough how important this is. Guesswork on location doesn't work. You need to locate the right size garden center in the right location. Prior to purchasing a site, you need to study traffic flows and the reasons people use those routes. The ideal garden center should be located en route to other leisure activities that your target group participates in.

Step Three: Develop and Aggressively Market Your Image

Image is one of the most critical aspects of your business, and you destroy it at your peril. It's built up of many facets, and to be successful you must project a consistent image to your customers and team at all times. Image is made up of:

- Visual appearance, both external and internal
- Range, quality, price points, width and depth of product
- Team member professionalism and service standards
- Store atmosphere, displays, signage, lighting, and fixtures
- Promotional activities targeted at your customers and potential customers.

As I have mentioned, the key is consistency of image. Unfortunately, customers make decisions on your image very quickly. It is often called the moment of truth. In ten seconds outside your garden center, a potential customer makes a decision on your image.

One of the world's leading experts on image is Bobbie Gee, based in California. Her book, *Image Game*, should be essential reading for anyone in business. Bobbie talks about the image wheel. This wheel identifies the key areas that make up a business image and the key areas you need to concentrate on.

Figure 13-2. Image wheel.

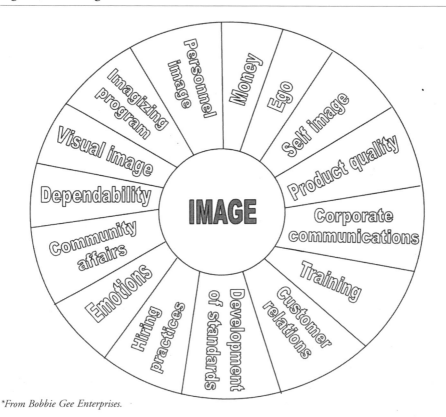

From Bobbie Gee Enterprises.

To be consistent you should develop daily and weekly image check-lists and ensure that a member of your team walks the garden center floor on a regular basis to check your image standards.

Weekly Image Checklist
How Good Are We?

Physical Appearance

	Extremely	Quite	Slightly one nor the other	Neither	Slightly	Quite	Extremely	
Dirty								Clean
Unattractive décor								Attractive décor
Difficult to shop								Easy to shop
Slow checkout								Fast checkout

Products Offered

	Extremely	Quite	Slightly one nor the other	Neither	Slightly	Quite	Extremely	
Narrow selection								Wide selection
Depleted stock								Fully stocked

Staff

	Extremely	Quite	Slightly one nor the other	Neither	Slightly	Quite	Extremely	
Discourteous								Courteous
Cold								Warm
Unhelpful								Helpful
Inadequate number								Adequate number

Prices								
	Extremely	Quite	Slightly one nor the other	Neither	Slightly	Quite	Extremely	
Lower prices compared to others								Higher prices compared to others
Low average average dollar spending								High average dollar spending
Large number of specials								Low number of specials

Advertising								
	Extremely	Quite	Slightly one nor the other	Neither	Slightly	Quite	Extremely	
Uninformative								Informative
Unappealing								Appealing
Unbelievable								Believable
Unhelpful								Helpful

Step Four: Plan and Implement the Optimum Ranging for Your Garden Center

The range of products you offer for sale must reflect your image and your target demographics. You must formalize a ranging plan that sets out clear objectives concerning expected sales, margins required, inventory levels, and expected shrinkage. It's easy for a garden center to become very wide and deep in the range of products it offers. But don't fall into the trap of having the most extensive range available. You need to have the best range available for your target market.

Step Five: Have an Effective Layout and Merchandising Plan

Before setting up displays, you should have an initial floor print or plan to allow you to keep on track. Your objective is to ensure 100% of people see 100% of product. See chapter 4 for more on this subject.

Step Six: Control Costs

You must invest in a superior point of sale system. Knowledge in today's retail world is power. The more valuable information you can obtain on the financial operations of your business and use to implement changes, the more effective you will be. Point-of-sale systems change rapidly. When you read this book, I'll guarantee that any examples I might give you here will be out of date. Do check constantly with local sources on how state-of-the-art equipment can help your business.

Step Seven: Promote, Promote, Promote

In future chapters I will discuss promotions. To capsulize what will come later: You must let your potential customers know you exist and that you want their business. If you do not, you will never reach retail heaven.

Book List

Gee, Bobbie. 1991. *Winning the Image Game: A Ten Step Masterplan for Achieving Power, Prestige, and Profit.* Berkeley, Calif.: Page Mill Press.

Chapter 14

Building a Team

Operating a garden center requires using the same skills as any other business.

If it is to be successful, you will need a team dedicated to making the business work. Successful businesses work when ordinary people do exceptional things. This only occurs when managers become leaders and the team feels it's part of the business rather than doing a job for a wage or salary.

Team building is essential, but not easy. It takes time, patience, and a considerable amount of skill at a managerial level. To be a successful team, you will require vision, effective recruitment, induction, motivation, leadership, flexible training, and marketing skills.

Teamwork is one of the keys to success. Building a business is like building a sports team; you need the right players with the right skills in the right place at the right time and with the right motivation. The team will decide if you win or lose. The team must know what the business goals are and which way they are heading. But to be successful, your team needs to be committed. This means there are a number of techniques you need to introduce to present the right company spirit.

- Understand how team members see the goals. They will not see them the same way as you do. You need to know how they think and also what their goals are. Keep an open mind and encourage them to provide their ideas on business improvement.
- Make sure you have the right people for the right job. This may sound logical, but a survey carried out by the University of Newcastle, Australia, in 2000 revealed that 30 percent of employees lacked the skills needed to do the job they were doing efficiently in over 61.2% of sample companies.
- You need to understand your team. You must know their strengths and weaknesses. Use their strengths, and train or reassign to improve on the weaknesses.
- Work with your team and provide a guide to what results you want. This may be a sales target per square foot or average sale per customer.
- Check performance levels on a regular basis. Focus on results and reward team members with praise and job enrichment, which is more rewarding than an increase in salary (assuming they are paid correctly for the job they are doing).
- Remember, people are motivated by responsibility, achievement, personal growth, recognition, and accountability.

Your aim is to have the best team in town.

Where Do You Start?

Recruiting the right team members is critical to your business success. I would argue that recruitment is one of the most critical tasks employers carry out, yet they are often not skilled in this area.

Many garden center owners are unshakable; they are no longer able to find good people to work in their retail outlets. They are convinced that the people they require just do not exist any more and lay the blame variously with education, lack of interest in retailing and horticulture by young people, and the existing pay structures. In reality, however, nothing has really changed. Effective salespeople do exist, as they always have. It is just a matter of recruiting the right people in the right way.

Analyze Your Company Needs

Garden center owners recruit people for one of the three reasons: their company is expanding and they need people to provide customer service to an expanding customer base, the company has an incorrect customer-to-staff ratio that is resulting in a lower average sale per customer, or someone has left the business and a vacancy now exists.

The golden rule should be not to automatically replace someone who has left. If someone leaves, you have an opportunity to review the whole structure of your team. It may be time to rearrange the team or work times and duties to allow the business to operate more effectively.

Always Write a Job Description

If a vacancy does exist, you should make sure you have an up-to-date job description, which covers the duties and responsibilities. It should be specific in identifying all the duties you would expect the person to per-form within your business. For example: "Increase the average sale to $_____ by using add-on selling techniques," "Set out a relay product category," "Handle complaints. . . ."

Decide on Personal Specifications

With the job description, you can then draw up a profile of what the successful applicant will be like. The job specifications will identify where it is essential the person is competent and other areas where it is desirable they are competent. Never recruit someone who is not compe-tent in all your essential duties areas. The essential and desirable compe-tencies should be listed as the following example shows:

Job: Garden Center Salesperson

Essential Competencies: Capable of identifying features and benefits of plants grown by gardeners in your neighborhood. Able to use effective, open conversation, capable of closing a sale, able to deal with customer complaints. Well-groomed.

Desirable Competencies: Capable of suggestive selling. Able to do relay management. Competent in sign writing. Able to build a promotional plant display.

When recruiting people, remember everyone is different. You need salespeople that will fit in with your business culture. People in selling tend to fall into one of the five category types:

People-Oriented Salespeople

These salespeople are always the customers' friends. They want to

The Attributes of Great Garden Center Salespeople		
1	Enthusiasm	Believe in themselves and in your center
2	Appearance	Look professional in the eyes of the customer
3	Initiative	Are self-starters
4	Diplomacy	Are considerate of others; say the right things at the right time
5	Product knowledge	Seek and acquire the utmost in product knowledge, enabling them to present a convincing case
6	Imagination	Paint colorful word pictures to help customers envision the end result
7	Pleasing personality	Are likable and warm
8	Health	Have healthy mind and body that overcome most obstacles; appear energetic to customers
9	Confidence	Have faith in their own ability and the courage of their own convictions
10	Capacity for work	Have an intense interest in our work as professional salespeople and put out a great effort
11	Alertness	Are watchful and lively, observant at all times
12	Friendliness	Have disarming warmth that tends to melt resistance
13	Clarity of expression	Are articulate and has large vocabulary; enunciate clearly
14	Tolerance	Exhibit patience under trying circumstances
15	Optimism	Inclined to take positive views
16	Honesty	Are fair and deals with integrity with both customers and fellow workers

*From Successful Selling (Australian Institute of Management, Western Australia).

understand the customers and respond to their wants and likes. They build personal bonds and use this to encourage the consumers to buy. They are ideal salespeople where you are dealing with high-ticket items and where it takes time for consumers to make a buying decision.

Problem-Solving Salespeople
These people ask numerous questions so that they can identify all of the customers' needs and can then match the product to their information.

They ensure the customers that they have made a sound purchasing decision that produces the maximum benefits. Their empathy and relationship skills are weaker than those of people-oriented salespeople are. Although they make excellent salespeople, they tend not to build strong ongoing relationships with your customers.

Take-It-or-Leave-It Salespeople
These salespeople place the product in front of the customers and believe that products sell themselves. They offer very little advice, as they assume the consumers have the knowledge to make a decision. This may work in some retail environments, but they are a disaster in a garden center, where most customers need assistance to make a decision.

Push-the-Product Salespeople
These salespeople are often on commission, or at least they give this impression to consumers. They take charge of the situation, do the hard sell, and pressure the customers so they can make a sale. If you employ this character in your garden center, you will have a very short life expectancy as a business.

Technique-Orientated Salespeople
Successful garden center salespeople get customers to purchase by motivating them using an equal balance of personality and product knowledge. They have the attributes we have already discussed along with product knowledge related to the consumers' gardening needs. They transfer this product knowledge to customers in a language that they can relate to and feel comfortable with.

Employ Personality over Knowledge
Retailing is a personality industry. It is extremely difficult, if not impossible, to improve a personality through training. On the other hand, if the employees have the right personality, it is comparatively easy to train them in product knowledge. So, your recruitment procedure should be aimed at selecting people with the right personality for your business. Consider using such personality checking strategies as:
- A surprise telephone call to the candidates to check their tone of voice and natural approach on the telephone.

- Passing a compliment to the candidates in the interviews and gauging their reaction.
- Getting team members to show them around the store and to report back on their personality in the more relaxed setting.

Advertising

Recruiting a new person means you will need to use some means of advertising. The most common methods are advertisements in the local newspapers or trade press, friends/relatives of existing team members, word of mouth in the local community, and promotion to schools. Some businesses find recruiting friends and relatives as the most desirable approach, as this can quickly build a team spirit, but others are against this as they feel it can cause an increase in staff pilferage.

Remember, you are not only advertising for a person; you also have the opportunity to promote your business to your market. As a guide, make sure your advertisement covers three important areas: details of your business, details of the job, details of the person you require. By doing this, you are being very specific with your targeting and will reduce the number of unwanted applicants.

Interview Professionally

The purpose of an interview is to determine if the applicant has the knowledge, skills, and personality to fit into your organization. The interview, however, is more than a conversation. It involves a range of procedures and skills with which all garden center owners should be familiar.

Conduct the interview

You have two aims: to get the information you need to reach a decision and to give the applicant the information they want. Have these documents on hand:
- Checklist of essential requirements
- Applicant's details (letter or application form)
- Job breakdown, including terms and conditions
  Consider using the following interview sequence:
  Introduction-in office
  - Welcome applicant
  - Ask one or two informal questions to get her talking and put her at ease

- Explain the stages: discussion/tour/discussion

Opening discussion-in office

- Work through the checklist of essential requirements, confirming points and asking questions
- Ask open-ended questions to get enough information to reach conclusions
- Probe or challenge on any points of doubt to get her to open up

Tour of garden center

- Make a further check of essential (technical) requirements by questioning about the enterprise and systems as you tour them
- Probe on any point of doubt, asking how she would solve particular problems or do things differently
- Explain the layout of the center

Concluding discussion-in office

- Make a final check of your list of essential requirements, asking questions if necessary
- Give any further explanation of the business and organization
- Discuss details of the job, using your written job breakdown
- Negotiate pay and conditions, using your written job breakdown

Close-in office

- Tell her how and when you will let her know if you are offering her the job or not
- Thank her for attending

Be professional in your approach

It is essential that you appoint the right person to a job, which is why the hiring of staff is a major responsibility for owners or managers. To be confident you're appointing the best person, make sure you follow the appropriate interviewing procedures and that you brush up on your face-to-face interviewing technique. *Just about Everything a Manager Needs to Know* (pp. 146-7 and 78-9) will prove invaluable in this regard.

Check the applicant's personal qualities

During the interview process, try to focus in particular on the personal qualities of the applicant in the following areas: personality, reliability, attitude to retailing, ability to work on own, judgment, sense of responsibility, team attitude, and communications skills. In particular, you will require a person who has an outgoing personality, someone who is capable of holding a pleasant conversation with complete strangers. Listen carefully, watch the interviewee's body language, and pay attention to your intuition. Remember, once you hire people, you are stuck with them.

Plan your questions
Questioning is a powerful tool and an essential ingredient in an interview of this type. Keep your questions simple, direct, and focused on a specific topic. Start with general issues before moving into specific detail. Where necessary, probe and be persistent if the answer given is vague.

Never employ second best
Never select "the best of a bad bunch." If you cannot find a suitable candidate from those you have interviewed, then you will be far better to not hire and to place another ad for the position.

Induct the New Person into the Team
It is unfair to put anyone directly on the retail floor without going through company policy, meeting the team, discussing your approach to customer service, or having a formal induction procedure. The induction should be formalized and carried out over the first week of employment.

Managing Your Team
Once you have recruited the team, you then have to manage the team to ensure you get the optimum results. Teams are successful if they know the management style is consistent. Nobody likes going to work worrying about what mood the boss is in.

Meeting Needs
Your job is to motivate your team, but we are all motivated by different things in our lives. I will guarantee that what motivates you is not what motivates your team. Every employee has basic needs at work and in their lives for survival, security, and comfort, and it is only when these have been met that you can motivate these team members. Your job is now divided into two areas. First, you need to ensure that you have created a working environment that satisfies your team's basic needs. When

you have achieved that, you can move to the second area, which is to provide opportunities to motivate your team.

Basic needs are housing, food, warmth, and clothing. All our basic needs differ; a single eighteen year old's basic needs will be different than those of a forty-five year old with three children to feed and a mortgage to pay off.

As a team leader, you have two aims: Create the right conditions to satisfy basic needs, and provide job opportunities to satisfy each person's motivational needs. A skilled manager can identify when a person's basic needs are not being met. Indicators of someone with a basic need problem include:

- constant expression of concern about the salary structure in your garden center
- excessive concern over job security
- need to have things spelled out to them; this may be because they have more important things to think about
- they will not take risks at work or in their social life
- they are often complaining about work conditions
- to you they look like they have no motivation; they do, but it is masked by their high basic needs.

If you have team members with a high basic need, they will require careful counseling. You will not motivate them at work until their basic need has been satisfied.

Motivational Patterns

Some of your team will be motivated by friendship, others by achievement, and others by power. Everyone has a mix of these patterns, but in the majority of us, one of these dominates. If you understand what the dominant motivational need is, then you can manage team members a lot more effectively.

Achievement-dominated team members

Achievement seekers get a lot of satisfaction by doing things themselves. They show a competitive spirit and take pride in their skills. They enjoy jobs that show fast results based on their input and are often happier working on their own than with others. You may set goals for these team members, but they will set goals that are even higher (assuming they are achievable). Achievement team members do not like close supervisory management styles. Leave them to do a job, and you will get better results and they will enjoy it more.

Friendship-dominated team members

The majority of your team will probably fall into this category. As you would expect, these are your "people" people. They do not like being left out of things happening in the business. They tend to have many friends and get involved with social events outside work. They like helping others and dislike working on their own. They often become the company "auntie" or "uncle," the person others are attracted to when they have problems.

Power-dominated team members

If they already aren't, they will be the leaders of tomorrow in yours or someone else's business. These team members enjoy influencing other team members and often give help even if it has not been asked for. These folks enjoy arguments and always aim to win, but if your business has a crisis, these team members quickly come to the rescue. Power people want recognition and status and will take on more responsibility to achieve these gains. They want to understand how the garden center industry works and how your business works.

As I mentioned, they are the leaders of the future. The key to success is to match the right people with the right jobs. Before you can do that you need to understand the motivational needs of individuals and select appropriate jobs accordingly.

> *Management Memo*
>
> **Leadership Functions**
> Your skill as a leader determines how good your team is. Leadership is a difficult and multi-skilled job. To be an effective leader you need to:
> • be focused on results
> • lead by example
> • effectively communicate with your team
> • be a successful delegator
> • give attention to individuals in your team
> • be able to build a team
> • be fair and consistent
> • be able to act decisively under pressure.
> —Ref: Leadership Skills ATB Management Skills Guide SMSC2

Training Your Team

People sell; products do not. You need efficient, professional, skilled people to make your business work. But recruiting people and keeping them is expensive and time consuming. A recent survey in Australia found it costs U.S.$5,000 to recruit and train a retail salesperson to a competent level.

You will therefore need a flexible training program that meets the needs of your team members. Some companies rely on universities, colleges, and other businesses to train team members prior to them joining the company. This may be desirable in some circumstances, but basically, you will need to train your own team.

Sending team members away on training workshops has been the traditional way of increasing people's skills. These do work if tailored to your team's needs, but they can be sporadic and often you have to take the opportunity when it comes along, not when you need it.

A successful training program for your business should consider a number of options. The following are suggestions based on my experience.

Management Training

The short course programs held around the States are an excellent means of upgrading the management skills of your team. I also lead a three-day garden center management program, which has been held in various parts of the world with a high degree of success.

The important thing is that if people attend these short course programs, they should report back to management and the team and be allowed to implement the relevant ideas they feel could help the business. Too often people attend short courses and then are not allowed to implement ideas. The result is a negative rather than positive effect on the business since these people feel their time has been wasted and that you do not care about their ideas.

Managers also need to keep up to date globally with what is happening to the garden retailing industry. This information can be obtained through magazines. Ball Publishing's magazine *Green Profit* is an ideal medium to keep people up to date and should be essential reading. You should also consider magazines from other countries. I find *Commercial Horticulture* from New Zealand to be a valuable tool.

Team Training

The team needs skills in how to sell, how to merchandise, and in product information. Team members are also constantly coming and going, so this needs to be as flexible as possible. The trend is to use various "self pace" media, where team members can learn skills at their own pace, in their own time, and still be recognized for the skills they have learned.

Improving selling skills

If public workshops are available and relevant, then team members should be encouraged to attend. Alternatively, companies such as Adland Horticulture in Australia produce self-paced "Selling Skills" manuals that are specific to garden centers and are available in the global arena. These manuals take the student through a step-by-step process of how to sell garden products. The student can do the workshop all at once or spread it over a period of time. They key to success is that it is overseen by the store manager, who takes an interest in the program and the trainee's progress.

Improving merchandising skills

My own virtual reality garden center on CD-ROM, *Millennium Merchandising* (produced in partnership with Select

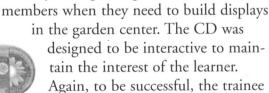

Multimedia), has proven to be a very effective way of improving the skills of team members when they need to build displays in the garden center. The CD was designed to be interactive to maintain the interest of the learner.

Again, to be successful, the trainee needs to feel the supervisor is interested and encourages her to implement the ideas she has learned. (The Adland manuals and my CD-ROM are available from our Web site, www.jstanley.com.au.)

Product knowledge

Learning about products has to be organized on site. If you need highly skilled horticultural knowledge, you will have to provide the time for people to learn. If you rely on them learning as they work, you will find it is a slow process.

The concern for many retailers is that they may have in excess of 10,000 SKUs and the problem is too large to tackle. You can make the task easier by dividing your products into departments and allocating each member of the team the responsibility of training the rest of the team the products in that department. If you select six products a week from each department and introduce these in your team meetings, you will soon find the overall product knowledge of the team will improve.

Ongoing Management

We have already discussed the first basic skills of a leader, to get a team together and then to motivate them. But you have to constantly strengthen the team and encourage self-development of each team member as well as the team as a whole. You should have an ongoing development program to enable team members to build on existing skills, learn new ones, and overcome their weaknesses.

Attitude is the single biggest difference between a successful salesperson and one that is not. Your role as an owner, manager, or supervisor is to ensure that your team has the correct positive attitude. This can be attained based on five key areas:

1. You recruit people who have the right personality.
2. Team members observe other retailers in action and learn from them. (Remember, they need to observe all forms of retailers, not just other garden center retailers).
3. Their previous experiences in retailing have been positive and fun.
4. They constantly attend well-structured training courses on retailing that keeps them in tune with the skills of selling.
5. The relationship they have with their peers at work and their relationship with management are satisfying and respectful.

Planning Your Routine

A motivated team expects management to plan effectively. An effective planner is able to control events rather than let events decide on how the day will be managed. In simple terms, planning is about your aims as a business and how to achieve those aims using the team and facilities you have available to you.

Some retailers will tell you that you cannot plan in a retail environment, as each customer has different demands and every day is different.

This is short-term thinking—a retail establishment can be planned like any other business. Planning is about organizing the main events, developing a short-term plan, managing your plan, and checking how well your plan is being implemented.

Plan main events

We all need to plan for the next year, and a wall planner is a valuable tool in your business. Use your wall chart to record events such as staffing levels, events, trade shows and events, training workshops, and key events in your business.

Short-term planning is concerned with getting tasks completed on a weekly and daily basis. To be an effective short-term planner, you need to consider this in three stages: First, keep a "to do" list, then put this list in a priority order, and finally draw up a work plan for the week or day.

A diary comes into its own when developing short-term plans, and you may wish to distribute diaries to all your management team to ensure they are encouraged to be efficient. The first priority when using a diary is to record key appointments and activities and then build your day around other priorities from your job list.

Identifying priorities is the real key. List the jobs and then rank them in priority order. With some jobs you may need to put a "to be done by" date next to them.

When looking at priorities, consider the following:
- Does the task need to be completed by a set date or time?
- If you do not complete the task, will it seriously effect sales?
- If you carry out the task earlier than planned, will you save time?
- If you do not do the task, will you be creating a health and safety concern for the business and the team?
- If you do the job earlier, will it be easier on the team?

Plans don't work according to plan

We work in an environment where you have to be prepared for the unexpected. But I still believe you can plan for the unexpected and build it into your planning process.

The main unplanned events in a garden center are going to be:
1. Bad weather: National and local weather forecasting gets more accurate each year. Bad weather can now be forecast ahead, and this enables you to plan "bad weather" jobs. Some companies

keep bad weather job lists in their staff room so employees know what to do when inclement weather strikes.

2. Changeable weather: This can be more of a problem, especially during a busy spring. It makes staff planning a lot more difficult. My local garden center has a team of standby team members. If the weather is bad, they are not asked into work. If the weather is positive for sales, then the team is called in.

3. Unpredictable customers: Some customers can take more staff time than is planned. If the customer is buying, then this could be a bonus. It is when customers take up staff time and do not buy that they become a problem. Set up a system where you can relieve team members who are finding they are wasting time with a customer. They key is to have a code that the team knows but the customer is unaware of.

4. Unpredictable supplier representatives: This is a simple one. You should have a policy of only seeing reps by appointment. If you do not, you will find they will waste your and your team's time.

Book List

Passmore, Neville. 2001. *Garden Center Self Improvement*. Perth, Western Australia: John Stanley Associates.

Stanley, John. 2000. *Millennium Retailing: Creative Displays for Profit CD-ROM*. Perth, Western Australia: John Stanley Associates.

Chapter 15

Making the Sale

Numerous books have been written on making the sale, selling skills, and sales closures, yet how often are you met with indifference as a customer when you go shopping?

Selling is one of those skills that does not come naturally to many people, and we constantly need to be reminded as salespeople of the basics. In this chapter, I will analyze what type of personality you need to be looking for when recruiting salespeople, what skills they require, and how they should handle various situations.

Setting Goals

Before we look at the technique of selling, it is important to remember that your objective is consistency in selling, based on a measurable performance. To achieve this, you must set standards and goals, which need to be in writing. When new team members are recruited, part of your induction process should be to introduce your standards and goals prior to introducing them to how you sell products within your organization.

When setting goals, keep in mind that they must be SMART:

- **S**pecific—Measurable, such as average dollar sale per customer or average units per customer

- **M**ilestones—Subgoals that will motivate your team

- **A**chievable—Realistic for all the team

- **R**ewards—Prizes along the way to acknowledge achievements and improvement

- **T**ime-based—Have a date when they will be evaluated, such as weekly, monthly, etc.

The Art of Selling

The skill of selling has not changed since the first markets were set up in Mesopotamia in Asia Minor thousands of years ago. The top salespeople then knew the same things the top salespeople know today. Selling is a skill with two distinct elements, and you need to be skilled at both of them. Salesmanship is about two things: Social interaction and selling a product or service. Social interaction involves impressing your consumer with the way your business is presented (the building, the stock, the parking lot), the way you and the rest of the staff are presented (how you look, what you do and say), and how effective the staff is as hosts (how capable they are at interacting with strangers). Selling something (the plants, products, and services) involves listening and asking questions to work out what your customer needs, removing any doubt your customer may have (by acting as a consultant or advisor), and closing the sale.

> ### *Management Memo*
>
> **Ideas from Larry's Shoes**
>
> Larry bends over backwards to ensure his customers look forward to a visit to his store. They can get a free cappuccino and a free foot massage on Sundays and holidays. Free shoe shines are on offer on Saturdays and holidays. New employees receive sixty-four hours of training before they go on the floor and have their own business cards, thank-you notes, and birthday cards to send to customers. There is a "walk test guarantee"-an exchange or refund up to thirty days. This shoe store sells the highest volume of shoes in America-you can guess why.

Selling is also about repeat business. Your aim is not to sell the plant, product, or service only once. You want to set the scene for selling a second, third, and fourth time. That is, you are looking for repeat business.

You want people to return to your store and become lifetime customers. The reason? It's easier to keep an existing customer than attract a new customer.

The discussion that follows tends to concentrate on retail outlets (stores, garden centers, etc.). However, the principles are still the same and equally apply to all work places and businesses. The selling skills that you need to be successful are always the same.

Professional selling is divided into three distinct skill areas, which everyone in your team should be trained in. First, everyone should be a host. This is the first priority, as customers want to feel welcome in your business. Next comes the role of the consultant. Consumers expect your team to know about plants and gardening, and a consultant will have the technical skills required in this area. Finally, your team member is required to be a seller and to know how to sell using pre-close and close questioning techniques so that she can successfully close the sale.

The Effective Host: Playing the Ten Seconds Game

Unfortunately, human beings tend to judge quickly, and our perceptions become our beliefs. Therefore, as salespeople, we have just one quick chance to create a first impression. Potential customers make decisions about a salesperson in ten seconds. It's what is often called the moment of truth. If the "vibes" are positive in these ten seconds, then a selling relationship may develop between both parties; if the "vibes" are negative, then the chances are a selling relationship is going to be exceedingly difficult to establish.

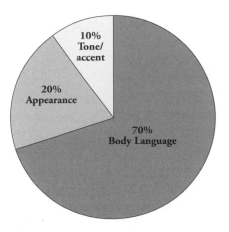

Figure 15-1. Customers make their initial impression of salespeople based on these characteristics.

When customers make their assessments of you, they judge your personality and attitude toward them. The three areas that are being assessed at a subconscious level are:

- Tone/accent—Is this person being friendly to me via the tone used in their speech?
- Appearance—Do they look professional?
- Body language—Are they positive and friendly to me?

You do not have control over a team member's tone or body language. But you have a large amount of control over appearance. Appearance standards should be part of your written policy, and team members should sign the policy at their induction to confirm they agree with the standard. It's essential that the team's appearance be at a consistent professional standard.

All team members who deal with the public should look professional and ideally should be provided with at least two staff uniforms. Some companies supply head-to-toe uniforms whilst others provide waist-to-head uniforms. The uniform should be safe and appropriate to the weather conditions and the tasks employees are expected to undertake. This often means that a business has to supply summer and winter uniforms. If you do not provide uniforms, it is essential that you specify the type of attire that should be worn with the uniform. This is especially critical when it comes to footwear, as safety footwear can become a key issue.

Some garden centers also provide back supports, which should be worn all the time when at work. These supports can become uncomfortable in very hot weather, but could save you from being involved in expensive procedures if a member of your team gets back strain.

Other businesses provide tools of the trade to help their team members look more professional. This normally consists of a pair of pruning shears strapped to team members' belts. Younger team members often find this helps with their credibility in front of customers.

Personally, I am a believer in name badges. A company that stresses the need for building customer relations should provide team members with name badges with first names only. My advice is that you make two sets of badges per person and you keep one set in the office. Sooner or later a member of your team will forget his badge, and the extra set in the office will be an essential item to maintain a consistent standard.

The moment of truth does not stop at your appearance (clothing, facial expression, and body language). It relates to everything you do, including what comes out of your mouth! Think about a party you have been to where you didn't know many people. What the host did and said when you walked in probably had a big impact on whether you had a good time, what you thought of the people there, and whether you would want to go back again.

When you are a salesperson in your store, then you are the host. Being a good host is an important element of selling. If you make a good first impression and are a good host, then the chances are the customer will want to deal with you, you will sell more goods, the customer will want to come back and be served by you in the future, and you could become his preferred supplier of goods.

As shown in figure 14-1, research says that 70% of what people perceive in the first thirty seconds of meeting is our body language. As a salesperson, you need to be aware of how your body language affects your relationship with people. Although much of your body language is subconscious, you can learn to change it so that the result is more positive.

The following table lists what good hosts and bad hosts do when they meet customers. Notice that many relate to body language.

Good Hosts . . .	Bad Hosts . . .
Approach the customers first or stop what they were going and concentrate on customers as people	Ignore customers and carry on working
Make eye contact	Look past people
Smile	Look surly, frown
Welcome the customer with a pleasant, inquiring voice	Do not welcome the customer, cross arms in front of the customer
Use a first sentence that is a social question, such as "Isn't it a lovely day?"	Use a first sentence that is a selling question, such as "How can I help you?"
Use positive body language, such as open hand gestures	Have hands in pockets
Face the customer squarely	Cross legs so they do not face the customer square on
Listen carefully	Don't pay close attention
Take a customer to products or tell customer how to find them	Point to products
Farewell the customer at the end of the conversation	Don't farewell the customer at the end of the conversation

When to help your customers

Your body language is important. But so too is the body language of the customer. Being a good host is based on observing your customer, watching her body language. This will be the clue when to approach your customer. Not every customer wants to be served. If you customer does not want to be served yet, then she will probably ignore your approaches and/or close the conversation down. For example, she may say, "I'm just looking at the moment, thanks." If this is the case, then leave her alone. Visit her again later when she may give you a different message.

If your customer wants to be served, then watch to see if she makes eye contact with you, approaches you, or smiles. She may also handle a product, put it down and then pick it up again; walk away from a product and then walk back to it; or look confused in front of a product. Think about what you do when you are shopping and want some help or are ready to purchase something.

Get into the habit of observing customers in your garden center. Learn to read their body language.

What do you say to your customer?

As a host, your first job is to open a conversation. This is something you do every day. The one thing that is different in your role as a salesperson is your aim. Your aim is to find out what your customers' needs are and then to satisfy them. The best way to find out what customers really want is through a conversation.

The Consultant: Finding and Meeting Needs

So far I have concentrated on making a good impression and developing skills you need to be a good host. The customers are in your store because they probably want to buy something. Part of your role is to make it easy for them and enjoyable. But your main objective is to sell something. So you will need to ensure that you and your team develop selling skills.

The steps that are needed to make a sale are: (1) find out what the customer wants by being a good listener and questioner; (2) remove any doubts the customer may have by being a good consultant—this means you need to know the features and benefits of the plants, products and services; and (3) close the sale.

	Type of Opener/ Question	Example	Description
		Types of Opening Questions	
		Key ✖ = should be rarely used ✔ = should be your most-common approach ❗ = should be used with care	
✖	Closed	"Can I help you?"	Encourages the person receiving the message to close the conversation down with a yes or no answer. If yes, then maybe a conversation will start. But you only have a 50 percent chance.
✔	Open	"How can I help you?"	Questions starting with how, what, when, where, why, and who are-called open because the receiver has to reply with something other than yes or no. The result is that you can start a conversation.
✔	Emotional	"Great! Those plants are one of my favorites."	The best salespeople are natural emotional salespeople. They find something positive to say to the customer that either compliments the customer or the products they are looking at.
✔❗	Probing	"How do you feel about . . . ?"	The word *feel* used in a sentence probes for an honest, emotional answer. Use probing questions carefully. You may offend some customers.
❗	Leading	"Lovely flowers, aren't they?"	Leading questions finish with "aren't they," "isn't it," "won't it," "didn't it," etc. This leads the receiver to agree with you. However, she may not agree. So, this type of question is a dangerous opener to use.

Becoming a good listener

There is a saying: "You have two ears and one mouth. You should use them in that ratio." This is a good motto for selling. You need to be a good listener. Unfortunately, many salespeople fall for the trap of talking too much and not listening enough. You need to train yourself to be a good listener and to convince the customer that you are listening.

Listening properly and asking open, probing, or emotional questions will allow you to figure out what your customer really wants. To listen properly to someone in a face-to-face situation you need to "listen" with your ears, your body, and your brain.

Listen with your ears

Make sure you can hear your customer clearly and that there are no loud noises. If it is too noisy or there are too many distractions, move somewhere else where you can pay undivided attention.

Listen with your body

Make sure that you keep regular eye contact with your customer, but do not stare. Stand up straight and face the person squarely. Stay about three feet away from her; this is a comfortable distance in our culture. Do not slouch, chew gum, jiggle keys or coins in your pocket, or keep looking over the customer's shoulder.

Listen with your brain

Make sure that you "switch on" to the other person (display empathy). Try to put yourself in the other person's shoes. It's not enough to just hear what the customer is saying. You have to understand what she wants, sometimes getting past what she's saying to what she really means. When listening, it's polite to wait for the customer to finish what she are saying. Do not jump to conclusions. Figure out the "big picture" of what the person needs. This will help with add-on sales.

Other listening techniques

To be good listener you also need to:
- Nod occasionally in agreement with the customer
- Verbally agree with the customer from time to time
- Keep to the same subject when you respond, and
- Use key word listening. This means you take the key word out of

a sentence you have listened to and use it in your response. For example, if your customer asks, "Are those shrubs over there with the red flowers camellias?" Your response could be, "Yes, they are camellias; they just arrived. They are a rich red, aren't they?" (Camellias and red are the keywords). When you use keywords, you offer confirmation that you have been listening, making your customer feel secure.

Listening on the telephone

To listen properly to someone on the telephone, you need to "listen" even more carefully with your ears and your brain. Again, make sure you can hear clearly. If there is too much noise around you, then shift to somewhere else, ask that the noise be cut down (don't forget to say please), or take the call on another extension. Because you do not have the backup of body language, it is more important to concentrate on what the caller is saying. Wait for the person to have her say, and keep notes. Then ask her questions so you can get a clear picture of what is needed so you can help.

Becoming an effective consultant

Customers come to your garden center for a number of reasons. Customers expect from you is accurate information and advice about the plants, products, and services that your store offers for sale. Customers do not expect you to have all the information in your head, but they do expect you to be able to source the right information for them. You need to be familiar with the plants, products, and services that your business sells and their features. This will help you to help your customers to make decisions.

Provide sound technical information

To be a successful consultant, you need to know how to obtain the information that your customers need and then pass it on in the appropriate manner. You may obtain information about plants and products from both inside and outside your workplace. Generally, information about services are from inside only.

After you find the information, you need to communicate it to your customers. The first clue is to use terms your customers understand. You need to talk the customers' language. If you do not, they will close down the conversation. This does not mean that you cannot educate the

Sources of Information	
Workplace sources	**Outside sources**
Catalogues	TV gardening shows
Package information	Other gardeners
Labels	Gardening magazines
Point-of-sale material	Nursery suppliers
Your colleagues	Garden books
In-store newsletters	Libraries
Leaflets from suppliers	World Wide Web
Product knowledge meetings	Botanical gardens
In-store reference books	Garden clubs
Your own product knowledge file	Other garden centers

customers in the use of horticultural terms—just take it easy. With experience, you will be able to gauge how experienced a customer is. Then you will know at what level to pitch the conversation and which words you can use with that customer.

Turn features into benefits

The real clue to passing on information in the right way concerns the features and benefits of plants, products, and services. Features are all about what plants, products, and services are and how they work. For example: How high it will grow? (plant). How long is the withholding period? (product). How much does it cost? (plant). You need to be familiar with the features (technical knowledge) to have credibility in the eyes of your customers.

However, most customers are not particularly interested in the features of the product. So, if you emphasize the features, then you are not relating properly with your customer. You run the risk of using jargon and overcomplicating the whole thing—and losing the sale!

Customers are more interested in benefits. Many customers may not be able to see the benefit in the features of products, so you need to be able to convert features into benefits. Benefits are what the product does for the customer, the reason for buying the item. Benefits appeal to the emotions of the customer. This will help them when they make a decision. For example: It screens the fence (plant). It provides a safe environment for the children (product). We can save you time (service).

However, there are some things to watch. Be aware that customers may become confused if you offer too many benefits. So, be selective; three is ideal. Each customer has different needs. You have to find out what each customer needs so that you can selectively provide a solution. You find this out by having a conversation with the customer. When people shop as couples, each person will have different perceptions of the need. You will probably have to talk to both people to work out what the needs are.

The contrast principle of add-on selling

Many retailers use the contrast principle of add-on selling, mainly because the great advantage is the customer cannot detect what is going on. Let me give you an example from outside the garden center industry. A gent goes to a clothing store to purchase a two-piece suit and a sweater. The salesperson uses the contrast principle of selling. He sells the expensive suit first and then sells a more expensive sweater than he would have if purchased alone. Why? The sweater is perceived as less expensive when compared to the suit. If the person had done it in reverse, then the sweater purchased may have been less expensive.

Research on this technique was carried out by Whitney, Hubin, and Murphy, and they state: "The interesting thing is that even when a man enters a clothing store with the express purpose of purchasing a suit, he will almost always pay more for whatever accessories he buys if he buys them after the suit purchase than before" (Robert B. Cialdini, *Influence: The Psychology of Persuasion* [Quill, 1993, p. 13]).

This technique works just as well in garden centers. Sell the patio furniture, large plants, trees, or other expensive items before you sell the accessories such as bedding plants, growing media, and garden care products. If you do, it will allow you to sell more expensive items.

Make Add-on Sales

Many people see add-on selling as pressuring the customer. In some circumstances, this may be true. However, in the horticultural industry, add-on selling shows that you care and are responsible. An effective salesperson will suggest items that will prolong the life or quality of the plant or product. Remember, you are the consultant. It's appropriate for you to make suggestions to the customer.

If you do not add-on sell, the customer may get home, realize that she doesn't have everything she needs and, most likely, will go somewhere else to get it. She may even be displeased with you because you did not suggest everything and caused her inconvenience. As people continue to become busier and have less discretionary time, they are looking for one-stop shopping, and your suggestions will save them time and energy. At the same time, you do not want to sell the customer something she doesn't need.

Add-on selling works best when you relate it back to your own experiences. For example, "When I plant these species, I always add a little. . . ."

There are a huge number of possibilities for add-on sales. Some examples of add-on links include:
- Rose bush and a flat of marigolds to repel nematodes
- Peach tree and copper-based fungicide to protect against peach leaf-curl
- Hose and hose fittings and a hanger

Selling up and selling down

In any range of plants or products there is often more expensive options and cheaper alternatives. If you add-on the more expensive item, then you are selling up. If you add-on the cheaper alternative, then you are selling down.

The Salesperson: Closing the Sale

Customer Doubt

People often do not make instant buying decisions. This is because of doubt. Customers need to have their doubts removed by a person they have confidence in, and this is where the salesperson comes in. It's their job to remove the doubt . . . and to make the sale.

Welcome customer doubts. If customers raise doubts, this normally is a clear indication that they want to make a purchase but they need a salesperson to remove those doubts and to help them make the decision. The presence of doubt is a positive opportunity that you should welcome. It often means that the sale is now close.

Here are some hints to help you deal with customers' doubts:
- See doubts as opportunities to make a sale. If you can remove doubts successfully, you will often find the customer will become loyal to you and your company.
- Keep calm at all times. Never let your frustration show. If you feel yourself getting agitated, quietly take some deep breaths to help you calm down.
- Never take any comments personally. Customers aren't being critical of you as a person; they have problems with the situation.
- Always be prepared: Know you products and develop the skills to deal with the customer.

Doubt may arise for a number of reasons. For example, the customer may not believe the product is going to satisfy her needs. Or she has unanswered questions or may not understand aspects of the product. She may require more discussion and may even need the approval of an in-store "qualified" person. Or she might have conditions that restrict or prohibit her from making a purchase.

This last point is important. Most people conceal the real doubts they have. For example, you often hear people say "I'll think about it," "I'll talk it over with my partner and get back to you," or "I'm just looking, thanks." These responses are often cover-ups. They usually hide the real reasons for not going through with the purchase. The customer is turning you off.

According to Jeffrey Gitomer in the book *Sales Bible*, the real reasons for doubt by customers are normally:
- I do not have the money on me
- I cannot decide on my own
- I do not understand the product
- I need someone else's financial approval
- I'm too rushed to purchase
- I don't trust your company
- You haven't convinced me yet
- I have a credit problem
- I want to shop around
- The price is too high
- I have a friend in the industry
- I have money, but don't want to spend it
- I have something else in mind
- I don't really need it at present
- I don't trust you

Your job is to try to discover the real reason for doubt in a customer. You may not be able to "solve" their problem, but at least you will know where you stand. If you do manage to discover the real reason for the doubt, then you may be able to take positive action to remove the doubt and make a sale.

John Wren, in his book *Yes, I'll Take That* (1998), recommends four steps when you are dealing with doubt:

1. Defuse any objections the customer may mention as to why she does not want to purchase anything. Do this by listening, showing empathy, and using open questions to try to discover the real reason for doubt.
2. Prove facts by using magazines, technical reports, testimonials, demonstrations, and any other material that is available to you.
3. Clarify to make sure the doubt has truly been removed in the customer's mind.
4. Refocus on the sale (for example, turning features into benefits) after having removed the doubt.

Building up your confidence

You must be confident to discover the real reasons for doubt. And the best way to build up confidence is by practicing. Role-playing difficult selling situations is an ideal way of developing the confidence to approach and deal with the doubting customer. It provides an opportunity to make mistakes and to learn from other team members. This is far better than bungling a real-life situation and losing the sale.

Role-plays can be undertaken in training sessions or in team meetings. If they are not already used in your workplace, introduce them so they become part of the work culture. All staff will benefit. If role-plays become normal practice, embarrassment will be minimized and people will not be reluctant to get involved.

Reject-and-retreat selling technique

Some retailers use this technique very effectively to increase the average sale per customer. The best way to explain this system of selling is to provide you with an example. Let's assume you are selling garden furniture, you have a range of prices, and you have to decide which to advertise in your local paper. You have a set for $350 and one set at $3,750. Most retailers would promote the low-priced set with the aim of selling up when customers come in. This may not be your best strategy.

In one piece or research carried out by G. Warren Kelly for Brunswick regarding billiard table retailing (*The Psychology of Persuasion,*

p. 47), he found the following: During the first week, customers were shown the low end of the line and encourage to trade up. The average table sale was $550. In the second week the customers were led with a $3,000 table and then allowed to shop the rest in declining order of quality and price. The average sale that week was over $1,000.

The second technique in the study is known as the reject-and-retreat technique of selling and can be used in the right situation in the garden center. It could be used to sell garden design, large plants, garden furniture, or garden makeovers. Give it a try—it may increase your average sale.

Selling skills: Close a sale

Once you have identified the customer's needs and offered a "solution," you need to obtain a commitment from her. That is, an order or money. This is a normal part of a transaction. A customer wants something. You give it to her. She pays. Everyone is happy.

However, some salespeople get embarrassed about collecting money. Don't be. Customers want to give you their money. Much of your effort is wasted if you fail to close the sale effectively.

The point at which you ask the buyer for money (or an order) is the close. It's important that you tackle closing the sale positively, realistically, logically, confidently, and with appropriate timing. Here are some clues:

- Always assume that you are going to make the sale. Let your whole tone reflect your confidence in the proposition and give the impression that you expect to sell the product.
- Use positive phrases. Never use statements such as "Would you like to have this?" or "Will this be enough?"
- Be persistent. Never give up at the first no, but be aware of the point when the sale is totally lost and further persistence will cause offense.
- Keep your body language positive and maintain eye contact
- Select the appropriate close technique to seal the deal.

Closure techniques

There are number of techniques that you can use to close a sale.

You should choose the technique that is most appropriate for a given situation. With practice and experience, you will work out which technique or combination of techniques to use.

Closure Technique	What to Do
Summary close	Sum up your sales story, particularly if you have been interrupted by customers, the telephone, etc., and then get down to quantities.
Physical close	Some types of promotion make a very positive "physical" close possible. For example, you may be selling a bonus offer to the buyer, and there is no more effective way of closing than actually giving them part of the bonus on the spot. "That's your bonus— just on this small order here."
Buyer's remark	The buyer will often make some remark that will give you a lead into the close. For example, "You were saying just now, Mr. Buyer, how popular this line has been recently. . . ."
Minor point	Very often the buyer has almost decided to purchase, yet requires a minimum amount of persuasion to get final agreement. A very effective method of closing in such circumstances is to check some point of detail with the buyer, such as, "Will you be wanting a copy of the order?" or "Let me see, . . . will you want it delivered to 23 High Street?"
Apparent concession close	Sometimes, part of a sale (order) may be too large or contain unacceptable sizes or colors. This may or may not be deliberately planned. An acceptable way to close is to seemingly give way on one part of the sale. For example: "The 5-gallon size seems too much for you, Mr. Buyer, so can we provide you with the 2.5-gallon and 1-gallon sizes?"
Verbal proof	This type of close is used when you quote the examples of other customers. For example: "I have a customer on the other side of town, and she felt this particular offer was ideal for her situation, which is very similar to yours."
Fear close	This close puts the point that the customer will be missing something if the sale is not closed now. You can stress that the deal is too good to miss or that if the customer does not take the product then, the opportunity will be lost. For example: "You know that this offer finishes at midnight on Friday?"
Isolation close	Very often you will attempt to close yet find that the customer says no to the sale. You should attempt to find the reason for not buying. This is an objection, so by addressing the objection in isolation, you can use it as an opportunity.
Alternative close	When using this type of close, you get the customer's acceptance by asking which of the two alternative orders is preferred. The buyer may then miss the fact that a third alternative—not buying at all— is also an option. For example: "Do you prefer the white camellias or the red ones?"
Assumptive close	Assume you are going to get the order and simply proceed to write it down, although care must be taken with the close to ensure the timing is right. This is a very effective close when well executed. For example: "I'll just get the order pad and take note of your details."

Making a sale when there's a line at the checkout

Spring is a hectic time of the year, especially during those precious weekends when the checkouts are ringing constantly. It's easy to just keep taking the money, keep filling the benches, and not worry about being a professional salesperson.

But, the principles are still the same. According to Michael LeBoeuf in his excellent book *How to Win Customers and Keep Them for Life* (Berkeley, 1989), the customers' needs and expectations have not changed. They still want "good feelings" as a result of visiting your garden center and are still looking for solutions to their problems. The more people that feel they have had the above experience then the more successful your business. It is critical to your success that they feel you have met their expectations during your busy time.

A salesperson is a problem solver. In the spring, you have to provide this with speed and efficiency to ensure you provide for customer needs and wants and build loyalty. But how often have you been in a retail store during their busy period and left without being spoken to and only purchasing what you planned to purchase before you walked in the entrance. As a business, the average sale is lower and the salespeople have not used their talents that they were employed to use.

During busy periods, the sales skills are different, but it is essential that:

- Every customer is greeted. This may only be with eye contact due to the volume of customers, but it can be and should be done.
- Checkout operators should always comment on the purchase being made by the customer. The major add on lines should be positioned near the checkouts to enable the operator to use suggestive selling techniques wherever possible.
- Every customer should have a farewell before the next customer is served. This makes people feel special.

Measuring your results

As salespeople become more proficient, a number of things will happen: They will gain confidence in selling and will enjoy the experience of dealing with customers. Customers will enjoy dealing with them and will come back to be served more often by them. And the average sale per customer will slowly increase.

Regular, on-going calculation of your average sale figure is one way of knowing how well you are going as a salesperson and business. To calculate your average sale figure, you (or your business) need to keep a record of every sale you make. This can be for a set period of time (a day, week or month), or it can be for a set number of customers (for example, twenty, thirty, fifty, etc.). Add up the total number of dollars of all the sales you made and divide by the number of transactions. (Do not include people who do not buy anything).

Measuring itself isn't important; what you do with the results is. For example, imagine the average sale per customer across the whole of the sales staff in your nursery is forty dollars. If your personal average sale is below that, then you need to analyze what you are doing. Are you using closed questions? Not add-on selling? Not listening carefully? Selling down (offering cheaper alternatives)? If your personal average is above forty dollars, well done. But do not get complacent. There's always room for improvement. Check that you always add-on sell, sell up (offer more expensive alternatives), form relationships with your customers, and pass on your ideas to your colleagues so their average sales can increase.

Book List

Baldwin, Ian, and John Stanley.1992. *The Garden Center Manual.* London: Grower Books.

Cialdini, Robert B. 1993. *Influence: The Psychology of Persuasion.* New York: Quill.

Flanagan, Neil, and Jarvis Finger. 1998. *Just about Everything a Manager Needs to Know.* 1998. Brisbane, Australia: Plum Press.

Gitomer, Jeffrey H. 1994. *Sales Bible.* New York: Morrow.

Leadership Skills. 1980. London: Agricultural Training Board.

Motivation. 1980. London: Agricultural Training Board.

Selective Interviewing. 1980. London: Agricultural Training Board.

Stanley, John. 2000. *Studies in Horticulture, Sell Plants, Products and Services.* Melbourne, Australia: Adland Horticultural.

Stanley, John. 1999. *Just about Everything a Retail Manager Needs to Know.* Brisbane, Australia: Plum Press.

Successful Selling. 2000. Perth, Western Australia: Australian Institute of Management.

Wren, John. 1998. *Yes. Thanks I'll Take It!* Auckland, New Zealand: David Bateman

Work Planning. 1980. London: Agricultural Training Board.

Chapter 16

Increasing Sales

Everyone who starts a business wants to be successful; few achieve their dream. The majority of retailers end up in the trudge of day-to-day retailing. In this chapter, we will concentrate on what you need to do to have a successful business.

First, we have to define what we mean by success. Success means different things to different people. To some it is an improved lifestyle, for others a healthier bank account, and for others a happy family life. In business, successful companies are looked on as those who are leaders. I am often asked who are the leading garden centers. They are the ones who are leading the industry globally.

What makes them leaders? These are the garden centers that are creating the changes in the industry. They have "retail heroes" who are from outside the industry, whilst other garden center owners have "retail heroes" from within the industry. This is not to say that people from our industry are not as good as those from without, but the "heroes" from other industries often bring new and exciting approaches from their experiences working with clothing, shoes, music, or with restaurants.

Successful leaders surround themselves with positive people who have like-minded dreams and passion for the industry. Every successful garden center I have worked with is totally customer orientated, and they often involve customers in the running of their business. Successful people realize they never stop learning and are often the world's greatest students. They do not know the answers, but know what questions to ask and of whom.

Do not get me wrong—successful businessmen know about their business. They know the lifetime value of their customers and are striving to increase the value in dollar terms they obtain from these customers.

Garden center shopping is different to supermarket shopping. Supermarket shopping for the majority of customers is a chore; garden center shopping should be fun. The successful garden center owner knows that it isn't the product that is the key to success, it's the "entertailing" (entertaining + retailing) experience that is the key to success.

Work on the Senses

Successful retailers know there is more to retailing than building their business on what customers see and hear. Success is about getting the ambience right to encourage the customer to linger longer.

Key areas in building on the ambience in your garden center include:

Lighting

Good lighting in your store can increase sales. All lights have a color temperature that can effect the shopping experience. For example, "warm" colors have a golden hue while "cold" colors have a bluish hue. Florescent tubes and light bulbs can increase or decrease the perceived warmth or coldness of your garden center shop.

The gift department in your store should have warm color, whilst you may get away with cold color in your garden care department. Florescent tubes all in a row send out the wrong message to your customer. They may light the shop, but they do nothing to get your customers to linger longer.

The level of light is also critical. If you want to speed customers up, you use brighter lighting in your store. The key is placing light fittings so you can change the ambience in your center for different effects.

Consider color filters to create interesting color themes or light control lenses to throw light onto walls through shaping the beam. Glare control devices can hide the light source, while a miniature projector can project images from slides onto your walls or ceilings.

Aroma

Smell is the most powerful sense, and smells can trigger strong responses in customers. Coffee shops and bread shops already use aroma very effectively. In your gift department you could use scented candles or oil burners to encourage customers to stay longer. Essential oils are plentiful; the challenge is which one to use:

- Orange is warm and uplifting.
- Lemon is crisp, sharp, and clean. Many supermarkets use it after 4:00 P.M. in their air conditioners to help de-stress shoppers.
- Ylang-ylang creates a feeling of exclusiveness and could be used around expensive products.
- Pine, cedar, and juniper could be used around outdoor products within your store.

According to Barbara Allpress, an aromatherapy lecturer at Wellpark College in New Zealand, the important tips for retailers are:

- Never use fragrant oils, as they are synthetic imitations. Always use essential oils from plant extracts.
- Put water in the bowl on top of the burner and then add four drops of essential oil. The heat from the burner will send molecules of oil into the air.
- Use the right oil for what you are trying to achieve.
- The power of smell is subtle. The customer should not be aware of it.

Music

We hate silence. In the United Kingdom when a survey asked consumers what lifted their spirits, the answer was music.

Get the music right in your store and you could increase your sales. But you need to know your customer demographics and play the right music at the right time. To speed shoppers up, you play dance music; to slow them down, you use music with a mild tempo. To encourage customers to linger longer, you should aim for music that has less than sixty beats per minute.

Do not let your staff select the music; members will inevitably select what they like, not what is right to increase sales. Once you have selected your music, you will need an industrial-strength CD player and a library of at least six four-hour discs, which may be obtained from professional music houses. Radio is not ideal, as you have no control over which songs are played and the commercial interruptions.

Focus on Strategies

In my work with garden centers, I have noticed a major difference between the leaders and the remainder of the field. In leading businesses, all the key members of the team are focused on increasing sales. Their mission in life is divided into two simple short-term and long-term strategies. The short-term strategies are (1) increase sales per square foot and (2) increase the average sale per customer. The long-term strategies are (1) create lifetime customers and (2) increase the value of lifetime customers. Compare this with other garden centers where full-time team members have no idea what their sales are or what they should be generating for the business.

I believe it is essential that every team member should be aiming to increase the average sale per customer whilst building a lifetime relationship with the customer. It is important that these two philosophies are brought together. Anyone can become a pressure salesperson and increase the average sale, but your aim is also to increase frequency of customer visits and lifetime value, which is a completely different approach.

To achieve the above, you need an understanding of customers and their changing habits and a system to measure success.

Think *for* Customers

Over the years, various authors have written books on customer service. The theme of these books has basically revolved around thinking like a customer. But times change, and customers and businesses change with the times. Potential customers have less time and are also getting information overload. If today you think like your customers, the chances are you are as stressed and confused as they are.

The modern garden center, if it wishes to grow its market share, needs to take a new approach to customer service. Today, managers and owners need to think for their customers, rather than like them. For some garden centers, this means training their team to think in a completely new way.

Let me give you an example. I recently carried out some work in Holland for a client. The Dutch retailer had analyzed his market and found that his consumers ate grapefruit at breakfast. His team agreed to move the grapefruits to the breakfast aisle and place them next to the cereals. The result was that grapefruit sales increased considerably, due to the retailer thinking for his customers.

When I mentioned this idea to a team in an Australian supermarket, they accepted that Australian consumers also eat grapefruit at breakfast, but the correct location for grapefruits was in the fruit department and next to the oranges. I failed in my attempt to get the store to test the concept. Why? The team was not prepared to think for their customers, and the result was no increase in grapefruit sales.

In today's hectic world, customers do not have time to think through the intricate details; they want you to do their thinking for them. This means getting away from your old category thinking and thinking about categories based on how customers buy and then managing the category in a way that helps the customer.

I worked with a group of garden centers where the trees were the responsibility of the plant manager and placed in one section of the garden center. The tree stakes were the responsibility of the "wood" category manager and were at the opposite end of the retail area. The category managers were happy, but the customers often left without a stake or were confused about where to find them due to the category management. The result was lost sales and disappointed customers.

I recently visited a paint retailer. When you purchased paint, he provided you with a checklist of items you needed to complete the job successfully. This was a simple but effective way of thinking for the customer. All the customer had to do was tick the checklist. This type of checklist could be used in many garden center situations to help customers through the project decision-making process. The key is to put the checklist on a notepad that your garden center team can keep in their top pocket. If you do this rather than having a handout by the checkout, it is more likely to be used.

Team training on how customers think and what information they need is critical. Too often sales teams take it for granted and assume the customers know more than they do. Plus, the team needs to realize that women buy and think differently than men do. Paco Underhill, in his book *Why We Buy,* identifies this exceptionally well. His research found that women generally purchased a portable phone based on one visit to the store. Men, on average, took three visits before they made the purchase. This was because sales assistants did not understand how men purchased portable phones. The men had to visit three times to understand the technical jargon, whilst female customers were happy to not understand the jargon and just make the purchase. Better training would have resulted in time saving for the customer and more sales for the retailer, a win-win situation.

Photo 16-1. It's simple and effective—make sure your stakes are merchandised by your trees, not just in the hard goods area.

As customers, we are often placed in situations where we do not understand the product and need comfort or reassuring statements on signage from the retailer. Airport bookstores tend to do this exceptionally well by introducing bestseller strategies through their signage. They know many people only read a book when they fly and their knowledge of what to read is limited. The consumers take assurance from bestseller signage; they believe a bestseller must be a good read and they will not be disappointed. The same strategy works in CD stores and liquor stores, but many garden centers miss the opportunity to introduce it to clients. The key is to think for your customers—as they get busier, they need you to do more thinking for them!

Measure Success

You need to let your team know that you measure success on a daily basis. The most effective way of achieving this is through the average sale per customer. The easiest way to achieve this is to place a white board in the staff room and ensure it is updated daily. This white board should be set up as follows:

Sales Target	
Average sale for today last year	$ _____
Today's target	$ _____
Yesterday's target	$ _____
Yesterday's actual	$ _____

It's amazing how this can increase motivation within a team. For it to be successful relies on management. They must do two things: first, they must keep it up to date, and second, they must reward the team when they hit the target. This does not necessarily have to be a financial reward, although I know companies that do. It can be as simple as a "Thank you, well done."

Increasing Customer Loyalty

To be successful means one of your aims is to make shopping easier for your customers, especially since gardening is a hobby and buying for hobbies should not be a stressful experience. Your product price is not the issue. It is perceived value that is the issue, which is a combination of price, time saving, quality, and convenience. Become a problem solver and provide the answer before your customers have even thought of the question.

Let me give you an example: A customer has become a loyal customer at your garden center, and over the last two years you have been tracking his buying habits. Every March he comes in and purchases twenty-five bags of growing media. You contact him in the first week of March and offer to deliver the twenty-five bags to his home and include a small gift of appreciation for his doing business with you. For this technique to be successful, you need to know your customers, track their gardening trends, and have a database that works for you.

Know Your Customers

The more you know about your customers, the more successful you will be, as long as you use the information at your disposal in the right manner.

Some companies will spend millions of dollars to get market research done on their customers. I believe you can obtain the majority of information you need by referring to horticultural magazines and in-house research using your own team. Start with the basics. You need to know the sex of your customers, the average sale, where they come from, how often they visit you, when they purchase, and how they found out about your business. All this information can be found out in a simple survey carried out in-house by your team.

The real key to success is to understand where your customer is now and to determine what their needs are in the future and then to provide for those needs before your competitor does. The key is to be one step ahead, not four or five. To express this another way, your business should be leading edge, not bleeding edge. Your aim is to have your competitors chasing you when it comes to trends.

Tracking trends is the real challenge; this is where you need to read lifestyle and gardening magazines as well as the commercial horticultural press. Kurt Fromherz of the Sunrise Marketing catalog summarizes gardening trends in a precise way.

Management Memo

"If customers have fun while shopping, they will spend more money."

Build-a-Bear targets children with interactive retailing. At the store, customers build their own personalized teddy bear. As a child is creating his or her very own bear, at a certain point in the process, a heart must be picked out. An associate instructs the child to rub the heart between his/her hands to make sure love gets passed on before it is placed inside the bear.

Can you put a dollar value on that experience?

Maxine Clark, Build-a-Bear's founder and chief executive bear, cites a 90 to 100% guest rating of the question "Did we make you smile during your visit?" What can we do in garden centers to achieve the same results?

Sell Solutions

Garden centers are in the service industry, and customers are looking for garden solutions. The company that can provide the most solutions gets the customers' confidence. Solution ideas include plant guarantees, shelf talkers on garden care shelves advising that it is time to use specific products, and "as seen on television" product talkers.

Sell Escape

In the U.S., Martha Stewart has become an icon in selling escapism to the public. In the U.K., Charlie Dimmock achieved the same position in gardening. Customers are looking for escapism, especially baby boomers, who are looking for comfortable nesting, fantasy, and creativity. The garden is the ideal escape. It's up to us to not sell plants, but to start selling escapism.

Sell Gardens

Group plants together and sell gardens. Most people have difficulty imagining concepts. It's our job to put those concepts together and sell the package. Leading, independent garden centers are doing this exceptionally well. For example, Lifestyle Family Garden Center in South Africa finds one of its busiest weekends of the year is in mid-winter, when it has a garden expo and converts the majority of its planteria into display gardens or gardens to go.

Keep Pace with Change

Gardening styles and lifestyles are changing at a rapid pace. Keep up with garden styles by visiting the major garden shows such as Chelsea Flower Show and Hampton Court Flower Show in the U.K., the Elleslie Flower Show in New Zealand, or the New England Flower and Garden Show and the Chicago Flower and Garden Show in the U.S.

Read the leading lifestyle magazines and ensure one or your team watches lifestyle programs. Home and Garden Television is a great channel for trends, and magazines such as *Martha Stewart Living, Better Homes and Gardens,* and *Southern Living* will keep you in touch with your clientele.

Communicate

The following chapters concentrate on communicating with your customers. Prior to reading those chapters, you should analyze how you are communicating now. Are you pushing (interruption marketing) or pulling (permission marketing)? Push marketing is radio, TV, and newspaper ads and mass-mail flyers; pull marketing is e-mails, newsletters, directed postcards, and loyalty or preferred-customer clubs. Traditionalists invest in pushing, while contemporary retailers are investing in pulling.

Garden center retailing is fun, and increasing sales is fun. But it does take dedication, commitment, proper systems, and a desire to be the best garden center in town. Ask yourself the following:

Look out for Signals of Poor Communication	
Signals to Improve	**Comments**
The team complains about lack of communication.	Establish why there is complaint. It may be valid (you do not give enough information), or it may be caused by frustration or lack of job security.
There is a flourishing grapevine of rumors (often inaccurate) regarding the state of the business and future intentions.	Unofficial communication channels flourish when official ones are weak or in times of uncertainty (change, recession).
There is confusion about responsibilities amongst the team.	Spell out each person's duties and authority clearly.
Sometimes people do not do things, even though they have been told.	Always follow up communications (particularly non-routine ones) to make sure they are carried out.
Sometimes people make silly mistakes, despite clear instructions.	Are you using two-way communications? Are you checking that they can do it? Are you following up to control performance?
Sometimes people fail to bring major problems to your attention soon enough.	Review your relationship with the team. Do you encourage them to ask for help? Have you spelled out when they should come to you?
People do not come forward with ideas for improvement and show little initiative.	Are you keeping the team fully in the picture? Are you trying to build communication?
The wrong message is often read into messages at the lowest level.	This suggests a problem of low morale or lack of trust. You will need to work at building trust and cooperation by being as open and frank as you can be.
Reference: A.T.B. Communications Workbook, U.K.	

- Is your company customer friendly?
- Have you a service strategy defined in terms of benefits to the customers?
- A well-defined promise?
- Have you a service strategy clearly communicated? Outside? Inside?

- Are your systems and procedures turned towards the customer?
- Have you measurable quality standards for all service areas?
- Are they communicated to all the members of your company?
- Are your recruiting, training, and promotions orientated toward customer service?
- Did you reward somebody for something really special that he/she did for a customer in the past twelve months?
- Did you deal with letters of complaints or praise? Rapidly (within twenty-four hours)? To the customer's satisfaction?
- Are your employees involved in the setting up of service quality standards?
- Do these employees participate in chasing errors through quality circles?

OK. You've made the effort to communicate, but are your communications effective? Use the checklist on the previous page to see if there is a need for improvement in your garden center.

Book List

Falk, Edgar A. 1994. *1,001 Ideas to Create Retail Excitement.* New York: Prentice Hall.

Konjoian, Peter. April 2001. "Retailing 2001: Are Your Customers on a Pedestal?" Ohio Florists Association Bulletin No. 857.

Quinn, Feargal. 1990. *Crowning the Customer: How to Become Customer Driven.* Dublin, Ireland: O'Brien Press.

Underhill, Paco. 1999. *Why We Buy: The Science of Shopping.* New York: Simon & Schuster.

Chapter 17

Getting New Customers

It is a real challenge to cut through the clutter and attract new customers. People are exposed to up to thirty thousand messages a day. These messages come via television, newspapers, radio, and dozens of other ways. By 2005, the average American will be exposed to a thousand messages online alone.

Getting a new customer is expensive and frustrating. The technique used is often called "interruption marketing." Interruption marketing gets its name from the fact that you are interrupting the life of an existing non-user of your business to tell them you exist and that they should visit you. But with all the messages people see each day, your new customer is becoming less and less tolerant of interruption marketing. You have to become more imaginative to get their attention, and, by the way, it will also become more and more expensive.

Most of us still rely on the traditional ways of interrupting our customers' lives. These are television commercials, radio commercials, press advertising, billboards, and mail drops. Do not reject them as a means of getting your message across. The keys are to plan your interruptions and to use your selected media constantly. The drip, drip system is effective, but it may take a long time before the customer actually walks to your front door.

Larger businesses that have larger budgets are now looking at what is called guerrilla marketing. Guerrilla marketing can often be the most expensive form of interruption marketing. It relies on eye-catching stunts to get the potential customer's attention. Let me give you some examples. During the Christmas shopping period of 2000 in New York, eight thousand wallets were dropped in Manhattan by a marketing company and contained the address of a Web site that they wished consumers to log into. In November 2000, in the same city, twenty car wrecks pouring with smoke crawled through the city to promote a new car-chase video game.

Remember, the key to success is to be noticed, but to be noticed in a positive light. The last thing you want to do is repel your customers.

Interruption Advertising Techniques

Interruption advertising can take a number of different formats. You need to select which one is most suitable for your garden center. The key is to "get different" to ensure you get noticed. You have four basic media to choose from:

- Ink—The printed form can be used to promote your business via newspapers, magazines, direct marketing, billboards, and other ink-based formats.
- Broadcast—Broadcasting includes television, cinema, video, direct television, and events. It revolves around the film media to get a message across.
- Voice—Radio is the most common way of using the voice, but street noise and other techniques may be considered.
- Net—This is the first interactive interruption advertising media. Net advertising is available via the Internet, kiosks, Web ads, and Net links.

For interruption marketing to work, you need a very clear understanding of your target customer and an ability to do things in a slightly different way. Your aim is to get your message through the clutter. You have to be smarter than your competition and come up with the unexpected. When advertising, remember that you still need to be truthful, decent, and legal, be responsible to the consumer and society, and conform to the principles of fair competition.

Before selecting the media to use, you need to decide how fast you want the "call to action" by your potential customer. For example, television, radio, and newspapers are aimed at a rapid-response (today), whilst magazines and cinema advertising are a "slow burn" option (the response time may be weeks).

You will also need to consider placement quality in the media you select rather than quantity. Your aim is maximum impact. Prime placement positions include the last advertisement during a television break, advertisements in high-view programs for your target group, and the inside cover of magazines. Before making a major investment in interruption advertising, it is important you experiment and test the media you are going to use before making large commitments and investments.

Advertising your business to new customers is an essential part of growing your business. The challenge is selecting the right avenue to use out of a plethora of different media. You therefore need to plan, measure, and monitor your advertising.

You also need to identify who your real target is. This goes beyond gender, age, income, etc. Marketers often use the acronym SPADE to focus attention on the real target:

Starter—The person who initiates the enquiry

Purchaser—The person who pays for the goods

Advisor—The person who influences the decision

Decider—The real authority on what to buy

End user—The consumer of the product

Consider the following example: It's spring, and Mrs. Smith (starter) phones your garden center to inquire about whether you sell garden shovels. Her husband (purchaser) drops into pay for it on his way home from work. He mentions that his neighbor (advisor) had seen your advertisement in the newspaper and had mentioned it to him. Their friend is a keen gardener (decider) and had phoned him and told your customer this was the best shovel on the market. He was buying it as a present for their son-in-law (end user), who has just moved into a new house.

A number of people need to be influenced by your advertisement! Before deciding on which advertising media to use, do your research. Contact advertising outlets that suit your audience. Ask for details on costs and for evidence on how effective they are at reaching their audience.

Which Interruption Channel?

Every situation is different. In a book like this, all I can provide is options for your consideration. You need to review your own situation and select the right media to promote your garden center to your selected audience.

Roadside Advertising

Many companies favor commercial advertising along main roads and highways. The regulations will vary with local governments, and you will need to check what you can do in your neighborhood.

There are four basic categories of roadside advertising.

1. Large freestanding signs and signs on overhead bridges. These signs can be 12 feet by 12 feet square or larger.
2. Signs on bus shelters, seats, city trashcans, and illuminated signs under street names.
3. Small local business signs placed in public areas and visible to passersby. These signs are a lot smaller than those in category 1.
4. Signs on private property other than your own.

Before you approach your local government on this type of advertising, it's important that you take a few steps to assist your application.

These are: (1) Decide on the size, height, legend, message, etc. that you want for your sign. (2) Identify your preferred location. If it is on someone else's property, get his or her permission. (3) Prepare a detailed drawing. This should also show the construction and fixing details. (4) Check if you need public liability insurance for the sign you wish to erect.

Television Advertising

Few of us can afford television commercials. Especially when you consider half a minute of time during the Super Bowl can cost up to $2 million. Airtime during regular primetime programming isn't nearly that expensive, but it is still a costly endeavor. Therefore, although as consumers we are exposed to a wide range of products and companies via this medium, it is a rare business that can afford to invest in this type of advertising.

But, do not neglect the television as a means of promoting gardening. Television lifestyle programs are all the rage. In the U.K., Charlie Dimmock became a celebrity through her television appearances on a gardening program called *Ground Force*. As a result, gardening boomed. Researchers found that at her celebrity peak, 30% of customers going to garden centers were doing so because of her presence on the small screen. The message is: Make sure you watch the lifestyle programs on television and ensure your garden center reflects what the viewers are watching.

Cable offers a more affordable alternative to network commercials. Check with local cable companies and see what rates are during cable access programs or for text ads on community message boards. The Weather Channel and Home and Garden Television also have opportunities for local advertising.

Radio Advertising

Radio advertising can be a lot more cost effective than television. It is also more targeted to specific customers. With the proliferation of local radio stations, you need to select the station most targeted to the demographic group that comes into your garden center. Of course, advertise during gardening programs to hit your target audience dead on.

Newspaper Advertising

For the majority of horticultural retail businesses, newspaper and magazine advertising is still the most popular means of interruption marketing. We therefore need to concentrate on how to use this media effectively.

Plan Your Print Advertisement

As I mentioned at the beginning of this chapter, your customers are confronted by thousands of advertisements every day of their lives, and your aim is to make yours the one that is noticed. That is not an easy task. However, by following some simple guidelines, you can take some important steps to give your advertisement a chance in the highly competitive retail world. Your aim must be to reveal the message you hope to get across to your target audience in a simple, logical, and effective way.

Plan an Effective Layout

A good layout embraces four essential factors: sequence, focus, simplicity, and eye appeal. Begin with these key components in mind and on completion of the advertisement, check that your layout reflects this essential formula.

Get Your Sequence Correct

To make sense in life, it's important to get things in logical order or sequence. In advertising, sequence is also important. When preparing your advertisement, try to make your advertising content capable of creating AIDCA in your readers when they follow this sequence:

Attention—Your advertisement grabs readers' attention immediately

Interest—If you do not get the readers interested, you have lost them.

Desire—Your advertisement must be capable of arousing the readers' eagerness to possess the product

Conviction—the reader makes a decision to purchase

Action—the reader actually takes steps to purchase

Focus Your Readers' Attention

Ask yourself, What is the most important part of my message? Whatever it is, that's what you want your audience to concentrate upon. There are a number of techniques you can use to accomplish this. For example: highlight the message, change the typeface, use color, a pointed finger, or arrows.

Keep It Simple

The KISS principle (Keeping It Simple Sells) applies to many aspects of the retail business, and simple eye-catching advertisements are always your best approach. The only catch is that a simple advertisement is not always as easy to achieve as you would hope. Indeed, you may need to design your advertisement a number of times to accomplish that desired simplicity. Remember also that space sells and readers will often overlook a cluttered advertisement.

Give Your Advertisement Eye Appeal

To attract and hold the attention of your target audience, your advertisement will need five components: an eye-catching headline and subheads, text, illustrations, white space, and your name, address, and logo.

Since our minds work in pictures, not words, pictures will help get your message across. We also prefer to read lowercased letters, not capitals, and we prefer the serif typeface, as used in newspapers (and this book). A printer can advise you on the best typefaces to use. Finally, make sure the advertisement is in keeping with the image you want for your business.

Adhere to These Proven Rules

Most newspapers and magazines have studios that concentrate on creating advertisements. If you lack confidence in this area, use their expertise. Even so, it's worth knowing a few simple rules so that you can draw up your own advertisements if required.

- Decide on your approach, either a hard sell or soft sell. Hard sell is price dominated; soft sell is benefits dominated. The decision will depend on your image, target audience, time of year, and product.
- Compile a checklist of what you would like to say in your advertisement. In addition to product details, this may include a map, telephone, fax, e-mail, and Web page details, parking facilities, years established, etc.
- Westerners read from left to right and absorb information quickly in a Z pattern. The major products you wish to promote must be in the path of the Z. The less important products are set off to the side.
- Place your name and address at the bottom of the advertisement; your objective is not to sell your name. The headline should be selling a product, service, or idea.
- A picture speaks a thousand words. Use illustrations and pictures to catch your reader's eye. Use copyright-free clip art that is available in computer software packages or clip art books. Newspapers often subscribe to artwork services, and manufacturers and suppliers often have illustrations that you can use.

Management Memo

Aim your advertising appeal at the basic human needs:
- Making money
- Saving effort
- Impressing others
- More leisure
- Self improvement
- The need to belong
- Security
- Getting something others can't.

Write Copy That Sells

Writing advertising and promotional copy is a skill. If it were not, we would be reading every advertisement we see. Good copy answers important questions that a potential customer is going to ask: Who are you? What are you trying to sell me? Why should I buy it? Why should I come to your garden center? Where are you located? When are you open for trade? You have to get this information across in such a way that the potential consumer will want to read your advertisement—and then buy. The following advice will help you do that.

Identify your USP

Every successful business has a USP, a unique selling proposition. You must identify your USP and be able to explain it to your target audience in a way that captures their attention and hopefully has them beating a path to your door.

Write a headline people want to read

The most important part of the copy is the headline. It must attract and hold the readers' attention. Headlines that work usually promise benefits to the readers and encourage them to read on. Your USP may be the focus of your headline.

For a headline to really grab the readers' attention, it should:
- Mention the reader and their interests
- Use current news if it is relevant to your message
- Provoke curiosity
- Promise the benefits up-front

If it is a product you are promoting, say what it does or how easy it is to use. Remember that price is not a benefit when consumers are making initial decisions.

List your selling points and benefits

Selling points are inherent factors about your business and your products. Can you identify yours? They will need to be mentioned in your copy. Selling points could include: biggest range of plants in the city, large parking lot, massive sale this weekend, thousands of items under the one roof, or you've been in business seventy-five years.

The benefits are what the consumer is looking for when purchasing products from you. For example: immediate home delivery, reliability and trust, or money savings.

Consumers always buy benefits over selling points, and you must highlight these in your copy.

Be creative, competitive, and located

Writing style is critical. You need to create a desire in customers to buy products at your garden center. You may need to write competitively—if your audience already has the desire to purchase, your job is to channel that desire into your particular location over any competitors'. And you may need to tell your hard-won consumers where you are; let them know how to find your store.

Successful copywriters adhere to certain basic rules, such as:
- Use simple and clear English
- Don't use long words or jargon
- Use local language
- Be credible and avoid half-truths
- Always use facts and figures
- Don't promote technology early on in your copy
- Tell it the way it is
- Don't use too many adjectives
- Don't try to be too clever
- After writing the ad, get someone else to read it and check it. It must sell and be error free.

Call the readers to action

Keep the AIDCA formula in mind when preparing your copy. Action must be stimulated. Your job is to ask the readers for their business. Tell them what you want them to do. For example:
- Pick the telephone up and speak to . . .
- Fill in the coupon and mail to . . .
- Visit the garden center and ask for . . .
- Fax your response to . . .
- Order now from our Web site at . . .

Many retailers will write excellent copy and then neglect to include a procedure for getting an order. You must remember: Your aim is to sell something!

Use a PS to drive the message home

Most people will read headlines, scan the text, and focus on the end. Research has shown that postscripts enjoy a readership as much as seven times higher than "body" copy. So, to boost the power of your message, to reinforce your major point, consider using a PS to sell product, stress

Management Memo

When you have written advertising copy, read it through and count how many times you have written *I, I'm* and *we* and how many times you have written *you* and *your*. You should have used *you* and *your* at least three times more than *I, I'm* and *we*. Your aim is to communicate with another person about them and their interests, not tell them about yourself.

benefits, or call the reader to action.

Examples of Garden Center Advertisements

When writing an advert for your garden center, remember that the most successful garden centers do not sell plants.

How many garden centers do you know who just promote their name, address, and products and end up solely competing on price?

Prices in an advertisement are effective; they give the customer something to go on, but do you want to sell on price? A top garden center is in that position because its customers know they will get consistent advice, service, and quality plants.

Figure 17-1. Price-led ad.

FRED'S GARDEN CENTER
Main Street, Yourtown

Chrysanthemums $2 each	Bedding Plants From $1 a pot	Trees $15 and up
Cottage Garden Plants $5 each	Groundcovers $4.50	Conifers $15
Vines $12.50 each	Roses $7.50	Pot Color $3 each

★Fred's
North St. | Main St. | Elm Ave.

Tel: (555) 555-1111
Fax: (555) 555-1112

Figure 17-2. Lifestyle ad.

Consider these two advertisements (figures 17-1 and 17-2) and see which one grabs your attention and which you would have glossed over.

Other Marketing Ideas

Advertisements in the media are not the only way to go with interruption marketing. There are several other ways to get potential customers to notice your business.

Coupons

Probably, the most popular means of promoting products in the U.S. is the use of coupons. The majority of coupons are based on reduced price incentives when redeemed in the retail outlet. Coupons really took off in the late 1980s, when manufacturers discovered how powerful they were at pulling customers into stores to purchase their product.

According to research by the manufacturers Coupon Control Center, 77% of Americans use coupons, although female customers use them more frequently than men do. Research by the above organization shows that coupon use increases as the economy declines.

Manufacturers produce coupons, as consumers have become less brand loyal and more price sensitive. They also find that coupons increase the buying power of that product by consumers and it means that the supplier has the control over the expiration date on the promotion. Plus, the supplier knows that the retailer will not absorb the price reduction and they can distribute directly to the consumer and create a demand at a public level.

As manufacturers have felt they have had less control over retailers, they have tended to gravitate to more use of coupons to build brand loyalty. This is specifically evident in the laundry product household cleaner and ready-to-eat cereal sectors of retailing.

Coupons come in different delivery channels. There are:

- FSI—Freestanding inserts. These are the booklet coupons you come across in your weekend newspaper. They account for about 80 percent of coupons distributed in the U.S.
- ROP—Newspaper run of press. These are actually printed in newspapers and are accompanied with a standard advertisement.
- Direct mail—These are distributed through the postal service directly to the consumer's home and can be very targeted. You could aim these directly at avid gardeners.
- Magazine coupons—This media has lost popularity by coupon producers but should target people interested in gardening.
- Merchandise-distributed coupons—Fertilizer and garden chemical producers often use this media. The consumer purchases the product and has a discount coupon on the pack for their next purchase. This is a very effective system, as the manufacturer has no delivery costs involved in the process.
- Specialty distributed coupons—These are coupons generated at the point of purchase and are more common in the supermarket industry. A coupon is generated to encourage substitution and is ideal to target for example gardeners who if they buy a rose get a token for rose food.

According to research carried out by NCH Promotional Services, the average minimum value for a coupon is $0.23, whilst most people required $0.58 coupons to encourage them to use them, although this depends very heavily on the type of product.

If you do use coupons as a promotion, remember to put a realistic expiration date on them, otherwise you could get caught with coupons that are out of date as far as you are concerned but you are obliged to accept.

Contests

My local newspaper, radio station, and shopping center recently teamed up to produce a crossword contest. The crossword was in the newspaper, the clues were on the radio, and the collection box was in the shopping center. This proved to be a huge success and had the whole town talking about it. There is no reason why a garden center couldn't team up with other lifestyle retailers and produce a similar competition.

People like some excitement, and contests are one way of creating that buzz. The keys to a successful contest are that it should involve the customer, increase sales, and provide the retailer with names and addresses for their database.

To ensure success, the prize has to be exciting enough to motivate the customers to participate. Although we live in a changed world, travel is still one of the biggest draws. In gardening, this could be: a visit to the Chelsea Flower Show, a visit to a television garden program, or a tour of the wholesale nursery and Disney World.

The contest should try and involve the consumer in being adventurous. Contests could include designing a garden, patio bowl, or courtyard, writing a horticultural poem, finishing a sentence, or naming specific plants—the list is endless.

When developing a contest, costs are critical. You need to figure the cost in prizes, media for promotion, entry forms, publicity material, judging expenses, and incidental cash. But the right contest can really catch customers' imagination and grow your business.

Special Events

Celebrities and special events can really draw in the crowds, but they do take a lot of preparation. People like meeting people from the media, and if you can combine a special and a celebrity, then you should be able to attract a lot of customers.

You will need a "wet weather" plan and a plan of action if the crowd draw exceeds your expectations. Do plan parking, food, and toilet facilities. In my experience, these are the areas that can turn a great event into a disaster.

Special events could include: a spring garden show, scarecrow competition, children's garden day, charity day, radio and television gardening programs at your center, apple days, pumpkin days, harvest festival, arrival of Santa Claus, and your anniversary celebration. You can probably come up with others too.

Sample Programs

Sampling is a very effective means of building traffic in the food and wine industries. Most of us cannot resist a sample of wine on a tour of the Napa Valley or tasting the cheeses at our local gourmet shop or supermarket.

Sampling is a lot more difficult to introduce into the garden center, but it still works. It can be used more effectively when promoting fertilizers than plants. My local garden center always offers a sample of fertilizer to start the plant off in garden and then recommends the fertilizer pack. If you can introduce a sample policy you will be surprised how it can help build customer loyalty.

Leaf Drops

I have recommended "leaf drops" to clients around the world. I will be honest—some have made it work exceptionally well, whilst others have found it difficult to justify in dollar terms. The objective is to mass mail "leaves" (promotional flyers in the shape of leaves) in the fall to local households. Potential customers are encouraged to come to the garden center and tie the leaf on their cart to obtain a discount. It's a different than a standard coupon and may catch the imagination of potential customers in your catchment area.

Advertising Budget

How much should you spend on advertising your garden center? Most experts suggest a starting point of 3 percent of turnover. If you are starting a business from nothing, this percentage could be far too low. If you are a really established business, you may argue it is on the high side, but it is a good starting point for a typical garden center.

Before spending, you need to plan and write it down. Write down what your company objectives are. How much you feel you should spend? How often and when should you invest in advertising? Now you can start planning your advertising budget for a full twelve months. Use last year's sales to look at next year's projected sales and the advertising expenditure you will need.

Once you determine how much you've budgeted for advertising, then you can decide where it is best spent. Do not look at the dollar cost of the advertising. Instead, look at the penetration rate cost. This is not easy, but you need to have an idea how much it will cost per customer. For example, a $500 advert that attracts two new customers costs $250 per customer. A $10,000 advert that attracts a hundred customers costs $100 per customer, which is a far more effective penetration rate and a sounder investment in your business.

The advertising and promotional planner on the following page was originally produced by Keith Banks of the Queensland Small Business Development Corporation and is a valuable planning tool for any garden center.

Word of Mouth

Your best marketing tool, however, is attracting new customers through referral marketing. This is ideal because it doesn't cost you anything, and word-of-mouth referrals usually come from sources new customers trust.

Mintel recently interviewed 7,000 European consumers and asked how they would promote a new product. Their survey revealed that 60 percent mentioned they would tell a friend, 44 percent nominated discount coupons, 30 percent wanted to provide free samples, and 36 percent would plan a TV advertising promotion. Bailey's Irish Cream research found 5 percent of additional sales came through advertising and a staggering 64 percent through word of mouth.

Using customer word-of-mouth advertising to promote your company and goods must be a winning strategy. Customers will also tell you the best means of advertising to them. Target marketing is critical, so why not ask current clientele how they obtain information and how they found out about you in the first place?

Promotional Planner	Month		Promotional Recorder		
Important dates and events this month	Day & date	Sales $	Competitor activity	Weather	Other events worth recording
	1.				
Next month	2.				
	3.				
	4.				
Traditional product (types) for promotion (to suit your industry)	5.				
	6.				
	7.				
	8.				
	9.				
	10.				
	11.				
	12.				
Sales Last year $_____ This year $_____	13.				
	14.				
	15.				
	16.				
Promotional Budget Last year $_____ This year $_____	17.				
	18.				
	19.				
	20.				
Product/service promoted and media	21.				
	22.				
	23.				
	24.				
	25.				
	26.				
Keep copies of ads	27.				
Sales promotions, displays	28.				
	29.				
	30.				
	31.				
	Trading days in month		Ideas for next similar promotion		
Take photos of displays	Stock purchased, stock sold, stock carried over				

Book List

Schultz, Don E., William A. Robinson, and Lisa A. Petrison. 1992. *Sales Promotion Essentials. The 10 Basic Sales Promotion Techniques . . . and How to Use Them.* Lincolnwood, Ill.: NTC Business Books.

Chapter 18

Getting Existing Customers Back More Often

As discussed in the previous chapter, interruption marketing is the technique used to get the customer to your premises in the first place. Permission marketing is the technique you use once you have attracted them to your business. It can be split into two: how you market to them while they are in your store, and how you market to them after they have visited your store.

In-Store Marketing

By entering your garden center, the potential customer has given you permission to become a host, consultant, and seller. You should have a structured corporate approach to the way you deal with customers in your business.

Greeting Plan

You should be a host to every customer that walks into your business. Many retailers argue that they do not have time, yet the world's largest retailer, Wal-Mart, greets every customer that enters their stores. Your customers should expect a greeting when they enter your business; it should be a matter of courtesy.

The key points in being an effective greeter are looking the part, using positive body language, always making eye contact, and, if the opportunity exists, greeting customers verbally. The greeting should be a sincere gesture. Not only does this make the customers feel welcome, research shows that shoplifting is reduced dramatically.

Relationship Marketing

Stew Leonard Jr. of the U.S. and Fergal Quinn of Ireland are recognized as two of the world's leading retailers. Although from different sides of the Atlantic Ocean, both have a key philosophy that many retailers ignore: The best consultants in your business are your customers.

Integrating customers into your business is called relationship marketing. In practice, it means actively involving customers in promotion planning, staff training, quality inspections, market research, and other areas. It is much more than customer satisfaction through good service. It goes as far as involving them in the decision-making process.

Consultant Philip Kitler defines five stages in relationship marketing:

1. Basic stage—This stage is when the customer is receiving good service from sales staff.
2. Reactive stage—At this point, the salesperson starts building a relationship and suggests the customer contacts him or her if they require additional information or have a problem.
3. Accountable stage—The company now takes responsibility to phone the customer to check the customer is satisfied with the purchased product.
4. Proactive stage—The customer is contacted on a regular basis (at least four times a year) often by a newsletter providing ideas on new products and useful hints.
5. Partnership stage—This is the point where a customer becomes a consultant to the business, often through customer forums.

Customers can be used in a number of areas within your business. A wholesaler can involve them in designing a new label and point-of-sale material. This strategy is successfully carried out by Bransford Nurseries (U.K.) and Proteaflora Nursery (Australia) and is constantly used by such companies as Reebok and Reader's Digest. Nuriootpa Nurseries, a South Australian wholesale fruit tree grower, recently used the public to help design labels and a promotional campaign.

Quality and image are critical. Consumer mystery shoppers can check standards of plant quality, image, and service. You can become "store blind" and walk past the obvious problems while your customers notice them quite quickly.

Invite customers to join your training courses. Normally they are flattered and will soon get involved and offer ideas from a customer's perspective. Looking for a good salesperson? Ask customers to recommend someone prior to advertising. Ours is an industry people would love to join. Western Australia's Zanthorrea Nursery is almost 100 percent staffed by ex-customers.

Customers can also help you plan promotions and advertising campaigns. And, as mentioned in the previous chapter, recommendations from existing customers are one of the strongest ways to get new customers in your doors.

Customers can be valuable, on-going consultants. They can help you develop your business and increase profitability. Why not start employing them to help your business grow?

The following ladder represents the progression customers should go through as they come to know your business. Obviously, we'd like all our customers to be advocates. But remember: if you upset advocates, they

Figure 18-1. Take your customer up the ladder of loyalty.

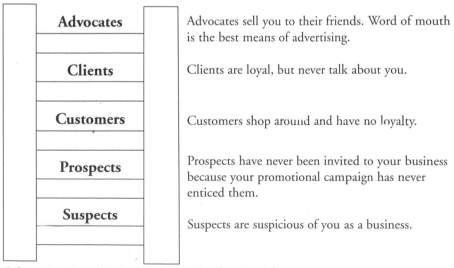

Advocates	Advocates sell you to their friends. Word of mouth is the best means of advertising.
Clients	Clients are loyal, but never talk about you.
Customers	Customers shop around and have no loyalty.
Prospects	Prospects have never been invited to your business because your promotional campaign has never enticed them.
Suspects	Suspects are suspicious of you as a business.

Reference: Janet Sernack, Design Management Consultants Pty. Ltd.

will decry your faults just as fervently as they had sung your praises. And bad word of mouth can destroy your business.

Out-of-Store Marketing

Marketing to your customers after they leave your store, not while they're inside, is what most people think of when they hear the term permission advertising. It's where consumers give you permission to market your products to them.

To do this successfully, you need personal details about your customers. The more details they are prepared to provide you, the more targeted you can be in providing a service to these consumers.

Permission advertising and marketing really took off when retailers had easy access to a computer and a reliable database program. Not all permission advertising and marketing needs a database, but most retailers will soon come to the conclusion that this will streamline their efficiency and allow them to communicate more easily to specific individuals. There are a number of reputable databases on the market. You need to select one that suits your needs.

The key is you need to know your customers. The better you know them, the more likely you are going to build a firm relationship with them and, as a result, grow your business.

Many retailers will tell you all you have to do is provide excellent service and provide what customers want. This is all very well, as long as you are aware that a lot of customers do not know what they want and customers' definition of excellence varies, as all customers are different. This means that the service you provide must be flexible to accommodate all types of customers.

The first step in developing your customer retention strategy is to analyze your existing strengths and weaknesses and to recognize the importance of customers in every task your team carries out. In analyzing your strengths and weaknesses, you have to ask, What do our customers care about? If you don't ask this question, you may not clearly understand your true strengths and weaknesses.

Authors often write about vision and that successful retailers have a customer service vision. What they really mean is that you have to be able to see the customer's role in everything you do and then ask, How does the customer benefit and what impact does this have on the customer?

Database: The Essential Tool

Customer relationship management is about having a mindset where you develop lifetime customers rather than one-transaction customers. You must look at each customer as an individual and provide for his individual wants. This is where your database is really valuable, especially if you have CRM (customer relationship management) software.

A fully integrated database is essential to any garden center that wishes to develop its relationship with customers. Some centers use databases exceptionally well, while others do not use them as effectively as they should.

The primary access to the database should be your customer's name, but you should also use other criteria, based on frequency of visits, categories purchased, annual spending patterns, and so on. The better the database, the more valuable information you can put on it. A well-planned database will start with personal details, address details, sales details, and customer history.

I recently worked with a garden center that had a garden club and database. It produced leaflets promoting the garden club and placed them in a stand just past the pay point. On the day I was there, nobody filled the leaflets in and the checkout operators did no promotion of the scheme. The customers who came in during that time were lost to the client's database. Once we encouraged the checkout operators to promote the scheme, we found customers were keen to become members, providing information for their customer profiles. Your aim should be to get all customers onto your database.

Management Memo

A recent survey asked senior marketers what they believe to be the most essential areas of marketing to focus on until 2005.
The results were:

Increased customer focus	59%
Innovation	34%
Quality	21%
Vision	15%
Integration	8%

—*Reference:* Smart Things to Know about Your Customers *by Ros Jay.*

Remember, knowledge is the key to being able to develop customer loyalty. With the knowledge via a database you can then start managing your customers. A database provides information for business analysis and is a source to be used for selective marketing. Once you have a database, you can decide what you need to know and find the best way to identify the data you need to obtain. With the correct search tools in your database, you should be able to analyze what your customers are buying and, ultimately, what is happening in your business. You'll know which customers prefer perennials or annuals, which purchase fertilizers, and which purchase garden décor items. Once you have developed a database, you can then develop your permission marketing aimed at individual needs.

How Do You Build Loyalty?

Every retailer is looking for loyalty. We have looked at the "hard" side (databases) to build loyalty, but you also need to develop the "soft" side (people skills). If you are going to succeed, you need a mix of high tech and high touch.

Customer loyalty is only increased when the customers' experience goes beyond what they expect. Your aim is to ensure the quality of your customer experiences is a source of real differentiation with that of your competitors.

Chris Duffy, the U.K. customer service guru, has a grid to identify the type of customer service you have to achieve, since satisfaction is not enough.

Customer Satisfaction Grid				
	How the Customer Reacts			
Brilliant	Wow	At Risk	Loyal	Raving Fan
How You Implement Customer Service	OK	Lost	Hedger	Loyal
	Ouch	Sabateur	Lost	At Risk
Bad		Ouch	OK	Wow
What Do You Do? **Bad** ⟶ **Brilliant**				

You have to aim at the loyal and raving fan boxes. If the customer says "ouch," he becomes very negative toward you and your company and can verbally destroy your business. If they feel you are OK, then loyalty is not an issue. You have to provide "wow" service.

According to Chris Duffy, to provide "wow," you must:
- Banish the bland. Always look for opportunities to provide a fun experience for your customers. My local garden center owner often bakes cakes and makes coffee to serve with her compliments on quiet days. On their silver anniversary, everyone wore silver, plus they encouraged their customers to dress up as well.
- Dare to be different. Always look at ways to be different. The only thing holding you back is yourself. Gardening is fun and creative; garden centers should be too.
- Think ahead of your customers. Try and foresee what the customer has not and then provide the solution. That may be a tree stake, fertilizer, or a substitute plant.
- Own complaints. Encourage customers to complain and then own the complaints. If a customer feels you own the complaint, they will become more loyal. Up to 90 percent of customers whose complaints have been resolved immediately to their satisfaction will become more loyal.
- Go beyond the call of duty. Charm your customers, and do more than they expect you to. The formula for success is Delight = Expectation + 1

Loyalty Cards, Smart Cards

Technology and telecommunications have taken leaps and bounds in directions not considered possible a mere decade ago.

Competition for customers has entered a different phase altogether. Interaction with current customers has become a necessity. For some, the club card/loyalty card has proven itself by increasing in-store customer spending.

Now brands find themselves in direct competition with retailers to get to know their customers better. With segmented analyses cross-referenced with data from other sources, combined efforts can achieve powerful predictive capability for all marketers. The future may be bright, it might be orange, but one thing is for sure: the consumer drives it. Interaction on a personal level—face to face, via direct mail but more likely SMS messaging and WAP—is the way forward.

> —Martin Williams. "Boot up your predictive power!"
> *Marketing and Business.* October 2000, p. 32.

Retailers have used loyalty cards for a number of years, but it is only now they are beginning to penetrate the garden center market.

Today, as a retailer, you need to maintain a meaningful ongoing relationship with your customers that also provides you with information that can help you help them. You need to identify your most profitable customers and understand how they spend their money with you. You need to know what your wallet share is of their gardening dollar.

This means that before you start manufacturing loyalty cards, you need a database system that is capable of combining relevant data on them as a person and what they purchase. You need to ensure you have the capability to obtain individual consumer data and to match that to transactional data information. Plus you need to ensure the customer is constantly kept up to date with the information that is relevant to them personally.

Consumers are non-loyal. They will shop a number of garden centers and may have loyalty cards from a number of centers. Your aim is to target your most loyal customers and increase your portion of their gardening dollars. Tesco's, the U.K.'s leading supermarket, now plans its buying and merchandising based on information obtained from its customers via its Club Card. That is really giving the customers what they want.

Keith Kirsten Garden Centers in South Africa have linked their loyalty card to other retailers. Customers collect points that they can use, for example, at the movies. Points earned at the movies can be used at the garden center. This card aims at targeting a specific lifestyle customer. This could be the way forward and may also earn new customers who attend movies but may not have heard of your center.

The Cost of Loyalty

I have come across garden centers who are completely dedicated to their loyalty card, whilst others have found it too expensive to implement. Tesco's and Sainsbury's supermarkets in the U.K. estimate a typical cost effective loyalty program costs 0.5 percent of sales. The main costs are up front in getting the program set up; overall operating expenses decrease significantly after launch and more people get involved in the scheme.

Remember, a loyalty program should not be offering discount to all your customers. It should be increasing your average sale by adding value to a specific segment of your customer base. That is far different than price slashing and discounting . . . and a lot less expensive.

What to Do with Children?

A common question that comes my way is, "Should we be providing facilities for children?"

Some retailers, believe it or not, are actually anti-children and place negative signs around their business to discourage younger shoppers and their parents. It's essential that you take a positive approach to this important market sector. Research carried out in Australia shows that the majority of today's gardeners were also keen gardeners in their younger years—they had gardens as early as at eight to twelve years old. We need to encourage the "tweens" age group to garden centers, as not only are they part of today's consumer market, but they are also the big spenders of the future.

Children fall into a number of different market categories based on age, and we should look at each age segment separately.

Management Memo

Child-Friendly Ideas for Your Garden Center

• A sandpit
• Stroller access
• Highchairs in your café
• Child-sized nursery shopping carts
• Baby changing facilities
• Display a "Breast-feeding mothers welcome" sticker
• Kids gardening club
• Children's garden
• Children's garden department
• Children's activity sheets
• Child-sized furniture and coloring equipment
• A pet zone
    —Reference: Ian Atkinson, "Child's Play . . . Kids in the Nursery." The Nursery Papers, *Issue No. 2000/14, Australia.*

The Zero to Two Year Olds

You're right—these are not consumers, but their parents are, and they prefer to shop in a store that is baby friendly. You therefore need to review your procedures and ask yourself if you are providing the facilities this market sector requires. These may include:

• Large parking spaces near the entrance where parents can easily extract a stroller from the car in safety. This parking space should be marked with a stroller sign, similar to those used for the handicapped parking spots.
• Changing facilities in a unisex toilet facility.
• You may also wish to provide complimentary disposable diapers and wipes as an extra service.
• Customers should be able to push a stroller around the whole garden center without being bogged down.

• You should have a company policy to carry out goods to parents' cars if their main concern is handling their baby.

The Three to Seven Year Olds

This is often the age group that causes most concern to retailers. Without strict parent control, they can cause havoc in a garden center. It's a brave retailer who chastises a parent for not looking after their offspring.

As a retailer, you have a responsibility to ensure displays are safe for your customers and their children. There have been recorded fatal accidents in garden centers where young children have overturned stone birdbaths and ornaments on top of themselves. Do ensure that you do a daily safety check of your retail areas. Some products have clearly written on them "Warning: Keep Out of the Reach of Children." If this is the case, then ensure these products are at least four feet above ground level, especially if they do not have childproof caps.

On a positive note, you should provide play areas for this age group. This will keep them out of mischief while their parents shop. If you do provide play facilities, do ensure the following:
- The play facility can be seen easily from around the center. Parents like to keep an eye on their children.
- It is secure, with a safe fence around it and a childproof gate and lock.
- It is clean. Children should leave this area as clean as when they went in.
- It has a surface that is safe and will not encourage bruised and damaged limbs. Some companies use mats, rubber mulch, clean wood shavings, etc.
- The play area is protected from the elements, especially sun and rain. If it is outdoors, it may need a shade cloth over the equipment.
- The area is supervised. Some of your team may need to be trained in child supervision and first aid. At least one of these members must be on duty when the store is open.
- The area is secure. Parents want to make sure their children will be there when they are finished shopping. Consider numbered wristbands or coded chips to ensure that children cannot leave with anyone other than the person who checked them into the play area.

• The equipment you provide stimulates your audience. Children have moved on from simple swings and slides. They are constantly exposed to more sophisticated play equipment at McDonald's and Disney, and they expect similar play areas wherever they go. If possible, tie it into a garden theme.

The Tweens

The most fashion-conscious consumer is aged between eight and twelve, and we can attract them into garden centers. Globally, one of the biggest marketing opportunities in our industry over the last few years has been to develop this market. This has taken the form of products and garden clubs aimed specifically at this age group. Some garden centers have created a children's department and position children's products as a separate category within this department.

Photo 18-1. This play area is simple yet stimulating to kids. Note the high fence to encourage kids to stay in and the soft sandy floor.

A wonderful way to reach children (and their parents) is to form a kids' garden club. The success of these clubs revolves around the enthusiasm and commitment of the organizer. It is my opinion that this should be delegated to someone in his or her early twenties who can still relate to your target market—and who has the energy to keep up with the kids!

Your children's garden club needs to be separate from any other garden club initiative you have. My local garden center has the "Bilby Club" (a bilby is a small Australian marsupial resembling a

Figure 18-1. The Bilby Club issues this newsletter to its young members. Inside are games, coupons, and contests.

rabbit). This club has a quarterly newsletter that is interactive, and they have regular meetings at the garden center. Children are encouraged to plant vegetable gardens, make hanging gardens in baskets, miniature gardens, funny pumpkin faces, Christmas tree decorations, and so on. Its objective is to encourage young people into the garden center, but also to ensure that their parents also frequent the garden center on a more regular basis.

Photo 18-2. Green Village Garden Center (New Brunswick, Canada) introduced a character to promote gardening to children.

Garden centers can also form close links with local schools to encourage conservation and gardening within the community. Invite schools to come to your center for a field trip, or offer to sponsor an after-school garden club. You may even want to donate or discount plants that the kids could use to spruce up the school grounds.

Teenagers

Once the majority of tweens hit their teenage years, you will find that pop stars and other entertainment holds sway over gardening. Do not be discouraged by this. Those young gardeners, if we have done our job right, will be back into gardening when they have married. The cycle will then start again.

Selling to Adults

Customers are a diverse lot, coming from various age groups, social backgrounds, and a wide range of experience. There are those who are time-poor and relatively affluent, the do-it-for-me group of customers, and those in the do-it-yourself (DIY) category. These groups have different needs, but the one thing you should do for both is to communicate—not sell—every ninety days, or once a season. You can communicate within your business and in their homes. Key communications tools include newsletters, thank-you cards, demonstrations, and how-to leaflets.

How-to Leaflets

Help guides or how-to leaflets are aimed at the novice user and the do-it-yourself market.

In providing this helpful literature, you educate your customers in the hope that they become advocates of your business and spend more money in your store.

Relate to your customers

Always design how-to leaflets with your target market in mind. These people often do not have technical knowledge, which is why they need the leaflet. So keep it simple, keep it attractive, and avoid technical jargon related to your industry.

Although pictures are easier to understand than words, text will also be necessary to get your message across. Use short sentences and bullet points or short numbered statements rather than lengthy paragraphs of text. For example, a garden center leaflet on container gardening might read:

Which containers should I buy for my patio?
When choosing your container . . .

- Consider the area of patio and the architecture of the site. If it is a natural look you are after, select stone or terra-cotta pots. If it is a modern environment, select plastic or fiberglass containers.
- Consider the size of plants you want. Select pots that are large enough for those plants.

Use words like *you* and *yours* when writing for the customer. Do not use language such as *I* and *we* when related to you as the retailer, for it sounds like you are dictating to your customer rather than holding a conversation with them.

Your leaflets should highlight the common questions customers would ask. For example: Where do I start? Which _____ should I select? Which _____ do I buy to get success? How do I put it together? How do I look after _____?

Provide extra information in separate boxes. The basic text is what the customer needs to know to be successful. Decide what additional helpful bits of information the customer should also know, and then highlight these items in separate boxes. These should-also-knows could include timesaving tips or fun ideas.

Include a shopping list

Remember your objective: to increase the average sale per customer. The leaflet gives you the opportunity to cross merchandise, add-on sell, and provide a complete package—including products available at your store—to do the job successfully. These additional products could be purchased now, in the future, or in stages. Therefore, your leaflet could include such lists as tools you will need to do the job, a shopping list to be successful, or items you will need to maintain value.

Readability and design

Ensure that people can easily read your leaflet. The most easily read type-faces are serif-based, i.e. letters with small feet (or serifs) such as this typeface, while san serif typefaces (those without serifs) are best used for headings and signage. Research by the Newspaper Advertising Bureau of Australia, below, supports this. The text was the same in the samples; only the typeface was changed.

Comprehension level			
	Good	**Fair**	**Poor**
Layout with serif body type	67%	19%	14%
Layout with san serif body type	12%	23%	65%

Color will help the customer identify your leaflet, as well as clarify certain illustrative points. Try using a different color for each leaflet. Make the cover of each leaflet very simple yet very distinctive. And of course, make sure that your logo and store identification are clearly recognizable to the customers.

Use in store

Do not place your leaflets on the counter, where they will soon become untidy. Leaflets need stands, and these are best positioned near the counter where your team can use the leaflets as an added-value tool. You can also place the leaflets next to specific products. So, as a supermarket would place a cheese recipe leaflet next to the cheese, a garden center would put a container garden leaflet next to the containers.

Make sure your team has read the leaflets, for the story they tell to the customer must correspond with that outlined in the leaflet. If not, you will end up confusing your customer and your store's credibility will be lost. Also make sure you've briefed your staff on the most effective way of using the material as a value-added benefit.

Demonstrations

Customers like to feel, taste, smell, touch, and generally get involved with products. The more interactive you can make their shopping experience, the more inclined they are to buy. One cost-effective method of introducing interactive retailing is through the use of demonstrations. These presentations usually relate to such activities as food sampling, tastings, cooking, gardening, and patio décor.

Apart from selling product, your aim with demonstrations should be to cultivate your customers so that they will come back to your store for further demonstrations on subsequent occasions. Have a billboard in your store highlighting the topic for next week's demonstration. If you can sell the promise, you may find that word-of-mouth advertising and reputation will become major marketing tools for you.

If you want to send a message to your customers that you are an interactive store with a vigorous approach to retailing, then demonstrations are an effective strategy to embrace—but your demonstrations must be worthwhile and regularly scheduled. For example, if you start organizing demonstrations for Saturday mornings, you must keep doing them every Saturday or run the risk of disappointing or even losing your customers. For this reason, demonstrations should not be undertaken lightly. They must be planned well ahead to make sure you attract the people and to ensure you have sufficient product in stock to sell during the event. Demonstration tables are available from most retail promotional supply companies. These look a lot more professional than the homemade variety and show your customers that you've put a lot of thought and effort into your demonstration program.

Demonstrators

Select demonstrators who are presentable and have personality, communication skills, and a flair for this type of work. They must be trained in all aspects of the product they are talking about. This means, for example, that if it is a food demonstration, then the instructor needs to be knowledgeable not only about the product itself, but conscious also of food hygiene regulations and should wear the recommended gloves and headwear.

Management Memo

Demonstrator Training

I strongly recommend that you put team members in a workshop prior to giving demonstrations to the public. This will strengthen the appropriate skills and help them to critically analyze their own abilities in this area. Get them to give a demonstration to the team before you let them loose on your customers. Public speaking is among one of the biggest human fears—second even to death according to several surveys. They are far better to overcome their initial fears in front of friendly faces rather than in front of strangers.

If you are using outside demonstrators, make sure they are wearing either the supplier's company uniform or your company's uniform. As far as your customers are concerned, they are part of your team and should look like it. Remember to debrief outside demonstrators at the end of the session. You may get some valuable tips on how to improve your store.

Demonstrated product

In the food industry, research tells us that 70 percent of customers will sample food provided by a demonstrator. The technique is highly effective, and if you position the demonstration strategically, 30 percent of those who have tasted will purchase.

Clearly the demonstration can be a major selling tool. It should be positioned in a wide aisle where people can stop and watch and talk without the feeling they are being hassled by other shoppers who are trying to pass them. Demonstrations are best located at least one-third of the way into the customers' shopping experience. This gives them sufficient time to become comfortable and relaxed in your store.

Many demonstrators place the product right next to them and, unwisely, nowhere else. Although some customers will purchase immediately while at the demonstration, others—particularly men—usually prefer to think it over for a few minutes without pressure or harassment from the demonstrator. So have product at the demonstration for the immediate impulse buyer, but also have a display ten to fifteen feet past the demonstrator for those customers who want to reflect on the purchase. Make sure this display is signed with a message such as "As demonstrated today by Mary."

Records

Keep a record of all demonstrations. Note when they were carried out, by whom, and the customers' reactions. Record the increase in sales of the product you were promoting. If your sales figures showed no improvement, you may have used the wrong product and/or the wrong demonstrator. You can make changes in future demonstrations and compare figures until you find the best demonstration.

Share your results with the product's supplier, as this will help both of you to build on the success of such demonstrations in the future.

Thank-You Cards

The market place today is very competitive in most retail sectors. With technological improvements, one's own customer base can be infiltrated by all types of other businesses offering the same products and services as your own.

The Internet and Web allow businesses to either set-up or expand without the need for a "shop front" to attack what may have been a niche that one considered their own.

Therefore creating customer loyalty is extremely important. If a customer is loyal to your business, your competitors have far less chance of poaching that customer on price or product. Providing you continue to offer a high standard of customer service (and we all know price is secondary to service) stock the products/services they want and create loyalty, you have that customer for life.

Of course, there are many ways to create loyal customers, e.g., the Thank You Cards; an important if not an essential element in running one's business. Those that do not have a high turnover of their client base spend a fortune on advertising and find it increasingly difficult to ward off competitors.

According to one garden center owner, "Our managers are constantly reminded that it is better and more cost effective to look after the customers we already have, rather than advertise for new customers."

Loyalty cannot be expected from customers, we must earn it. We must give the customer respect, offer the right advice and treat the customer as if he/she were the only customer we had. The customer should be made to feel important at all times and the shopping experience should be a pleasant one.

By doing all of these things we will get to "know" our customers as if they were "friends," thus creating loyalty which in turn contributes to a solid foundation for our business to survive and grow.

—Gary Crofts. "Thank You Cards Australia."

Newsletter article,

Hugall & Hoile Ltd., Australia.

Thank-you cards give you an opportunity to network with other retailers. We have a garden center client who sends thank-you cards and gifts. If a customer has spent, for example, $950, he will receive a complimentary meal at a local restaurant as a reward. The restaurant provides these to the garden center on the understanding that the person awarded the meal will bring friends. On average, the restaurant picks up two paid meals on very visit.

Newsletters

Over the last decade, company-to-customer newsletters have grown tremendously. The newsletter concept was developed by the wine industry as a means of communicating regularly with their customers. Nowadays, car companies, hardware stores, bookshops, and a host of other retailers and suppliers produce newsletters.

In the garden center newsletters fall into three categories: in-house newsletters used by large companies for internal communication, wholesaler newsletters aimed at retailers, landscapers, or resellers, and retail newsletters aimed at the public.

In-house newsletters

In-house newsletters should not replace staff meetings, but rather should be an addition to them. Their aim should be to keep people in touch and will ideally contain a mix of business and social matters. Management should have a say on what is included but might not necessarily have control of the publication. Newsletters tend to vary in publication times from once a month to quarterly or annually.

The content of in-house newsletters could include:

Business Matters	Social Matters
• New product releases	• Introduction of new staff
• New merchandising techniques	• Weddings, births, and birthdays
• Financial statement on business	• A staff member profile
• Projected business plans	• Social calendar
• Changes in the marketplace	• Family interest
• New equipment purchased	• Training courses attended
• Managing director's statement	• Social and sports
	• Team member achievements of
	• Local community events

Retailer-to-consumer newsletters

With the development of direct or target marketing, the newsletter has become one of the most effective means of building loyalty between retailers and their customers. The aim of the retailer newsletter is to increase the average spend by existing customers, either by encouraging them to come to the nursery more often or to spend more on their normal visits.

A newsletter or magazine shows your customers that you care about them and are not just interested in selling to them. It is also a means of building on goodwill in the community and is certainly one of your most effective forms of advertising. You will find your customers will start collecting the newsletters and pass them on to friends, extending your customer base.

Writing a retailer newsletter is not easy. It should be factual but entertaining and only softly sell the company and products. It can be as small as two sides of a single sheet or it can be a proper garden magazine with color photographs. Successful magazines may attract trade supplier advertising, which helps pay for their production. A garden magazine or newsletter can be written in-house or by using an outside writer or company. My experience is that most businesses can cope with producing only about four newsletters or magazines per year.

There are several tips to keep in mind when writing your newsletter.

A professional publication will impress your customers, while one with mistakes could actually hurt your reputation.

- Ensure the copy is well written.
- Keep the presentation looking professional.
- Do not hard sell; include plenty of ideas.
- Remember, most of your readers will be women—keep it feminine.
- Ensure the writing is relevant to the season.
- Keep in stock what you are writing about and merchandise it prominently. This may sound obvious, but it is the area where many retailers let themselves down.
- Keep the material light-hearted.
- Do not use jargon—most of the readers will not be horticulturists and will be confused or put off by terms they don't understand.
- Use plenty of illustrations and/or photographs.
- Have a set format for your newsletter so that it is easily recognized.
- Be consistent in your mailings. Once you have set a mailing time scale, keep to it.

According to research carried out by Brad Entwhistle, Image 7, Western Australia, the way you write the newsletter is critical to its success. Customers do not have time to read journals. The newsletter has to be read in seven minutes (the average person reads two hundred words per minute), otherwise even your keenest advocate will lose interest. Brad's formula for success is that the newsletter is no longer than four pages, set out as follows:

- Page one—Lead story, big picture, three-hundred-word maximum, no editorial from the boss
- Page two—Second lead, two articles in columns
- Page three—Profile page
- Page four—One-paragraph stories

Selling to Seniors

Some retailer consultants call them silver tops, but whatever term you use, the retired population is growing and is looking to be entertained. This market sector is more affluent than it has ever been and is having a major influence on today's retailing.

It is also a nostalgic market sector. They can remember the perceived "good old days" and wish many of the elements of that bygone era would come back. They are Internet literate, but when it comes to gardens, they prefer an old-fashioned look. As a result, we are seeing growth in David Austin's old-fashioned roses, herbs, scented plants, and old-fashioned perennials.

Seniors are also looking for extra facilities. It's this market that has helped promote refreshments in garden centers, and retirees are often the mainstays in garden clubs run by garden centers. The key is that they have time, are often lonely, and are looking at your garden center as a means of filling time and for social interaction. Do not be discouraged by this. They are more affluent and will spend on the right types of garden products.

Book List

Jay, Ros. 1999. *Smart Things to Know about Customers.* Oxford: Capstone Publishing.

Stanley, John. 1999. *Just about Everything a Retail Manager Needs to Know.* Brisbane, Australia: Plum Press.

Stanley, John. 2000. *The Nursery and Garden Center Manual.* Epsom, New Zealand: Reference Publishing.

Williams, Martin. October 2000. "Boot up Your Predictive Power!" *Marketing and Business Magazine,* p. 32.

Chapter 19

Shrinkage

Your aim is to sell everything you buy, but have you noticed you often purchase a hundred units of an item and end up selling only ninety-two? What happened to the other eight units?

This missing number of units is called shrinkage. The fewer the missing units, the higher your net profit. Therefore, part of your management strategy should be to measure and control shrinkage. Some shrinkage is a natural part of running a business, but other shrinkage is a reflection on the way you manage and control your business.

So what has happened to those missing units? They could have disappeared via a number of different avenues, and in this chapter we will discuss shrinkage and the management strategies you need to put into place to minimize them. It's a sobering thought that in some businesses you can double the net profit by bringing in a shrinkage policy and measuring it.

The majority of shrinkage comes from three key areas in your business: incorrect management procedures, customers, and team members. Are you ready for the shock? U.S. research in retailing reveals most retail-

ers operate on 2 percent shrinkage, and this can be divided up as follows:
- 51 percent: team members stealing product
- 24 percent: customers stealing product
- 9 percent: Incorrect receiving procedures
- 7 percent: damage to product
- 5 percent: accounting errors
- 4 percent: incorrect pricing

Shrinkage in garden centers can be as high as 4 percent due to the perishable nature of plants. Even 4 percent may initially seem a small amount, but a 2 percent saving of shrinkage over a year is equivalent to one week's turnover during that year. Or, look at it another way: Say a plant sells for $50.00 and has a gross profit of $5.00; if one item is stolen, then you need to sell ten more to break even!

You will not eliminate shrinkage entirely, but you can reduce it. Some shrinkage is uncontrollable and will happen whatever procedures you introduce to your business. Accidents and product damage will occur, but don't worry about it because it is out of your control. It's the shrinkage you have control over that you must concentrate on.

The only way you will reduce controllable shrinkage is to put management procedures into place, train the team so it is aware of the shrinkage, monitor your shrinkage constantly, and introduce team incentives to reduce shrinkage

I often argue with retailers that there is little difference between dry goods retailing and perishable goods retailing. The principles are exactly the same. It's just that in perishable retailing your management skills need to be sharper. But I do accept that when it comes to shrinkage there are some major differences that we need to address.

Many garden center operators will rightly argue that plants are a perishable product and, therefore, shrinkage is inevitable. This is true, but it still has to be managed. Shrinkage of plants compared to 'dry' goods will be higher, but it still has to be managed and be at an acceptable level.

Plant shrinkage still comes under controllable and uncontrollable factors.

Controllable Factors

The weather. Some plants, for example, may not be completely hardy in their first year outdoors. If you are aware of this, you may use frost protection over the plants in the garden center to reduce plant loss.

Always check the quality of plants when they arrive at your garden center. Check for pests, diseases and the type of growing media. Diseased plants or growing media lacking food will soon affect your shrinkage ratios.

Plant care is a key factor. Plants that are looked after carefully will clearly look healthy longer. Your plant manager needs to be aware that he has control over a high dollar value and lack of attention to detail can be a costly mistake.

Plants may be used to enhance the landscaping around your business. If this is the case, make sure this is recorded. This will enable you to factor this in when doing your end-of-year accounting.

Arrangement Pricing Table		
Plants Used	**Wholesale Price**	**Accumulative Total**
1.		
2.		
3.		
4.		
5.		
Accessories Used	**Wholesale Price**	
1.		
2.		
3.		
4.		
Labor Cost		
Total Production Cost		$
Gross Profit Required	____%	$
Retail Selling Price		$

Plants are also often selected to be used in mixed patio bowl arrangements. Again, make sure this is recorded in a book. Whilst on this topic, can I ask that you cost out this operation accurately? I have often come across wrongly priced patio containers due to a lack of accurate recording.

The table on page 261 will help you get a realistic price structure for made up arrangements. Note: Figure the amounts at unit cost and add the gross profit at the end of the calculation.

Discounts. Plants can be discounted because a customer is buying in bulk or you believe it will increase the stock turn. Whatever reason, it again should be recorded to ensure that your figures are accurate at the end of a given product life cycle.

Replacements under your guarantee policy. Do make sure you record what you replace, to whom, by whom, and why you need to replace the plants. It's critical that you keep a record in this area of management to ensure you keep guarantee replacement under control. Too many replacements means problems with your supplier or with your care.

Uncontrollable Factors

The weather. Occasionally the weather throws climatic factors at us that we have no control over. An unexpected storm, cold spell, or heat wave can do extensive damage to plant material. The unexpected will happen, but your aim is to keep these events to a minimum.

Hidden pest and disease factors. I had a client recently who purchased what looked like perfectly healthy camellias. After a few weeks, a disease became obvious. There was no way the grower or plant buyer could have anticipated this happening. It is rare, but it is an example of uncontrollable shrinkage.

Incorrect Management Procedures

Generally, 25 percent of shrinkage comes from incorrect management procedures. There are some key areas you need to address to reduce this wastage:

It's a proven fact that retailers who do not check deliveries correctly have more incorrect product counts from suppliers than those who do check. You should have a receiving procedure that ensures deliveries go to a specific location in your garden center and that product is physically counted and matched to the invoice prior to signing off. Don't be harassed by delivery drivers who challenge you because they're in a hurry.

Your job is to ensure you get what you ordered.

Shrinkage can also occur due to accounting errors. A regular check on stock versus what the computer says will allow you to pick these up as quickly as possible.

Always double check pricing. Incorrect pricing can result in a loss of dollars.

Customers

I have worked with many businesses where I have been advised that their customers do not steal. Yet 24 percent of shrinkage is due to theft by customers. Young and middle-aged women are more prone to stealing than any other demographic group. Young women tend to steal cosmetics and other health and beauty items and are not a real concern to us in garden centers. Middle-aged women are part of our target group, and a small percentage, given the opportunity, may steal from your business.

Do not have a policy where you look at everyone as a thief. With that attitude, you could put all of us off shopping at your garden center. But do put in systems and policies to reduce your risk.

Deterring Thieves

As a retailer, you have to accept that products will be stolen from your center, and you need to introduce strategies to minimize the opportunities for a thief. Luckily, the biggest fear of thieves within this group is embarrassment, and this can work in your favor.

For this reason, many companies introduce a "self-observance" system where customers can watch themselves. Self-observance systems include large convex security mirrors placed in strategic locations, and security monitor screens connected to cameras are an ideal deterrent and should be used in your garden center.

Management Memo

Security Systems Used in Retailing
1. Closed circuit TV (CCTV)
2. Floor safes
3. Lockable display cabinets
4. Observation mirrors
5. Cables, locks, and clamps
6. Plainclothes detectives
7. CCTV linked with electronic funds transfer at point of sale (EFTPOS)
8. Trial shoppers stealing
9. Uniformed guards
10. Electronic tags
11. Merchandise alarms
12. Observation booths
13. Dye tags
14. One-way glass on offices

Here are some other suggestions:

- Greet every customer. Companies where team members make eye contact, smile, and say hello as customers come into the center have half the shoplifting of those who do not acknowledge customers as they enter.
- Place products that fit easily in pockets (e.g., seed packets) in positions where team members can keep an eye on them from key locations in the garden center.
- Don't place products between the cash point and the parking lot. If you do, you are encouraging customers to load the car without paying.
- Keep small, expensive products in secure locations. Ensure they are still visible to the customer, but cannot be readily picked up.
- Ensure everyone has attended a training workshop on shrinkage and how to apprehend customers.

The most notorious position for shrinkage is the checkout. Richard Burns of Intercept Security Services provides a checklist of precautions for retailers to introduce at this location. This includes:

- Always check the price of all products that arrive at the checkout damaged or with missing or swapped-over price tickets.
- Always keep the cash register closed between transactions and locked if it's unattended.
- Always inspect all items, especially where a customer can place small items in big items. A common trick is to hide small items between two stacked empty containers.
- Always block checkout aisles that are not in use. You may want to put a display on wheels that you can roll out when it's needed to block the aisle.
- Be extra careful when a large bill is tendered for a low-priced item. Get into the habit of counting out the change as you hand it to the customer.
- Wrap and seal expensive dry goods, such as gift lines, and attach the receipt to the outside.
- If boxes look like they have been tampered with when they arrive at the checkout, then always check the contents.
- Put add-on sale products at the checkout in a position where team members can observe them.

If you've implemented the above strategies, you have dramatically reduced your chances of being shoplifted. But your center is not theft-proof. You still will have people stealing, and you or a team member will have to take action. Your team should know how to apprehend a shoplifter, especially as professional shoplifters use some ingenious methods to hide products. The following are some ideas of how to deal with shoplifters:

While still inside your garden center, team members should approach the person suspected of taking product as a potential customer. Always approach from the front, greet, and use a service approach. For example, "Good morning. If that is a gift you are purchasing, I can gift wrap it for you." The person will either buy the item or put it back.

Only apprehend a person if you are 100 percent certain they have stolen and when he or she has left the garden center. The law is complex, and the last thing you want is a customer taking legal action against you. You are making a citizen's arrest, and you must have actually seen the person remove the product and hide it. Keep an eye on the shoplifter at the times and be confident the person has not dumped the product somewhere in the garden center. You must be confident that he has not paid for the product and he has left the garden center.

My advice is that you never approach a person on your own. Take a colleague and use words like, "We believe you have a product in your possession which is from our garden center and has not been paid for. Will you please accompany us back to the garden center so that we can discuss the matter?" Do not physically touch the person, and conduct the interview in a private office. It's best to get the police to handle the matter from this point.

Employee Theft

As retailers, we often get concerned about shoplifters and what they are stealing. This is a serious problem, but, alas, you also have to remember that a large amount of stealing that occurs in a garden center comes from team members. Overall, 51 percent of shrinkage comes from employee theft. It's your biggest challenge, and the one we would like to forget, as we trust our team.

I am not suggesting that all your team is stealing—or even that 51 percent of your employees are—but there is a minority of team members who, given the opportunity, will steal. This will cost you dearly.

Internal thieves have the opportunity to steal either cash or product and the first priority as a business owner is to accept it goes on and that you are not immune. Every business should have a theft control strategy to minimize theft in the business; this strategy should include:

- Screening of new employees when they join your organization. A thorough pre-employment screening conveys a message to all your team that you are concerned and that you expect the highest integrity from each member.
- Introduce business procedures that deter theft opportunities. These include requiring team members to delegate selling to other team members when it involves making a sale to family or close friends.
- Staff bags should be left in a secure area, and all sales to staff should be recorded.
- Do not let your team members just take plants home because they have deteriorated in quality. Record the plants as a loss, and charge your team members a nominal price for them. If you don't, you may find some team members neglecting plants and then creating new landscape gardens using your plants.

Finally, do not get over-concerned with people stealing from you. If you have sound management strategies and an aware and trained team, your shrinkage will be an acceptable percentage of your business. It only becomes a problem when management is weak.

Book List

Stanley, John. 1999. *Just about Everything a Retail Manager Needs to Know.* Brisbane, Australia: Plum Press.

Chapter 20

The Role of the Buyer

Many people would argue that the most important person in your organization is the buyer. If the buyer makes a bad judgment, then it could cost you a lot of dollars. If her judgment is accurate, then she can make you very rich.

In the past, the buyer's role was relatively simple. A supplier dropped in, you purchased what you liked, and you sold it. Times have changed. The supply and retail chain has become more sophisticated, especially since the appearance of large box stores with garden departments. This means we have all had to become more professional in dealing with each other. Negotiation skills are now critically important if you are going to be an effective buyer.

A buyer needs to know the product, local buying habits, pricing, stock control, and the best sources of products. He or she needs to have skills in negotiations, communications, and financial controls. Hence, there are not a lot of people in the marketplace that can be classified as professional horticultural buyers.

I believe the most important skill a buyer needs is the skill of negotiating. Negotiating is the process by which we create agreement on a specific issue between parties with different views. In horticultural buying, one party wants to normally sell as much product as possible at his price. The other party needs to negotiate the right product mix at the right price to enable him to sell it within a given period at an acceptable profit.

Although we negotiate everyday of our lives, many people have a fear of negotiating. This may be due to cultural differences, fear of losing or looking the fool, not having all the facts, or just human nature, which is to avoid things we are not comfortable with.

In negotiating, the skill is to concentrate on what you want, but normally you start the process by asking for a different position. Negotiating can result in a lose/lose outcome, a win/lose outcome, or a win/win outcome. A professional negotiator aims at a win/win outcome, where both sides win. This is a benefit to both companies and builds loyalty. Your objective should be a preferred supplier–preferred retailer relationship. In most situations, to achieve this you need to use the give/get principle.

The Give/Get Principle

When applied to negotiations, the give/get principle provides for a better chance of success. The principle simply means that both parties enter the negotiations willing to give something in return for receiving something. To be a successful negotiator, you have to be prepared to give something to the other party. Remember, when you give concessions, you should ensure they are valuable to the other party but are cheap to you.

As a horticultural buyer, you may use the give/get principle as follows:

Retailer Concession	Supplier Concession
Exclusive product release in your store	Train the retail team in your product
Preferred sales position in store	Supplier provides merchandise stand without charge
You recommend their product to your customers	Complimentary consultancy session

It's worth considering what are the characteristics you feel are important to be effective. The ideal buyer will be a good listener, communicator, professional looking, have positive body language, and know the product. A successful buyer will have honed his questioning techniques;

good questions enable you to get the answers you need to make informative decisions.

Some tips are:

- Start the process by using open-ended questions. This will enable you to control the conversation and get the facts you need early on in the transaction.
- Use direct questions when appropriate.
- Do not use questions as a means of intimidating the other person.
- Always ask the other party how she feels the transaction is going.
- Don't ask leading questions. You may end up with a win/lose situation.
- Keep asking until you get the information you need to make a sound decision.
- Ask "What if?" It gets the other person to explain their intentions.

The Buying Process

A successful buyer uses a four-step process when dealing with a supplier.

Step 1: Preparation

Before you meet a supplier, write down your objectives, your reference points for the negotiations, and what you want to have achieved post negotiations. This is why it is advisable to only see suppliers by appointment. A supplier who just "drops in" because he was passing by knows he has the upper hand before he starts the process. If you are going to establish a partnership, you need preparation time. Also, plan the place, duration, and strategy of the appointment. To take the initiative, set the time and agenda and let the other party know.

Decide beforehand what concessions you would like and what concessions you are prepared to give. Get all the facts, as this will build your confidence. Know what your bottom line is.

Step 2: Present Your Opening Position

At a meeting, forget the past experiences (which may be difficult). Be diplomatic, smile, and read the other person's gestures, body language, and posture.

Conflict is an acceptable part of negotiations, but hopefully it's part of the normal negotiation and never gets heated. Structure your argument based on: where you have been before, what the team thinks, how you see the situation at present, and a comparison of differences.

Remember, the give/get principle. Plus, you will need to handle objections. Listen, do not interrupt, appreciate the other person's point of view, and identify objections. Counter objections with desirable features and benefits.

Step 3: Negotiate to Reach an Agreement

Negotiate as little as possible and only on what are, for you, minor issues. At the same time, do not abuse your power; be modest, listen, and get the other party used to your plans. Take the other party's objectives into account, and do not get into a price negotiation—this is where we all often lose.

Step 4: Close the Negotiation

There are indicators of when you have been successful in a negotiation. You need to know the clues so you close the negotiations at the right moment.

Look for these signs:
- The counter-argument fades.
- The difference in positions gets very small.
- Other party starts talking details.
- You are given a personal invitation to visit their establishment.
- The other party offers to draw up the contract.

How to Buy Effectively

Retailing is the process of buying and selling products. To be successful, you need a policy that enables you to buy the right product at the right price at the right time, which then allows you to sell it as soon as possible at a profit. Many businesses work on a system where they calculate a 1 percent increase on the buying price for every month the product sits on the shelf or bench in the garden center. All of which means that the buying process is critically important for retailers. Get it wrong, and the result can be a loss.

Develop a Positive Relationship with Suppliers

You are your suppliers' customer, and the relationship you have with them should be the same as the one you have with your own customers. It is a relationship built on trust. So you should select suppliers you can depend upon when it comes to price, quality, value, and timely delivery.

Select Your Suppliers Carefully

Your customers select their retailers carefully, and you should select your suppliers with the same care. You often have a choice between buying directly from a manufacturer or from a wholesaler. Whichever avenue you source, your decision should be based on such considerations as:

- The type of product you are buying
- The origin of the product
- The size of your business
- The proximity of the suppliers
- The supplier's policy on buying
- The financial status of the supplier and yourself
- Price

Suppliers can be contacted in a number of ways—via the Internet, by visiting cash-and-carry wholesalers, attending trade fairs, group buying or co-operative buying, central office buying, or through representatives visiting your store.

Retailers today have a wide choice of suppliers offering similar products. To help you make the right decision as to which supplier to use, a decision-matrix can prove useful. Consider the following example provided by John Berens (from *Journal of Retailing* 71/7). Score each supplier who you believe has the same priorities as you. The supplier with the closest weighting to yours is the one to select.

Your Suppliers' Priorities Weighting as You See Them							
		A	B	C	D	E	F
Suppliers can fill orders	5	3	4	4	2	0	1
Mark up adequate	4	2	4	3	0	1	2
Customer requests you stock it	1	1	2	4	3	0	0
Supplier supplies fashion changes	3	2	3	4	1	0	0
Supplier helps promote	2	1	0	3	1	2	2
Supplier delivery policy	6	0	1	3	4	3	0

Plan Your Purchases

Buying has to be planned and the astute buyer will use the following formula:

Planned purchase at retail price = planned sales + planned reductions + planned end-of-month stock - planned beginning-of-month stock

Remember that "planned purchase at retail price" is not how much the buyer can spend. Once you have this figure, you will then be able to calculate a buying price and a budget for your buyer. The chart on the next page will help you plan your purchases.

Ask Questions before Accepting Bulk Discounts

Suppliers often supply discounts for early bird buying and bulk buying. Before taking up such offers, you will need to consider such questions as: Is it a slow moving item for you? What extra costs of handling and storage will you need to add? What is the financial cost for you to carry this stock for a longer period? Do you have the storage space? Will you sell the entire purchase? Will the supplier guarantee the goods? What assistance will the supplier provide to help you move their product on to the customer?

Management Memo

Research in the United States shows that retailers look for the following in selecting a supplier:
* Responsiveness to specific retailer needs
* Commitment to follow through
* Flexibility
* On time delivery
* Integrity and honesty
* Good communication

Consider Central Buying

Larger organizations often rely on central buying using specialist buyers who, in theory, should be able to select better deals as they are specialists in their field.

Buying Options

Life was so much easier in the past. You received a nursery catalog and visited your local trade show, and you had a complete picture of what stock was available. Today, the options are a lot more extensive, plus a global marketplace means products do travel around the world before they get to your garden center. As a buyer, you need to be in tune with a number of different avenues.

Purchase Planner	Aug	Sept	Oct	Nov	Dec	Jan	Season total
1. Planned BOM stock	$197,919	$225,168	$243,811	$254,233	$243,880	$232,825	$251,500
2. Planned sales	48,273	54,919	59,466	55,268	87,100	44,774	349,800
3. Planned reductions (total of a + b + c below)	5,971	3,379	4,159	5,493	3,054	7,317	29,733
(a) Markdowns	5,247	2,915	3,267	4,664	1,748	6,645	24,486
(b) Shortages	483	549	595	553	871	448	3,499
(c) Employee/other discounts	241	275	297	276	435	224	1,748
4. Planned EOM stock (BOM stock for following month)	225,168	243,811	254,333	243,880	232,825	251,500	—
5. Planned retail purchases (items 2 + 3 + 4 - 1)	81,493	77,301	74,047	50,408	79,099	70,766	433,114
6. Planned cost purchases (initial markup is 44.3% so cost is 55.7% of item 5)	45,392	43,057	41,244	28,077	44,058	39,417	241,245
7. Planned cumulative initial markup (44.3% of item 5, or item 5 - 6)	36,101	34,244	32,803	22,331	35,041	31,349	191,869
8. Planned gross margin (item 7 - 3)	30,130	30,505	8,644	16,838	31,987	24,032	162,136

The Wholesale Catalogue

This may come in the form of a traditional paper catalog or a CD, but is still a major reference point for identifying what product is available in the market. Catalogs give you the opportunity to comparison-shop in the comfort of your own office.

Plantmarts

Plantmarts have had a real impact on the market in recent years. The concept is relatively new to the U.S. but has been established for a long period in Holland and then refined by the Australians.

A plantmart is basically a one-stop shop. As a buyer, you go to one site and can see nursery stock from a number of growers. You can then order and have one delivery, but from a mixed number of growers. This enables you to compare quality, quantity, promotions, and prices at one site and then plan your stocking levels and save on delivery costs. Plus, it gives you an opportunity to "top off" your stocking levels on a regular basis. This saves you spending capital on stock that will be slow moving in your center. Many retailers like this system as it ensures that they maintain fresh-looking stock, and as a result, they can increase their stock turn.

Management Memo

According to the Australian Trade Show Bureau, surveys of those attending trade shows have revealed that:
• 60 to 70 percent of attendees expect to make a purchase of an exhibition product within two months of the trade show.
• 60 percent of all attendees do make a purchase within twelve months of the show.
• But 83 percent of trade show contacts are never followed up by a representative from the company within the next twelve months.

Sales Representatives

Putting a salesperson on the road is becoming more and more expensive, but many businesses still rely on sales representatives visiting your business. Make sure they make an appointment prior to visiting you. You need to plan for such a meeting to maximize the opportunity, as discussed previously.

Trade Shows

Trade shows are getting bigger and as a result are becoming places for looking at stock rather than buying stock. Suppliers do use trade shows as an opportunity to

launch new plants and promotions and, therefore, these
are ideal opportunities to
familiarize yourself with new
concepts and discuss them
face to face with a company
representative. Before going
to a trade show, make sure
you have plenty of business
cards and a pad of paper and
pen to enable you to make
relevant notes.

Photo 20-1. Trade shows are fabulous ways to
get an overview of the market, talk to sales
reps and company executives, and get hands-
on experience with the products you may want
to buy. Ball Publishing's booth at the Ohio
Short Course is a busy spot, where people can
leaf through the books they see in the catalog.

Due to the size of trade
shows, my advice is to plan
whom you must see prior to
entering the show. I would
then walk the show quickly
and make a note of new companies, products, or promotions I need to
look at. I would then go back to the start of the trade show and plan my
tour of "must see" booths. At the end of the show, you need to take time
to list all the follow-up situations when you get back to your office.

The Web

More and more suppliers and growers are using the World Wide Web as
a means of introducing their products to retailers. As far as the retailer is
concerned, this is quick and easy and can be done at any time of day,
such as after closing or on weekends. As long as you trust the supplier,
this is a cost-effective way of buying stock.

Open Days

Many growers have open days to allow you to inspect stock. These are
often combined with training sessions or social gatherings. This is an
opportunity to meet colleagues and growers in a relaxed atmosphere. It's
also an opportunity to discuss promotional opportunities with growers.

Contract Growing

Larger retailers around the globe have the opportunity to form contracts
with growers. A contract is where the retailer stipulates how many plants

he will purchase over a given period of time and at what price. The advantage is the retailer has a guaranteed supply of a unique product to his specifications. The disadvantage is that if he doesn't sell the stock due to bad weather or changing trading patterns, he still ends up paying for the plants.

Branding Issues

Earlier in this book, I discussed the fact that your garden center is your brand. Various growers are developing product brands, and as a buyer you need to be aware and prepared for plant and product branding and how it fits into your buying process.

Dry goods branding has been around for many years and names such as Scott's and Miracle-Gro have become household names. The latest challenge has been in plant branding. Companies such as Herb Herbert International have branded a whole category, herbs, internationally with huge success. Global branding is on the increase. Ball Horticultural Company and Anthony Tesselaar International have branded the My Favorite range of easily grown color plants for release around the world.

20-1

Figure 20-1. Plant brands are becoming more common. Flower Fields, Proven Winners, Simply Beautiful, and My Favorite (pictured) show up in garden centers across the country.

Brands are more than labels on a plant. We have grown up with brands in our lives and have come to trust specific brands. It has taken a long time for branding of plants, mainly due to the inconsistency of growing plants and the historic makeup of the wholesale industry. But with improvements in growing techniques and global networking by growers, this is all changing. Branding will be focused to specific customer needs, rather than promoting a specific company. The aim is to relate to a customer's lifestyle rather than promote a grower. As a buyer, you need to consider: Does this brand complement my image? Does it detract from my company brand or enhance it? Does the brand reflect my customer's lifestyle? Is the grower consistent in supplying the brand?

The brand issue, I feel, will be one of the major challenges and opportunities in our industry over the next few years. Start thinking about it now so you are prepared down the road.

Chapter 21

Coffee Shops in Garden Centers

by Anne Sugden

You have no coffee shop, but you'd like to open one. What processes must you go through to start proceedings?

Start with a discussion of the people who make decisions in the company. Decide what you want from your business. Is it successful? Is it profitable? Are you proud of it? I ask these questions because if the answer is no to any of these, then you should not even be thinking of starting along the route of a new business. And, yes, that's what a coffee shop will mean—a completely new business.

So, here we are in your discussion having agreed that all is well elsewhere. What is there to discuss? Why do we want a coffee shop? Is it to give service to customers? Is it to make a profit? Is it to add to the store and encourage customers to linger longer? Is it to give customers a reason to visit the store because your store has something to offer that other stores don't?

These are the kind of questions we should be asking and hopefully all agreeing that a coffee shop should have quality, consistency, good value for the money, giving the kind of service that you feel matches the rest of your store and that your customers know and like.

Finance

There are two things that are essential at this early stage: First is access to the money required for this new venture and second is planning permission from the planning office in your community.

Money can be raised from a number of different sources; chapter 3 discusses some ways of financing your business. Adding a coffee shop will be a major expense, and new coffee shops always cost more money than you have budgeted for. The costs can escalate if you are not totally clear on precisely what you want!

Planning

Planning permission can be more difficult than raising money. It depends where you live, what kind of land you want to build on—greenbelt, residential, and so on—so a good architect who knows his way around the planning office is an asset at this stage. Do not start building before you receive a permit. It is not unknown for a jurisdiction to issue an order imposing removal of work done to date.

The time waiting for zoning approval may be the time that you need to go out to contract for the construction. Unless the architect specializes in catering, it is better to rely on a catering consultant for advice and assistance with kitchen and counter designs, as this is a specialist area. A professional will be able to advise the easiest and most successful way of putting together a drawing and coordinating the planning application along with the architect. You will save money, the consultant will process the job faster and more efficiently than you could, and you will save yourself a lot of hassle. Let others take the strain—that's what they are there for.

Ensure that whoever is managing the project (please check legal requirements that may apply to certain types and sizes of operation) furnishes you with a full schedule of operations and a chart of time frames showing when each phase of the work should start and finish. It often happens that the project is not completed within budget and/or time frame agreed. If this is likely to result in lost sales/income and added costs, you should seriously consider ensuring that adequate and appropriate penalty clauses are included in the contract to help focus the mind of all those involved!

Design

The style of service you want to provide will affect the design of your coffee shop. So before hiring your first sketch, decide what kind of service you want to give.

Is waitress service what you want for your shop? This method can give great service and—if the service is speedy—can lead to very satisfied customers. Waitress service is very appropriate for an up-market store where customers want to sit in a restaurant rather than a coffee shop. It's a more formal experience. However, this style of service can be expensive in payroll. You tend to need more staff, as at least one person is busy taking and delivering orders and another person is needed in the kitchen to prepare and cook the food ordered. With waitress service, there is usually no food on display and since customers cannot see what the food looks like, impulse buys are harder to make. Since everything happens in the kitchen and the wait staff are not involved in the preparation of food, they tend to be less aware of what they are serving and cannot sell as effectively. The design of the kitchen will be quite different if you chose waitress service, and that's where you should be clear on what you want and then use the professionals to achieve a super job.

If, on the other hand, you think you would like a self-serve counter, with lots of lovely food displayed for customers to select, then you require a totally different type of kitchen layout and counter setup. The staff costs are not as high, and customers sit in their seats for half the time that they would with waitress service. You may think that this is insignificant, but it is very important. Consider a busy day with customers lining up to go into your coffee shop. There is definitely no way that you can politely rush customers with table service. If your store gets very busy at peak times, then a self-serve style of service is better for the customers, as they are served faster. They can also see the food and tend to make larger purchases, buying more cakes and extras than they would if they could not see or help themselves to it.

When discussing what equipment you require with your professionals, make sure they know precisely what you want to achieve with your coffee shop. The positioning of the equipment will denote whether the food is prepared in the kitchen and therefore served by the staff to the customer's table. If your design enables the staff to remain at the counter to meet and greet customers, have food well displayed, and serve from the counter without going into the kitchen, then you will have a very efficient system. Meanwhile, the kitchen can be dedicated to food preparation, cooking, and baking.

Seating

After concentrating on your kitchen design, you need to turn your mind to the eating area. "How many seats?" is the most frequently asked question. It's not necessarily the number of seats, but also the configuration of the tables. You need a combination of twos and fours, some round but mostly square, as they take up less space. Less than forty seats is not viable. If customers come in ones or twos, which often happens in quiet periods, even if you have twenty tables, you can only seat thirty people at the most. This is because people do not like sharing tables! A good number is sixty to eighty seats, depending on the size of your store and your projected turnover.

Ambience

It is essential that ambience, lighting, decoration, color scheme and flooring, crockery, cutlery, furniture, and uniforms all compliment each other and the rest of your store so that it becomes easily integrated into one unit. Choose seating that is comfortable, light to lift, and easy to clean. Plain, simple lines are best. And if chairs have arms, they should fit under the tables to make more room. Tables should be adjustable (where floors are not even), not too heavy, easy to clean, and very stable. Seek the advice of your architect or an interior designer, but, remember, you don't have to follow their suggestions slavishly if you are not entirely happy about any of them. After all, it's your operation and your money; you may as well have it as you wish.

If you have a system where food is displayed to the customers, then highlight the food rather than the furnishings. The food is what you are selling, not the fixtures and fittings.

Catering Equipment

Having gotten the designers and builders underway, you need to go out to bid out three catering companies. Your professional catering consultant will be able to help put the equipment schedule together, but it's critical that you choose a menu before selecting equipment. Remember that catering equipment companies will be keen to encourage you to buy all kinds of different equipment to fit every eventuality; there is no advantage to this random selection. Far better to focus on your menu, buy the right equipment, and add specialized pieces of equipment as and when you want to expand your menu. You may purchase, rent, or lease the equipment, so investigate the various options and choose the best for your circumstances.

Menu

This is an opportunity to carry out a customer survey to discover what your customers would want and expect from your coffee shop service. This can also help you to know where your main competition is and why it's popular.

The menu should be enticing and different in order to give your customers reason to visit your establishment. It's better that it is not too complicated or expensive to prepare and serve. It is essential to cost your menu correctly and accurately to maximize your profit. It should be costed at a minimum of 3.5 times above cost (this includes sales).

Recruitment and Selection

Selection of appropriate staff is essential to the success of your operation. The way that advertisements are worded can influence who applies. Think carefully about the wording. Write what the job entails and what you can offer. It's not necessary to include salary; this can be discussed when you get to the interview stage.

Catering is demanding physical work, and your staff needs to be aware of and maintain the highest level of customer care while working well under pressure. Both you and they must be aware of all local and national legislation referring to the preparation and sale of hot and cold foods and ensure that such laws are adhered to. Make sure that you have planned a training program *before* you open and that all staff is appropriately and effectively trained. Training should commence with induction, then the specialist food hygiene, safe food handling, customer awareness, and care and sales techniques. Follow up with refreshers about a month or two after you have opened and regular training thereafter.

You should allow about one week for the initial training and incorporate team-building exercises, as most, if not all, your staff will probably never have met before. Thorough work on team building will lead to a strong cohesive group that will be capable of managing well under pressure.

When selecting for interviews, remember that the job the applicants are doing currently will influence how they approach the job you are offering. For example, if the applicant is working in a waitress-style restaurant, then she may not be familiar with a self-serve style coffee shop, and vice versa. The past and present experience will have an effect on how potential employees will do the job.

When interviewing, adhere to the criteria that you require from the position. Explore vague answers and make sure the *interviewee* knows what you are looking for at the end of the interview. It could save you being dissatisfied later. When you have made your decision, check references and offer the position if the references are satisfactory.

Food Costs

So here you are—it's opening day! The register is ringing, customers are buying, and your staff is working. Congratulations! You have achieved stage one of your coffee shop enterprise.

The next step is to manage your new business without being involved in the day-to-day aspects. Manage at a distance by seeing what is happening, tasting the food, talking to customers, and, most important, looking at the figures.

I mentioned food costs in the menu section above, and this issue is complicated. You must keep on top of these costs and not assume that they are static. Even if what you pay for the food products remains constant, myriad other factors will influence the final cost.

Figuring Food Cost

You should aim for about a 30 percent food cost for your coffee shop. The following formula will help you determine what you need to price a food item at to achieve this goal:

Cost of portion $\times$ 4 = selling price, including sales tax

Controlling Food Cost

Food costs can only be controlled when the problem is known. Read and understand the stock sheets, and make sure that staff members who need to can do the same. The answer is usually evident if you understand what the numbers are supposed to look like. Once you identify the problem, you can take the appropriate action to bring costs back in line.

The following list includes areas that you can control. If one of these is a problem, your business will not be as profitable as it can be. If several are out of control, you may soon find yourself closing your coffee shop.

1. Theft
   A. Cash
   B. Stock
2. Portion control
   A. Over-portioning to customers
   B. Over-portioning to staff
3. Waste
   A. In preparation
   B. Overproduction, food not being sold and having to be thrown away
   C. Incorrect storage
   D. Receiving stock in poor condition
   E. Food drying out in hot plate or while on display
4. Staff meals
   A. Staff eating more than the agreed allowance
   B. Staff eating high-cost food items
5. Pricing
   A. Incorrect prices being charged
   B. Items not being charged for by cashier
   C. Incorrect pricing of new recipes, functions, etc.
6. Purchasing
   A. Purchasing food stock at high prices, i.e., vegetables, fresh meats, breads, and emergency purchases through petty cash
   B. Purchasing unauthorized products with high food costs
7. Deliveries: Make sure that you, your manager or other responsible person checks every delivery personally. Check for:
   A. Incorrect quantities being delivered, short delivery
   B. Stock not received at all, but you are being charged
   C. Substitute product at a higher cost being delivered by supplier

8. Sales mix: Producing and selling a high percentage of products that have a high food cost
9. Recipes: Recipes not being followed, resulting in higher usage of raw food items
10. Stocktaking: Incorrect stocktaking may produce a high food cost if stock is not counted or excluded from the closing figure

Other Costs

Food costs are not the only ones to keep watch over. Employees and overhead must be kept in line too, or else your business will be in trouble. Wages should be 25 percent of turnover. Overhead should be approximately 20 percent of turnover.

If you keep to these guidelines, and have good food and good service, you should see steady profits in your coffee shop.

About Anne Sugden

Anne is a catering consultant who works with garden centers around the world. Anne can be contacted at:

Anne Sugden
Anne Sugden Enterprises
Well House, 1 Victoria Street,
Haslingden, Rossendale, BB4 5DL
United Kingdom
Telephone: +44 1706 223718
Fax: +44 1706 830169
E-mail: annesugden@aol.com

Chapter 22

Benchmarking:
Its Role in Your Garden Center

Operating your garden center without measuring your success is exceedingly dangerous. You need to measure how your business is performing against a reliable standard. To do this, you need set formulas and the correct figures.

Benchmarking your business is less common in the garden center industry than in many other retail sectors, but this does not mean it is less important.

The data you require for benchmarking can come from a number of different sources. The main sources are:

1. Your own historic records. It's relatively simple to compare your performance for one month compared with the same month in previous years.

2. Group performance indicators. If you belong to a garden center group, the group may share certain financial data and produce group performance figures. This gives you an indication of how your business is performing compared to your colleagues.

3. Association indicators. Organizations such as Garden Centers of America provide benchmark figures on how the industry is performing nationally. Again, this is valuable information, but

remember that it does cover a wide geographic area and a multitude of different businesses that are all structured differently. These figures will give you a ballpark figure to help you steer your business.

4. Research units, universities, colleges, and private research organizations are often commissioned to produce development reports on the garden industry. These reports are valuable, but do make sure you know where they were done and how the sample figures were generated. Obtaining benchmark figures from one geographic location and adapting them to yours can be helpful, but also misleading if not used correctly. Whatever benchmark figures you do come across, check when the figures were produced. The last thing you want is to benchmark your business against figures that are, for example, twelve months out of date.

The sophistication of your benchmarking can vary greatly. I have some clients who only monitor average sale per customer, whilst others monitor everything including sales per square foot for every plant and product category sold. The key is to only benchmark in areas where you will use the information to improve your business. Don't get drowned in figures that you do not know what to do with.

What Are the Essential Benchmark Areas?

It's easy to fall into the trap of gathering measurements from the garden center industry, averaging them, and then comparing your figures with the average statistics. This is misleading, as often the average business is failing. You need to identify the top third of businesses, average those, and then use those as a yardstick. This will provide you with a better picture of how you are performing.

Your aim is to measure key profit indicators within the garden center industry. If you are performing below the standard, then this process will force you to ask questions about your performance. It may be you have a unique location, demographics, product mix, or management style, or your garden center is simply performing poorly. Benchmarking will not give you the answers, but it is a business tool that will force you to identify problem areas and ask pertinent questions of yourself.

The key benchmark areas are:
- Sales per square foot of retail space
- Average sale per customer
- Sales per full-time team member (or equivalent)
- Sales returns as a percentage of total sales
- Markdowns as a percentage of sales
- Wage costs as a percentage of sales
- Stock turns during the year

When you begin, you will probably just benchmark your business. As you become more confident, you will benchmark different product categories, i.e., bedding plants versus shrubs.

Knowing How to Measure

You should contact your trade organization for assistance and information relating to benchmarking within your industry sector. To obtain a benchmark figure in the key retailing areas, apply the following equations:

Sales per Selling Square Foot

$$= \frac{\text{Total dollar sale}}{\text{Number of square feet of selling space}}$$

Do not include parking lot, office space, or other non-retail areas in this equation. Include aisleways. It's exceptionally valuable if you can do this in each product category, as it allows you to identify your profit and loss merchandise areas.

Average Sale per Customer

$$= \frac{\text{Total dollar sales}}{\text{Number of customer transactions}}$$

This tells you how good your merchandising and selling strategy is. The information should be available to your whole team.

Sales per Full-Time Team Member

$$= \frac{\text{Total dollar sales}}{\text{Number of full-time members equivalents}}$$

The key is to look at full-time equivalence, so group part-timers' hours into full-time employee equivalence. If you do not, it is very difficult to compare one store's figures against another's.

Sales Return as a Percentage of Net Sales

$$= \frac{\text{Returns in total}}{\text{Total of transactions}}$$

This will provide you with a customer satisfaction report based on return of goods, not on human relationships with your team. For example, a high goods return may reflect on your quality control.

Markdowns as a Percentage of Sales

$$= \frac{\text{Markdowns}}{\text{Total Sales}}$$

This lets you know how much you're selling at discount.

Shrinkage as a Percentage of Sales

$$= \frac{\text{Inventory shrinkage}}{\text{Total sales}}$$

This will provide a shrinkage figure that then needs to be marked against customer theft, team member theft, or administration errors.

Labor Cost as a Percentage of Sales

$$= \frac{\text{All payroll expenses related to selling}}{\text{Total sales}}$$

This tells you the cost of doing business with your present team.

Stock Turn during the Year

$$= \frac{\text{Total retail sales per year}}{\text{Retail value on inventory held at any one time}}$$

This tells you how often you turn your products during a twelve-month period.

Interpreting the Figures

The value of doing this exercise comes when you interpret the figures. The following table provides you with a guide on benchmarking.

Benchmark	Above Top Third in Industry	Below Top Third in Industry
Sales per selling square foot	Well done.	You have opportunities. Review your product mix, merchandise, display, and signage strategies.
Average sale per customer	Well done.	Review your sales training. Your team is not add-on selling, selling up, or communicating with the customers as well as could be done.
Sales per full-time equivalent	You may need more team members. They may eventually burnout.	You could be overstaffed, have the wrong people selling, or your training program needs to be reviewed.
Sales return as a percentage of total sales	Customers are dissatisfied. Finding out why is urgent.	Well done.
Markdowns as a percentage of sales	Are your price strategies correct? Are team members selling professionally?	Well done.
Shrinkage as a percentage of sales	Analyze your shrinkage policy as a matter of urgency.	Well done.
Labor cost as a percentage of sales	Is your training effective?	Do you have enough team members to service customers properly?
Stock turn during the year	Well done.	You are overstocked or have the wrong merchandise mix.

Departmental Performance

Generally, retailers look at the performance of the whole business, then departments, then individual products. In the garden center industry, historically, we have looked at overall business performance and individual product profit levels. As profit is made from the sale of a complete range of products within a department, all achieving different levels of

Management Memo

Ian Baldwin has worked with U.S. garden centers as a consultant over the last twenty years. He believes that in order to return a pre-tax net profit of 10 percent on sales volume, garden centers must consistently achieve a gap of 26 percent between their actual gross profit margin and their total retail labor costs, both expressed as a percentage of sales. For example:

Sales	100%
Cost of goods	- 54%
Adjusted gross margin	= 46%
Total labor costs	- 20%
Gap	= 26%

*Ref: "Across the Pond"
by Ian Baldwin in* Nursery Man
and Garden Center Magazine,
February 26, 2001, p. 14

profit, you need to analyze the performance of departments to get a true picture of how your business is performing.

This type of report, in our industry, is probably best done seasonally. There are three steps that need to be completed before the report can be finalized.

First, you should keep a record of all purchases made by the department for the season. Detail the supplier's name, date of delivery, invoice number, and the amount of the invoice. You should also record any returns to suppliers.

Next, at the end of the season, do a physical count of all stock. This should include all stock on the shop floor and any relevant stock that is being stored in reserve. Ideally, do this when the garden center is closed. The first time you do this, you will also have to count the stock at the beginning of the period.

Last, record all sales from the department for the season. Once you have all these figures available, it is a simple matter of completing a performance report for the department. This report will allow you to identify any problems in the department and compare one department with another. When you complete it on a seasonal basis, you will be able to control stock and space allocation more accurately and put remedies into place to minimize losses. Used correctly, this is an essential tool to analyze the health of a department.

Each department contributes profit to your garden center; however, it's not always the department with the highest sales that makes the highest contribution to gross profit. To calculate a department gross profit contribution, you first need to calculate what percentage of garden center sales come from that department. This is known as the department sales contribution. For example:

	% Gross Profit	**% Store Sales**
Bedding Plants	30	20
Perennials	35	15
Conifers	45	4
Shrubs	33	15
Garden Care Products	25	15
Trees	50	2

Once you have calculated the department sales contribution figures, you can use the following formula to calculate the department's contribution to the total garden center.

$$\text{Department gross profit contribution} = \frac{\text{Department sales contribution} \times \text{department gross profit \%}}{100}$$

Using the information for the shrub department above, we see the department is contributing 15% of total garden center sales with a gross profit of 33%

$$= \frac{15 \times 33}{100} = 4.95$$

If we go back to our original example garden center, we now have the following information:

Department	**Sales $**	**Sales Contribution**	**Gross Profit %**	**Gross Profit Contribution**
Bedding Plants	20,000	20	30	6
Perennials	15,000	15	35	5.25
Conifers	4,000	4	45	1.8
Shrubs	15,000	15	33	4.95
Garden Care	15,000	15	25	3.75
Trees	2,000	2	50	1
General	29,000	29	40	11.1
Total	100,000	100%		

Using these figures in our example, we now have some valuable information to use in our business. It's clear that bedding plants and perennials contribute for higher gross profit to the business than, for example, trees and conifers. The questions you can now ask yourself are:

1. Have we allocated the correct space to each product category?
2. Does our promotional campaign reflect where profit comes from?
3. Do we have the correct pricing structure for each category?
4. Does management time for each category reflect where the money comes from?

Benchmarking is a relatively new tool to our industry, but one that will become more commonly used as the industry develops. The sooner you use it, the sooner you will make positive, profitable changes to your business.

Book List

Stanley, John. 1999. *Just about Everything a Retail Manager Needs to Know*. Brisbane, Australia: Plum Press.

Chapter 23

Electronic Commerce

compiled by Linda Stanley

E-commerce is much more than just ordering goods from an online catalog; it's a totally new way of doing business using the Internet. E-commerce involves using information technology as an integral part of your company's business operations to improve communications and facilitate transactions with all of your business's stakeholders. The entire e-commerce transaction—which begins with the provision of raw materials, manufacturing, distribution between all stakeholders, wholesaler transactions, retail transactions, and at the retail level may include catalogue shopping, ordering, payment, and delivery tracking—can all be done electronically. As with any major change to the way you conduct your business, adding an e-commerce capability requires careful planning and the learning of a new skill set.

There are two principal types of e-commerce: (1) business-to-business transactions (B2B) between manufacturers and suppliers and (2) business-to-consumer transactions (B2C), or electronic retailing. B2B is the most common of the two, as business computerization and the transfer of business documents between companies was already happening in the 1980s, long before the widespread use of computers in the home.

Despite the shakeout that happened with Internet startups, both B2B and B2C e-commerce are growing rapidly and will lead to profound changes in the way we conduct business, in household practices, and in society itself. An upheaval in traditional business practices has already begun, with Web-based companies supplying directly to consumers where traditional manufacturing companies have supplied via a chain of distributors since the industrial revolution. For example, Dell is a computer manufacturing company that sells directly to consumers, while Compaq and Hewlett-Packard have an established, or legacy, chain of supply that they are committed to working through.

Unfortunately, many B2C companies do not take full advantage of the Web's potential as a customer service tool. Some do not because they aren't aware of just how powerful a business tool the Web can be. Some fail because they're slow to respond to customer needs, and yet others fail because they don't develop an efficient process for capturing and quickly delivering the information and services that customers want from the company's Web site. Many companies find the potential cost of developing a complete e-commerce application too daunting; others develop a site but leave out some of the key functions that make e-service really "click." Companies with poor e-service strategies lose customers since Web users get frustrated quickly and go elsewhere.

Only a few years ago companies regarded their Web sites as electronic brochures, a site on the Web that gave visitors information on products and services, along with a phone number, address, and details on how to contact the company. This sort of site is called "brochureware," as it's basically an electronic company brochure. Today, however, visitors to Web sites expect much more from a site than company information. Visitors today expect to be able to purchase products, have questions answered, and receive support.

So in order to assess how e-commerce is going to affect our own businesses and to create effective strategies to deal with it, we first of all need to look at the trends that are occurring at present. According to Kalakota and Robinson in their book *E-Business: Roadmap to Success*, today's trends can be divided into four primary areas, namely consumer trends, service trends, organizational trends, and enterprise technology trends. For the function of this book, we will look at the first three.

Consumer Trends

Speed of Service

The first major consumer trend defined by Kalakota and Robinson is speed of service. This trend indicates that consumers are more time-pressured than ever before and, as a result, hate delays of any kind, especially delays in being served. So speed of service becomes a key reason why consumers will deal with certain companies and not with others. In order for a company to succeed, the company must reduce the amount of time a consumer spends searching for, selecting, ordering, paying for, and receiving the order.

In this era of busy, time-poor customers, the Internet offers a convenient timesaving solution. The Internet allows customers the ability to conduct their purchasing of required goods at all hours of day, seven days a week (24/7). It means that customers can shop at a time to suit themselves without having to wait for service. If a company does not make purchasing goods easy and convenient for their customers, if they don't make it easy for customers to do business with them, then the customers will go to someone who does.

Self-Service

With the rise of the mass production, mass marketing, and department stores, personal and personality service became things of the past. For too long now customers have had to put up with poor service and slow business experiences. More and more customers now prefer to serve themselves in order to speed up the purchase process; Kmart and Meier have self-service checkout lanes, and I'm sure many others will follow. The lack of personality service means there is no incentive to linger in the retail establishment. Customers will prefer to serve themselves and leave as quickly as possible.

I noticed an interesting exception to this trend last year in Italy. In the countryside there were very few self-service stores of any kind; most of the stores were small family businesses. A customer entering one of these businesses was engaged in a long conversation by the storeowner. The social interaction between the storeowner and the customer was the primary and most important function of the visit; selling a product was secondary. Italian self-service stores have not been able to compete within that high-service environment.

E-commerce is a big enabler of self-service, and market leaders are giving customers the opportunity to serve themselves online. However, to serve customers well, companies must integrate and streamline their internal processes and systems, which is no easy task.

Convenient Integrated Solutions

Shopping has become a low priority for today's time-starved consumers. They want easy, convenient, one-stop shopping whenever possible. They buy integrated software packages, not separate stand-alone packages. They buy from one-stop life-needs providers (Wal-Mart, Target), one-stop lifestyle providers (The Gap), and one-stop life-path providers (Toys "R" Us). The aim is to make shopping more convenient for the customer by selling more related products to the same customer from the one site.

Since customers want fewer shopping trips and integrated services to solve their one-stop shopping requirements, garden centers today must look at the lifestyle of their customer base and analyze how they can become one-stop garden lifestyle providers.

Service Trends

Integrate Sales and Service

The average company today loses half of its customers every five years, and it costs five to ten times as much to obtain a new customer as it does to keep an existing one.

To improve the retention rate of our customers, companies need to manage customer relationships more effectively. The computer age provides the technology to allow us to do that. A database of customers is just the beginning; we need to learn to develop and manage our relationships with our customers in order to tailor our service and offerings to each customer. Technology enables us to cross-sell and up-sell to our existing customers, based on their purchase history. However, the relationship doesn't end there—customers want service before and after the sale. Good customer relationships are the key to business growth, and we retailers need to learn and track customers' needs, behaviors, and lifestyles in order to create specific value offers.

Amazon.com is an excellent example of customer relationship management. Amazon creates a database based on purchase history. Once you have purchased one book from Amazon, they recommend to you books that other customers who have bought the same book have also read. Your subsequent book purchases continue to help them build a profile of your areas of interest. Before long, they have a very accurate profile of your interest areas and are able to offer you books or products that are of extreme interest to you. This not only helps Amazon to sell more products, but this creates very strong loyalty among customers. Why buy elsewhere when Amazon knows exactly what you like!

Make Customer Service Consistent and Reliable

As our customers' time becomes more and more valuable to them, they become less and less tolerant of inefficiencies and delays in customer service. As the speed of service increases, customer expectations for prompt and efficient service grows higher. The customer service process must be friendly and easy to use, and customers must have a single point of contact with the company—they should never be shuffled from one company representative to another.

Provide Flexible, Convenient Service Delivery

The goal today is to provide reliable service and quick delivery. In the world of hectic schedules, home delivery will become increasingly important. This means that companies need to develop a speedy, effective, and flexible system of order fulfillment.

Organizational Trends

Contract Manufacturing

A trend toward specialization means that companies must concentrate on doing what they do best and contract out the rest. The aim is to move from a capital- or asset-intensive company to a knowledge-intensive company through contract manufacturing or outsourcing. Companies are using technology to separate marketing from manufacturing, production from distribution by developing contract partnerships. This allows companies to improve on what they do best. It frees up more time for innovation in marketing and for more frequent updates of products, it reduces overheads, and it clearly defines cost boundaries.

Outsource

Outsourcing is delegating business processes that are not your core competencies to an external provider so that you can concentrate on your core competencies in order to improve overall business performance. Marketing, finance, human resources, information technology infrastructure, even product development or manufacturing can be easily outsourced to specialists who have levels of proficiency that you might not be able to afford if you tried to hire them full time.

Increase Process Transparency and Visibility

Customers today want to have access to product information, pricing, availability, and order status. An example of process visibility is the United Parcel Service (UPS) tracking system, where, via the Internet, customers can track the progress of their air and ground parcels. The more open and visible a company's processes appear, the greater the customer retention and the stronger the long-term relationship.

Continuous Innovation and Employee Retention

Employee retention is now being recognized as critical to a company's long-term success. The trends here are to offer employees better incentives that are dependent upon productivity and are tied in to continuous improvement, with promotions being earned and based upon proven ability. A company commitment of productivity incentives must be made to employees in order to encourage more self-motivation. A self-motivated workforce will seek to continuously improve processes and themselves.

E-Service—The Answer to Today's Trends

Having looked at the trends that are telling us our customers want quick service, self-service, convenient service, easy service—it is easy to see why the twenty-four-hour-a-day, seven-day-a-week (24/7) facility we know as the Web has so rapidly evolved into such a popular medium. The Web is now used by companies to buy, sell, recruit staff, solicit bids, make referrals, and support customers and forge closer relationships with them. It is used by customers to buy goods and services, sell items at auction sites, communicate with family and friends, carry out their own research on products or items of interest, join chat forums, or complain about a company's poor service.

While the Web and the e-service it has enabled are great ways to meet our customers' needs, it's very easy to lose customers if we do not fully and immediately respond to those needs. We have just seen that a large part of the Web's appeal to our customers is the ability to get instant gratification. When visitors come to a Web site, they want to find the information they seek to solve a problem or make a purchasing decision, and they want to find it fast. In 1999, visitors to Web sites were prepared to wait twelve seconds for a Web site to download; by 2000 they were prepared to wait only three or four seconds before giving up and moving on to another site. This means that enormous pressure is being placed not only on Web designers to create sites that are quick to download and easy to navigate, but it also puts pressure on content contributors to anticipate and meet the needs of visitors to the site. This means meeting the needs of first-time visitors as well as regular customers, so the range of information that must be provided to meet that breadth of diversity can be potentially enormous. A Web site today must be highly responsive to the needs of visitors, or they will go elsewhere.

There are a couple of important areas to consider:

The needs of your visitors. Many business owners still think of their Web site as an electronic brochure or an advertisement for their business. If they are not frequent users of the Internet, they may be unaware of the experience today's regular Web user has come to expect. A Web experience today may include chat rooms and highly interactive sites that generate expectations of interaction and response. Companies have to provide the content on their site to satisfy the expectations of their visitors.

Cost constraints. Even if a business's Web development team understands the need to build a highly responsive Web site, there may not be the funds available to construct such a site in-house. There also may not be sufficient competently trained staff in-house to track and respond to frequently asked questions that have come into the company via the Web site. There are, however, a number of Web development companies who provide cost-effective packaged solutions designed to track and manage visitor contact and inquiries.

What Are the Benefits to My Business?

The benefits of e-commerce are many:

Faster service. When customers can get the answers they want on a

Web site, it increases customer satisfaction and gives the impression that the company who owns the site is a company that is responsive to its customers' needs.

Increased traffic. A site that customers find useful is more likely to have repeat visitors. This type of site is more likely to get "bookmarked" by visitors so that they can quickly return to the site again at a later date.

Continuous trading hours. An effective Web site provides your customers with a 24/7 facility to obtain answers to queries, browse catalogs, or order product. And you can provide that all at a fraction of the cost of a traditional service facility.

Improved access to information. The Web enables visitors to find information quickly. It allows companies to publicize their business via their own Web site. And it allows visitors to join in discussion groups with their peers.

Effective communication. The Web affords you the opportunity to build a better relationship with your customers and suppliers with the aid of technology such as e-mail and online newsletters.

Opening of new markets: The Internet opens up new business opportunities to extend your customer base and permits access to international expertise to improve your business.

Improved client service. E-commerce allows the development of personalized marketing programs designed according to customer interests by using electronic databases. It also enables the dissemination of information on your products and services on your Web site, which facilitates interactions with individual customers.

Mass customization. The Internet can provide retailers with a more efficient and profitable means of processing orders and configuring products so that each product suits the specific needs of each customer. This, in turn, allows retailers to optimize their inventory management practices.

Reduced costs. Depending on the size and nature of a retailer's existing operations, the Internet can offer potential cost savings to retailers through lower inventory, transaction, customer service, administration, and communication costs. According to Greg Gianforte of RightNow Technologies, when customers can help themselves at a Web site instead of having to call a help desk for information, savings can range from ten to forty-five dollars per incident.

Enhanced market research. By using online surveys, Internet chat groups, and online feedback forums, retailers can obtain data on their customers' preferences, ideas, and attitudes, and can conduct their own market research to improve service and product development.

Value-added applications. The Internet provides retailers with the vehicle to capture customer information and place it in a relational database. This is one of the most powerful aspects of the Internet, as that information can then be used to provide value-added services to customers. Using a relational database, retailers can offer customers other related or linked products or services based on a customer's particular preferences or buying history. Web site links can also be provided to other Internet sites that may be of interest to a customer.

How Do I Get Started?

There several steps involved in the *connectivity* of a business. The first step, according to InfoEntrepreneurs.org, consists simply in getting connected to the Internet and to electronic mail. This will make it possible to deal inexpensively with suppliers, clients, and employees and will provide access to an entirely new information medium. You can obtain an Internet address from an Internet service provider (ISP).

The second step is to establish a promotional Web site for your company, which will allow you to display your products and services. You have the choice of developing and accommodating the site internally or assigning these tasks to an ISP. If your company involves several locations, then you may want to build an *intranet*. An intranet is like a private internal Internet, where part of the site is only accessible to employees. You may be large enough to need an *extranet*, which is like a private Internet that is only accessible to business partners.

Subsequent stages consist of developing the interactivity of your Web site in order to take orders and process payments online. Last, depending on the size of your business, comes the development of e-commerce enterprise models and the sharing of information resources with trading partners to create expanded *virtual businesses.*

Building Your Web Site

Whether you build your Web site in-house or use a professional to build it for you, there are a few steps to consider.

First, consider first what sort of site you want for your business. Do you want a complete service site for your customers, an online store, or do you just want to provide information about your company?

Next, sit down and sketch a rough layout for your site, beginning with your home page. Your home page should have your basic business information and links to the other pages of your Web site. Think of your site as a pyramid, with each layer containing more specific information. Consider what detail will encourage your customers to buy your products or visit your store.

Graphics and images can add appeal to your site, but they can also make it hard to use. If a graphic such as a map showing how to get to your store will actually help your customers, then go ahead and use one, but avoid unnecessary images, photos, and graphics, as they can make your site too slow to download. Use them carefully and thoughtfully, especially on the home page.

Once the Web site is built, you need somewhere to put it. That means finding a Web hosting service. There are many to choose from, and some will promise what they cannot deliver. Ask other business leaders which service they use and if they would recommend it.

Register your domain name. If you fail to register your own business domain name, someone else who sees a commercial advantage will. So if someone is going to own your trading name(s) on the Internet, it should be you. In 2001, more than sixteen thousand domain names were registered every day. This means that your chance of getting the domain name you want is diminishing every day—so don't delay in registering.

Remember then that your Web site needs to be updated regularly. Check regularly to ensure your links still work, and update the information on your Web site on a regular basis.

Structuring Your Site

How you structure your Web site is the decision of your corporate strategy team and your Web design team. The Working Group on Electronic Commerce has created a useful list of basic things to keep in mind when you are planning out your site.

1. Tell your Web visitors who you are, display your company name, legal identity address, and full contact information including telephone, fax, and e-mail address on your home page. It gives visitors are deeper sense of security to know that

there are several ways that they can contact you should they need to.

2. Give customers as much accurate and truthful detail as possible about the products and services that you offer, keeping the information in as plain and simple language as possible. Provide a catalog of items for sale. Electronic commerce software is available that enables customers to secure orders online using credit cards. However, provide customers with an alternative to entering credit card details on line, such as a phone or fax number, as some customers may feel more secure using an alternative.

3. Make sure your ordering process is as easy and simple as you can make it for your customers. Web users recognize the visual image of a shopping cart—this is a good symbol to use on your Web site. Once customers have chosen their products and placed them in the shopping cart, use a "send to checkout" or other easily understood button to send the products to the order form and finalize the order.

4. Repeat customers may prefer to set up an account facility with a password to create a faster ordering process. This is something you should consider.

5. Clearly define all of your terms and conditions that apply to a purchase, making sure you list the full price, any shipping charges, taxes, customs duties, delivery arrangements, any shipping limitations, any warranties, as well as your cancellation, return, and exchange policies and any associated costs. Place these details in an easy-to-find place, and provide customers with a way to print a copy out for their records should they choose.

6. Be clear about the level of security you provide on your Web site. State who provides the security and briefly describe how the security works. If your security service provider has a Web page, you should consider putting a link to it on your Web site.

7. Declare your privacy policy on your Web site. Tell your customers how you plan to use the personal customer information you collect. This will become an invaluable resource for your business, and it will allow you to build a close relationship for marketing purposes with your customers. Customers are more

willing to provide personal information if they know it will not be sold to others.

8. To reassure prospective customers, consider having a reputable third party endorse your business. There are a number of Internet approval programs that offer a range of services from simply verifying that your business exists to comprehensive auditing services.

Choosing a Web Design Company

Once you have decided to build a Web site and have thought through what you want your Web site to do for your business, then it's time to find someone to build it for you. If you don't have an in-house team to build the site for you, then you need to carefully choose a Web design and development company. A poorly designed Web site cannot only cost you a lot of money, but it can also lose you a lot of customers and damage your reputation. So it is important to do as much research on finding the most appropriate company to build your Web site as you did on figuring out what you want your Web site to do for you and how you want it to function.

Thoroughly research each prospective Web designer's work, ask around, and look at the work they have already done so you can evaluate their suitability and their potential to fulfill your needs. If you require ongoing maintenance and support or training, can they meet your needs? Would you prefer a small company with whom you can work individually and on a one-on-one basis, or would you rather work with a large company that has an established reputation but with whom you may be just another client?

Arrange a face-to-face meeting with the prospective Web developer to ascertain whether you can work together. In the meeting as you are talking to them, find out if they listen to your needs, talk your language, and whether they understand your industry. Most important, evaluate whether they share your vision for the site or if they want to build their own pet project?

Finally, ask for references from past jobs, and check them out. Ask past clients if the prospective Web developer met their needs, met their deadlines, whether they were responsive to suggestions, fully answered questions, worked within the budget, and listened to their customer.

Once you have decided on a company, make sure your contract or agreement with that firm includes a clause assigning complete, unquestioned ownership of every aspect of your Web site to your business once the Web site is completed.

Checklist of Issues for Web Site Development Contracts

Drawing up a contract with your chosen Web site developer will help to ensure that all your goals are met and you both know exactly where you stand with each other. The contract with the developer should cover the following key areas, including ownership and intellectual property rights, the development process, functionality of the finished product, possible problems that may arise and any measures required to correct them, covenants of the developer, confidentiality, and other provisos. The following is a checklist for the types of issues you will need to consider in a contract.

A. Ownership and intellectual property
- Who owns what in relation to content, screens, software, and information. Ensure the develop is working on a "work for hire" basis under the copyright act.
- Ensure that your company owns the rights to screens, graphics, domain names, content, code, and all other software, programming, etc.
- Ensure the developer does not infringe on anybody else's copyright when developing your site.
- Determine who is responsible for obtaining rights, licenses, and other permissions in relation to graphics, audio, or other material to be used on your Web site.
- Display relevant copyright notice on your Web site.

B. Development agreement
- Determine a budget for the site, as well as a timetable for the development. Include time frames for progress payments and other required milestones.
- Ensure any changes to specifications do not incur additional costs.
- Ensure developer provides documentation for all software used.
- Include a training clause for the developer to train your team on how to use the software and the site.
- Ensure the developer has the responsibility for transferring the site to the company's server.

- Make sure you have the right to reject the site if it does not meet your specifications.

C. Site functionality
- Maximum download time for any Web page.
- Consider the user-option for a low-graphics, fast-loading Web site.
- Site compatibility—ensure it is compatible to the latest browsers, especially Microsoft, Netscape, and AOL.
- The site will integrate with the company intranet.
- The required number of users will be able to access the site simultaneously.
- The company can modify the site without interfering with operations.
- Security procedures are specified and put in place.

D. Problems
- Ensure the contract states that it is the developers duty to rectify any problems, bugs, failed links, and include a maximum time for correction of the problems.
- The developer must ensure that the software used is free of viruses or other disabling devices.

E. Covenants of the developer
- The developer must comply with the laws of the country.
- Ensure the use of your company logos and trademarks are not used without your written permission, before, during, or after the development of your site.

F. Confidentiality
- Obligate the developer to keep confidential all of your proprietary information.

G. Other
- Include clauses to cover how disputes will be handled and who will pay what costs.

Developing Your Web Site Strategy

The Web has changed the way companies and customers communicate with each other. Traditionally companies sent information to prospective customers by way of advertising and direct mail. Today the flow of information has reversed, now customers seek out the information they want from the company of their choice via the Internet.

This affords small companies like garden centers, nurseries, and land-scapers equal opportunities with the larger conglomerates to market to specific sectors. A Web site strategy has to be developed to make the Web site into an attractor of your chosen market segment. Your Web site must not only be an attractor, but it must have the ability to allow interaction with existing and prospective customers.

Types of Attractors

Richard Watson et al. in their book *Electronic Commerce: The Strategic Perspective* have analyzed a large number of sites and their ability to attract visitors. As a result, they have grouped sites into categories based on their ability to attract customers. These categories are not mutually exclusive, and in many cases the categories can overlap with one another. The following are Watson's categories:

Entertainment park

Web sites in this category offer entertainment while engaging customers in activity. The Web sites are interactive and challenging and often use games or contests in order to market products and enhance corporate image. These Web sites seek to create an image of an exciting, dynamic and friendly corporation. Two examples on this category are Disney's site (www.disney.com) and the Kellogg Company site (www.kelloggs.com). Both allow children to choose and color a drawing and to play games.

Archive

Archive sites allow users to unveil historical aspects of the company. This method seeks to reinforce the image of a trusted and well-established company. Examples of companies using archive pages are Ford (www.ford.com/servlet/ecmcs/ford/indcx.jsp?SECTION=ourCompany& LEVEL2=heritage), Boeing (www.boeing.com/companyoffices/history/ indexf.html), and Hewlett-Packard (http://www.hp.com/hpinfo/ abouthp/histnfacts.htm). These sites allow users to discover historical and technical information.

Exclusive sponsorship

An organization that provides exclusive event sponsorship can use its Web site to attract a large volume of visitors over a short time frame (the period leading up to and during the event). This type of Web site must provide up-to-the-minute information. An example of this type of Web site is Coca-Cola (www.coke.com), which gives details of Coke-sponsored events.

Town hall
The town hall is a community venue where people go to hear speeches and participate in seminars. This type of Web site is a virtual town hall where speeches and seminars can take place. However, the difficulty is keeping interested participants informed of what is coming up next. An example is Tripod (www.tripod.lycos.com), which is a resource center for college students.

Club
The club is a virtual meeting place where visitors register or become members. These Web sites are interactive and can serve to increase company loyalty, enhance customer feedback, and improve customer service through members helping other members.

Gift Shop
These Web sites generate bursts of traffic using giveaways such as digital images (www.kodak.com), recipes (www.ragu.com), coupons, and software upgrades or shareware.

Freeway intersection
This type of Web site provides advanced information processing, such as search engines, news centers, portals (AOL), or electronic malls and can generate huge traffic flow. The goal can be to create a one-stop resource center such as Yahoo! or AltaVista.

Customer service center
Many organizations now use their Web site to provide services to their existing customers, such as parcel tracking, balance checking, answering frequently asked questions (FAQs), as well as opportunities to sell products and services to new customers.

Choosing Your Own Strategy
A horticultural organization may want to choose a primary attractor strategy of a customer service center, to provide a service to existing cus-

tomers with an access point to a product catalog with an ordering facility and a FAQ facility. However, there may be times when you will want to incorporate other attractor items into your site such as a gift shop and tips on how to plant that special plant or what to do in your garden in fall.

You may sponsor a local sporting event, and that may be a point of interest for other local customers, or you could start up a club for your customers and have a "members only" section on your Web site.

Develop your Web site marketing strategy in conjunction with your corporate marketing strategy and marry the two together. Decide who your most profitable customers are and design your Web site with that particular sector in mind. Build in a variety of stimuli that will create interest for that sector, concentrating on creating sufficient interest to encourage repeat visits from your most profitable group of customers.

Figure 23-1. Van Hage's Garden Center has a monthly tasks page at www.vanhage.co.uk.

Making Your Web Site Service Successful

An effective Web site is very achievable. Greg Gianforte of RightNow Technologies has surveyed effective Web site practitioners and come up with eight basic attributes to make Web-based customer service work:

Make sure your Web site "listens"

Your Web site should be your ear on your business. It should listen for both explicit and implicit clues to how your business is doing from your Web site visitors. Explicit messages are clear requests for specific information. Implicit messages are patterns of usage that indicate a difficulty in finding a particular type of content. An effective Web presence needs mechanisms to be put in place that will ensure your company listens and responds to both types of online customer interaction.

Give customers what they want

Once your Web site is set up and listening to what your customers want and you are providing it on your Web site, remember that the content must also be provided quickly. Recall one of the most important trends that we discussed earlier—visitors don't want to wait; they want answers immediately. Delays in delivering customer-driven content can be fatal. Your Web site should capture customer requests and use that information to enhance site content for future visitors.

Make response mechanisms easy to find and easy to use

Make sure the "Contact Us" button is easy to find, and if it launches an e-mail screen, ensure it advises the visitor when they can expect a reply. Make sure you also give visitors a phone number so that if customers really need to talk to a human being right away, they can call.

The "80/20" rule

While we should always make sure that Web site content is as comprehensive as possible, remember that, on average, *80% of Web site traffic will target 20% of your content.* In other words, a small amount of content can handle most of the business, provided you have put the right content there. It's wise to get the most important and pertinent information up and operating efficiently; you can then add to it over time as dictated by customer needs.

Get "pushy"

You don't have to always rely on customers coming to your Web site to get them the information they need. By offering e-mail options, you can "push" information to your customers. A good way to do this is to ask visitors to your Web site if they would like to receive information on specific items of interest or be notified when there is a special offer. This type of "push" mechanism allows you to use your Web site and build an ongoing electronic relationship with your customers.

Respond fast

Don't make the mistake of being too slow in your response to online information requests from your customers. Once customers have been disappointed by how slowly their question has been answered, they are unlikely to try again and may even become disillusioned about the company as a whole. So, if you're going to offer an e-mail contact mechanism on your site, make sure the customer receives a reply within twenty-four hours.

Track religiously
A large percentage of site visitors tend to ask the same limited set of questions, so it's critically important to track requests for information as they come in. Tracking of requests enables site managers to analyze where to direct time and efforts, allowing resources to be applied more effectively. E-commerce applications can perform this tracking automatically and will rank information based on the past needs of customers.

Automate as much as is economically viable
All the tasks required to create a really responsive Web site—such as assimilating and analyzing visitors queries, developing appropriate content, and displaying it in a user-friendly manner—and handling Web mail communications can be very labor intensive. As site traffic increases, so do these tasks. As a result, sites often become victims of their own success, as the volume of communications exceeds the resources available to support the communication. So it's important to use effective automation tools that are scalable in order to meet rising demands. Automation tools significantly increase the return on investment, as good applications automate site maintenance and knowledge-collection tasks.

Assess the Effectiveness of the E-Service You Offer
On page 314 is a short self-assessment test from RightNow Technologies that you can do to ascertain how effective your level of service on the Web really is.

Promotion on the Web
The Web provides an ideal means of marketing products and services as well as maintaining your corporate image. Make sure your Web site defines your image, and remember that when your customers see your Web site and not your business, your Web site becomes your business. Here are a selection of promotional opportunities that could be incorporated into your Web site.

E-Service Self Assessment	Yes	No	Don't know
1. Can your customers quickly find answers to their most frequently asked questions on your Web site?			
2. Can they easily check on the status of the response that they previously requested?			
3. Do you respond to all customer e-mails within one business day?			
4. Does the knowledge content on your site grow dynamically and automatically based on customer input?			
5. Is the most useful and/or commonly requested information presented to visitors first?			
6. Do customers have an easy way to get to a human support staffer?			
7. Do your customers consistently return to your site to get information? Do you have any way of determining whether or not they do?			
8. Can you generate reports detailing the support activities that have taken place on your site on a week-by-week basis? Do those reports help you determine the return on investment (ROI) of the site?			
9. Do you give visitors the option to have updates sent to them automatically by e-mail?			
10. Are you consistently using your Web site to capture and publish useful information that's currently only in the heads of your best staff?			
11. Have you off-loaded telephone calls that could be handled without human intervention to your Web site?			
12. Do customers ever praise your company because they found your site especially helpful?			

E-Mail

E-mail can be used as a quick and easy means of communication with your customers, club members, or employees. However, sending unsolicited e-mail (spam) to customers will only serve to annoy them and will not help to increase their loyalty to your company. *Always obtain customers permission first,* and always provide a method for customers to opt out of receiving any more e-mails from you. Remember that your customers are short on time, so avoid using large or inappropriate graphics in your emails—they waste time and bandwidth downloading and can irritate your customers. If you have something to say, say it within the e-mail, don't use an attachment if you can avoid it. Attachments slow down the information retrieval process, and it's easier for your customer if they can read what you have to say in the contents of the e-mail.

Press Releases

When something of interest happens within your organization, such as sponsorship of a sporting event or the winning of an award, post it in a press release on your Web site as well as in your community newspaper. Newspapers often edit your press releases, whereas on your Web site you can tell your story the way you want it told, and in full.

Hyperlinks

Hyperlinks are a key Web facility; they allow visitors to jump quickly from one Web site to another. Be careful though that you do not encourage visitors to leave your site and jump to another site, never to return. Use hyperlinks thoughtfully, as they could be a useful tool for your customers, providing links to special interest areas. Put yourself in your customers' shoes, and think of how you can help them find what they want and how they can find you from other sites they might be visiting. A hyperlink from your registered association to your Web site may help your customers find you.

Logos

To reinforce your company image in your customers' eyes, Richard Watson recommends putting your corporate logo on each page of your Web site. Depending on the design of your logo, it may be suitable to be used as a page direction indicator—back, forward, up, down—or it could be animated to catch the user's eye and reinforce the corporate image.

My company's logo, pictured here, appears on every page of my Web site and on all communications from my company.

Getting Found on the Web

Making sure your Web site comes up on the first one or two search pages on the Web is something every company wants to achieve. However, search engines search in different ways, and each directory lists companies differently, so it is difficult to ensure your Web site come up with a top ranking every time.

Meta tags are HTML (HyperText Markup Language) labels, and they are usually placed in the header of a Web document. Meta tags contain primary keywords and descriptive information and are used by search engines to rank search results in order of relevance. A good search engine ranking is vital, as research has revealed that most people do not look past the first couple of pages of results from a search.

To see how meta tags are used and to figure out how to improve your search engine ranking using meta tags, go to a search engine like Hotbot (www.hotbot.com) or Google (www.google.com) and type in the words that you think a visitor might type if they were looking for your site. Then go to the first half a dozen sites that the search engine lists and have a look at each site. Go to View, then Source on your browser, and it will display the HTML coding on the site. Study which meta tags the sites have used. You should be able to determine the relationship between the meta tags used and their ranking by the search engine. From this study you will be able to determine what meta tags would be beneficial and yet specific to your site.

Janice Reynolds from AllBusiness has suggested some things that you can do to help get a good site ranking:

25/255 rule. Always use keywords that best describe your business more than once in the first 25 words of each page you submit. Many search engines only use the first 25 words (or 255 characters) of a submitted Web page.

Title. Be sure to use a title tag for each page of your site. The title can have the most impact on your search-engine ranking. While there is no specific science to deciding on a title, use about five descriptive words that form a catchy headline and remember to keep the title simple and to use keywords.

Meta keywords. Always include at least two words that best represent what's on your page. Put yourself in the shoes of someone searching for this page: What keywords would they use?

Meta description. In addition to keyword meta tags, include a one-sentence description of your page. The description meta tag is an indispensable tool in your battle for search-engine ranking.

Comments. Some search engines ignore meta tags and instead look for comment tags. So in addition to a description meta tag, you should also include a comment tag that contains the same one-sentence description as the description meta tag.

Alt. Search engines cannot read nor index graphics. So if you include important information inside a graphic, be sure to also include that text in an alt tag, otherwise the information will be ignored.

Horticultural Web Sites

The horticultural industry is already incorporating the benefits of integrated electronic commerce solutions in B2B and B2C transactions. It's useful to look at what is already being done around the world so you can assess the possibilities of what can or should be done on the local scene. Software companies across Europe have targeted the Dutch horticultural industry to develop Internet tools and e-commerce solutions, while the Canadian government has assisted Canadian companies to become Internet active. Have a look at the following, and other sites, to see what is currently happening on this planet.

Business to Business (B2B)

B2B sites such as www.echorticulture.com and www.growit.com are some sites offering a variety of B2B e-commerce solutions with transaction management systems tailored to the needs of the horticultural industry. Registered participants in marketplace communities can trade with each other to more efficiently buy and sell products, reducing search and transaction costs and improving profitability.

In the Netherlands, there are a number of companies providing e-commerce services, among them Infogroen and Greenweb. Greenweb (www.greenweb.nl) has produced the Green Valley e-commerce trading site (www.greenvalley.nl), which brings together thirty independent Dutch growers.

LogiVert (www.logivert.com/) is a software development company focusing on ornamental nurseries and garden centers. It offers a number of software programs including a plant labeling system and a catalog building system.

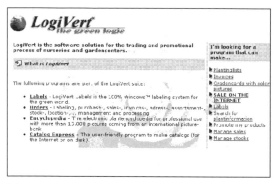

Figure 23-2. LogiVert's Web site, www.logivert.com, offers B2B solutions for the green industry.

Another European B2B site to have a look at is the French site Green Avenue (www.greenavenue.com), which claims to be the first Web hosting/software company in Europe to invite tendering for plants and flowers on the Internet. Sellers can register free, promote their products, and access invitations to tender. Buyers also register free and search for plants by looking at a range of grower Web sites and catalogs. This is not a full e-commerce Web site, as buyers and sellers must negotiate transport logistics, costs, and other details separately. Other sites to check out are www.floweraccess.com, www.flowerweb.com, and www.fpn.nl.

At Plantarium 2000, the International Nursery Stock Trade Fair, which was held in Boskoop, the Netherlands, in August 2000, Bruce McTavish, president of the Canadian Nursery Landscape Association, outlined the steps taken by the CNLA to build a Web site and develop a high-speed searchable database of members' inventories to assist with marketing nursery products throughout North America. The Canadian database, accessed through www.canadanursery.com, currently contains six thousand different plant species and varieties and is playing a significant role in increasing the ability of the industry to communicate over vast distances and to increase sales for Canadian nurseries.

The Canadian Nursery Landscape Association president also stated that members were using e-mail for bidding, order confirmation, sending availability lists to customers, and responding to customer complaints. Some nurseries use digital cameras to capture images to send to distant customers. The digital images allow customers to see and approve plants before shipping; it's a tool that is especially useful in supplying high-end landscape projects to distant markets. The next step will allow nurseries to send real-time video from their fields direct to customers by linking digital cameras to cell phones. This would permit direct picking of specimen plants in real time by customers.

The Canadian Nursery Landscape Association is currently exploring methods of promoting retail and landscape members directly to the public. As a pilot study, the province of British Columbia has launched a pilot Web site that lists the services of all landscape and retail members, searchable by city, geographic area, and the service required.

Business to Consumer (B2C)

B2C sites to have a look at include sites such as Plant Delights Nursery (www.plantdel.com), an online source for high-quality garden perennials, and Garden Community (www.gardencom.com), which contains over a hundred garden directory categories to find garden nursery sites for wholesale and retail trade, with free gardening newsgroup access, garden books and garden magazines, and the Cactus and Succulent Plant Mall (CSPM; www.cactus-mall.com), an Internet resource with regularly updated information on cactus and succulent societies and suppliers of plants, seeds, and literature on cacti and succulents. The CSPM has developed and hosts Web pages for more than 120 cactus and succulent organizations worldwide. It also aims to maintain as complete a list of Web pages and other cactus- and succulent-related Internet facilities as possible.

Figure 23-3. Plant Delights Nursery's home page features a picture of their latest creative catalog cover.

In the United Kingdom, Greenfingers.com, Crocus.co.uk, and egarden.co.uk are excellent sites directed to the consumer. E-garden, apart from selling practically every kind of plant and garden accessory, also offers free advice online from gardening experts. Crocus will design your garden for you, help identify and choose the right plants, and then deliver them to your doorstep. It will also provide trained horticulturists to plant them for you and then e-mail you through the year to remind you to prune your roses, trim your wisteria, and separate those bulbs. Grogrow.com, Dig-it. co.uk, and Birstall.co.uk are also excellent Web sites.

Have a look at the type of content being offered to consumers. You will see the style of Web sites and what they are offering vary greatly. Put yourself in your customers' shoes, think like your customers, and then innovate. The goal is to obtain repeat visits, so sites must be interesting, enticing, and offer customers reasons to keep coming back.

At Plantarium 2000, the president of the European Nursery Stock Association, David Clark, expressed his view that the Internet would allow businesses to update catalogs and availability lists on a daily basis. He felt that in time, as far as horticultural retailing was concerned, one or two market leaders would emerge and that the online gardener may be tomorrow's garden center customer. Online ordering will reduce lead times between ordering and delivery, virtually eliminating the time required to process orders and to print labels, delivery notes, and invoices. Significant savings would result while service for the customer would improve at the same time.

The Jargon Explained

There is an enormous amount of jargon in electronic commerce and the computer industry. To help you understand what tech-heads are talking about, here is a list of common e-commerce terms with a brief explanation of the meanings.

Acquisition. The second stage of the customer service life cycle, during which the supplier helps the customer acquire a product or service.

Attractor. A Web site that continually attracts a high number of visitors.

Authentication. The process of confirming the identity of a person or source of a message.

Banner. An advertisement that usually covers the bottom or top of a Web page.

Bot (short for robot). A program that operates as an agent for a user or another program or simulates a human activity.

Browser. Client software used on the Web to fetch and read documents on screen and print them, jump to other documents via hypertext, view images, and listen to audio files.

Client. A personal computer running an application that can access and display information on a server.

Client/server computing. A combination of clients and servers that provides the framework for distributing files across a network.

Computer network. An interconnected system of computers.

Cyberspace. Another name for the Internet and other forms of electronic communication.

Data access control. A method of controlling access to stored data.

Decryption. Conversion of encrypted text represented by characters into a readable form.

Digital cash or money. An electronic form of money that is parallel to notes and coins.

Discussion list. A group of e-mail users who have all subscribed to a listserv to share their ideas on a particular topic.

Domain name. Another name for the server computer address.

DNS (domain name service). A system that keeps up with all Internet addresses.

Download. The process of moving software or data from a central computer to a personal computer and saving it on disk.

Ecash. An electronic payment system that can be used to withdraw and deposit ecash over the Internet. It provides the privacy of cash because the payer can remain anonymous.

EDI (electronic data interchange). The electronic exchange of standard business documents between business partners.

Electronic document. An electronic form of a printed document.

EFT (Electronic funds transfer). The electronic movement of money.

Electronic publishing. The electronic presentation of text and multimedia.

Encryption. The conversion of readable text into characters that disguise the original meaning of the text.

Extranet. An electronic connection using Internet technology linking business partners to facilitate greater coordination of common activities.

FAQs (frequently asked questions). A list of frequently asked questions relevant to the particular Web site, along with answers to the questions.

File transfer protocol (FTP). A protocol that supports file transfers over the Internet.

Firewall. A device placed between an organization's network and the Internet to control data access.

Frame. A section of the browser window in which a Web page can be displayed.

GUI (graphical user interface, pronounced "gooey"). An interface that uses pictures and graphic symbols to represent commands, choices, or actions.

HTML (Hypertext Markup Language). A language used to create Web pages.

Hypertext. Links to other Web pages or Internet resources.

Internet. A worldwide network of computers and computer networks in private organizations, government institutions, and universities, over which people share files, send electronic messages, and have access to vast quantities of information.

Java. A platform-independent, object-oriented application development language.

LAN (local area network). A computer network that is restricted to one geographical area.

Listserver. A program providing a set of e-mail functions that enables users to participate in electronic discussions.

MIME (multipurpose Internet mail extension). A protocol that is widely used for the interchange of files.

Multimedia. An interactive combination of text, graphics, animation, images, audio, and video displayed by and under the control of a personal computer.

Newsgroups. A vast set of Internet discussion lists.

PDF (portable document format). A form of electronic document created with Adobe's Acrobat Exchange that can be easily shared with anyone who has an Acrobat reader.

Private key. An encryption key that is known only by the person sending and receiving encrypted messages.

Protocol. A formal set of rules for specifying the format and relationships when exchanging information between communicating devices.

Public key. An encryption key that is known to all persons who share encrypted communication with a particular person who holds a private key.

Routing. The process of determining the path a message will take from the sending to the receiving computer.

Search engines. Software that has been developed to enable Web users to search for Web pages that contain desired topics.

Secure server. A Web server that provides users protection from having their messages read while being transmitted over the Internet.

Server. A computer on the Web running an application that manages a data store containing files of text, images, video clips, and sound.

SET (secure electronic transaction). A system for ensuring the security of Internet financial transactions.

Smart card. A card, containing memory and a microprocessor, that can serve as personal identification, credit card, ATM card, telephone credit card, critical medical information record, and as cash for small transactions.

SSL (secure sockets layer). A program layer created by Netscape for managing the security of message transmissions in a network.

Stakeholder. Some person or group that can determine the future of an organization.

URL (uniform resource locator). A standard means of consistently locating Web pages or other resources no matter where they are stored on the Internet.

Web page. A special type of document that contains hypertext links to other documents or to various multimedia elements.

Web page address. The Internet address at which a Web page is found.

Web searching. The process of searching for Web pages of interest using a piece of software called a search engine.

World Wide Web (WWW). A body of software, a set of protocols, and conventions based on hypertext and multimedia techniques that make the Internet easy for anyone to browse and add contributions.

Book (and Web Page) List

AllBusiness. "Checklist of Issues for Web Page Development Contracts." http://www.allbusiness.com/cmt/information/general.jsp?fname=610. Available as of November 8, 2001.

Canadian Office of Consumer Affairs. 1999. "Your Internet Business: Earning Customer Trust." http://strategis.ic.gc.ca/pics/ca/merchant.pdf. Available November 12, 2001.

Gianforte, Greg. "The Insider's Guide to Customer Service on the Web: Eight Secrets for Successful E-Service" RightNow Technologies, www.rightnowtech.com.

Holden, Greg. 1998. *Small Business Internet for Dummies.* Foster City, Calif.: IDG Books.

Kalakota, Dr. Ravi and Marcia Robinson. 1999. *E-Business: Roadmap for Success.* Boston: Addison-Wesley.

Watson, Richard T., Pierre Berthon, Leyland F. Pitt, and George M. Zinkhan. 2000. *Electronic Commerce: The Strategic Perspective.* Fort Worth, Tex.: Dryden Press.

Index

A

Abraham, Jay, 9
add-on products, 197-98
  contrast principle, 197
  displaying, 61, **61**, 81
  encouraging, 211
  labels, using to promote, 155
advertising (to new customers). *see also* marketing
  costs and budget, 103, 232-34
  for recruitment, 176
  target audience, identifying, 221
  types of
    billboard, 222
    client-response, 10
    contests, 231
    direct mail, 232
    events, in-store, 231-32
    free samples, 232
    Internet, 220
    print, 220, 223-29
    radio, 220, 223
    referrals, 233
    television, 220, 222-23
Allen, Ken, 4-6
ambience, in-store, 208-9
anchoring, consumer trend toward, 8
archive-style Web sites, 309
aroma, using in retail areas, 209

B

backending, 10. *see also* add-on products
banks, communicating with, 37-38
benches, for plant displays

building, 73-74
  custom-designed, 75
  types and positioning of, **71-74**, 71-75
benchmarking
  assessment areas for, 288-90
  data sources for, 287-88
  department comparisons, 291-92
benefits, selling features as, 196-97
billboard advertising, 220
Blooms, 6, **61**
boutique floorplan design, 48, **48**
brand, defined, 156
branded business image, developing, 34-35
branded products, selling, 155, 276-77
breakeven point, 98-99
building permits, obtaining, 280
business plan, parts of
  description of your business, 34
  executive summary, 30
  financial strategy, 36
  industry analysis, 33-34
  introduction to your business, 30-33
  mission statement, 30-33
  objectives, 33
  personnel strategy, 36
  pricing strategy, 35
  retail strategy, 35-36
  sales and marketing strategy, 34-36
"butt brush" concept, 50
buyer, negotiation with suppliers by, 267-70
buying vs. starting a business, 23-24

C

About John Stanley

John obtained his horticultural qualifications in the United Kingdom and after working in the industry for a few years became a lecturer in nursery practices and garden center management at Merrist Wood Agricultural College near London.

His first visit to the U.S.A. was in 1976, when he was awarded a three-month scholarship to study horticultural retailing and marketing in this country. On his return to England, he formed Nursery Business Consultants with Ian Baldwin, and they became regular consultants to the industry in the U.S. and Canada.

In 1988, John changed his business name to John Stanley Associates and moved to Perth, Western Australia, and now has clients in seventeen countries. His clients are small as well as international operators in countries as varied as the U.S., Canada, India, Turkey, Indonesia, South Africa, Germany, the U.K., New Zealand, and Australia.

John is a sought after conference speaker around the world due to his entertaining way of presenting innovative ideas. John gives solutions where other speakers discuss the problems.

Also an accomplished author, John has written several books, including *The Modern Nurseryman,* three editions of *The Nursery and Garden Centre Marketing Manual,* two volumes of *John Stanley Says, Just about Everything a Retail Manager Needs to Know,* and the forthcoming *Think for Your Customers.* He is also co-creator of *Creative Displays for Profit CD-ROM,* an interactive 360° virtual tour through a garden center.

John is married to Linda, and they have four daughters. Horticulture remains strong in the family, with one daughter, Lisa, becoming a recognized landscape designer, and another daughter, Jenni, keeping everything in order in the John Stanley Associates office.

John can be contacted via e-mail at sales@johnstanley.cc or through the Internet by visiting www.jstanley.com.au.